THE ECONOMICS OF
GOVERNMENT REGULATION

Theory and Canadian Practice

This book may be ordered from:

THOMPSON Educational Publishing, Inc.

Publishing for the Social Sciences and the Humanities
11 Briarcroft Road, TORONTO, ONTARIO M6S 1H3
Telephone (416) 766-2763 / Fax: (416) 766-0398

THE ECONOMICS OF
GOVERNMENT REGULATION

Theory and Canadian Practice

JOHN C. STRICK
The University of Windsor

Thompson Educational Publishing, Inc.
Toronto

Requests for permission to make copies of any part of the work should be
mailed to: Thompson Educational Publishing, Inc., 11 Briarcroft Road,
Toronto, Ontario, Canada M6S 1H3

Canadian Cataloguing in Publication Data

Strick, J.C., 1937-
   The economics of government regulation

Includes bibliographical references.
ISBN 1-55077-005-5

1. Trade regulation. 2. Trade regulation - Canada.
3. Industry and state. 4. Industry and state - Canada. I. Title.

HD3612.S77 1990   338.9   C90-093685-1

ISBN 1-55077-005-5
Printed in Canada.
1 2 3 4 5   94 93 92 91 90

Table of Contents

PART TWO
CASE STUDIES IN GOVERNMENT REGULATION
IN CANADA / 117

PREFACE

R egulation is a major policy instrument used by government to constrain and direct the economic behaviour of individuals and business. It places limitations on economic freedom in the common interest. Certain characteristics of regulation distinguish it from other instruments of government policy. This book is more specific in its treatment of both the theory and application of regulation than most existing books which cover regulation but which tend to treat this instrument as part of a wider scope of public policy.

This is a concise presentation of the economic principles, theories, issues, and policies of government regulation. The text includes extensive analysis of the applications of regulation in Canada. The book is specifically targeted to university-level courses on government regulation. It does not, however, require extensive training in economic theory and would be suitable for students in related disciplines.

In Part One, the basic elements of microeconomics are applied in the presentation of government regulation in theory. Liberal use is made of geometric economic models to review market structures and to analyze market failures and government regulatory policies in a variety of market situations. This section reviews some of the theories attempting to explain the rationale of regulation, examines the impact of regulation on the economy with emphasis on the costs of regulation, and describes the trend of regulatory reform and deregulation.

Part Two consists of detailed case studies of the Canadian experience with government regulation and deregulation. The cases cover a mix of regulated areas which illustrate a variety of features of regulation. The areas selected include: *airlines and telephones*, two monopolistic industries traditionally subjected to regulation but which have experienced deregulation; *broadcast and paycable television*, a regulated industry in the sensitive area of Canadian culture; *financial institutions*, a competitive industry that raises problems because of its diversity; and, *pollution*, an area of social regulation that has international relevance. Other applications are briefly covered in various parts of the text and include agriculture, rental housing, patented medicines, and general wage-price controls.

PART ONE

ECONOMIC THEORY AND ISSUES IN GOVERNMENT REGULATION

1

INTRODUCTION TO REGULATION

The literature on government regulation contains numerous definitions of regulation. Some definitions are relatively narrow and restrict the concept to cover only specified government actions, while others are very general and cover practically everything government does. Government activities range from the provision of goods and services directly to the public in such areas as defence, health and welfare, and transportation, to the passage of laws and issue of rules and directives to provide order in economic and social affairs. Government in turn finances these activities through compulsory taxes, fees, and other forms of finance. It is useful for analytical purposes to distinguish between government policy instruments; that is, to identify government actions which take the form of rules and controls directed at economic activities and to distinguish them from other government actions such as those designed to provide goods and services directly to the public and those designed to control social and moral behaviour.

Regulation Defined

The definition of regulation adopted in this book follows closely that employed by the Economic Council of Canada in its studies of regulation.[1] Regulation is defined as government imposition of rules and controls which are designed to direct, restrict, or change the economic behaviour of individuals and business, and which are supported by penalties for non-compliance.

This definition contains a number of basic characteristics of regulation which serve to identify and to differentiate regulation from other instruments of government policy.

First, the emphasis of regulation is on economic behaviour as opposed to social or moral behaviour. Economic behaviour relates to production, distribution, and consumption activities in the economy. Consequently, regulation as defined in this study does not involve social and moral issues such as crime,

---

[1] The Economic Council of Canada has defined regulation as "The imposition of constraints, backed by the authority of a government, that are intended to modify economic behaviour of the private sector significantly." Economic Council of Canada, *Responsible Regulation: An Interim Report*, November, 1979 (Ottawa: Supply and Services Canada, 1979), p. 43.

which is subjected to the Criminal Code, civil rights and freedoms, obscenity, etc.

Second, regulation affects choices of producers, distributors, and consumers. Rules and constraints established by government frequently result in narrowing or limiting the range of choice in these various areas of economic activity. Choices which would normally be determined by free market forces are influenced or modified through an administrative process. The choices most frequently affected, and the manner in which they are affected, include: (a) prices of goods and services and factors of production—effected through price regulation and controls; (b) the production of goods and services—influenced by the establishment of entry restrictions, requirements or rules governing conditions of service, standards for working conditions, and standards for pollution emissions; (c) the quality and attributes of goods and services—controlled through the establishment of content standards, restrictions and prohibitions on various harmful products, etc.; and, (d) the distribution and marketing of goods and services—effected through rules relating to advertising, labelling, weights and measures and other rules concerning the disclosure of information.

In the above areas, regulation serves to restrict choices primarily in the production and sale of goods and services. Producers and distributors are not free to act as they please but must abide by the constraints, restrictions, and specifications established by government. For the most part these choice restrictions are designed for the protection of the consumer and society.

The third characteristic of regulation found in the definition is the imposition of rules supported by penalties. The latter may vary in severity and may take the form of fees and fines, loss of licence or charter, and in the most severe case, jail terms. To the extent that regulation is enforced under the threat of penalties for non-compliance, regulation is coercive in nature. A large proportion of the rules and directions which are categorized as regulatory in the definition above involve coercion as opposed to government policy instruments involving inducements or incentives.

A fourth basic characteristic of regulation, although not unique to regulation, involves the administration of the rules by a commission or agency with authority based on statute. A large proportion of government regulations are administered by agencies established by legislation with responsibility to interpret and administer the rules contained in the legislation. In the process of interpreting the provisions of the basic statute, the agency may establish more detailed regulations, which might be considered a form of subordinate legislation.

Finally, regulation may be distinguished from other government activities in that regulatory activities for the most part do not involve the provision of direct benefits to society. There are many government activities and programs in such areas of health, welfare, education, defense, and transportation, which provide goods and services directly to the public. The benefits from these activities affect directly the welfare of individuals. Similarly, government ownership and operation of business-type enterprises in the area of energy, transportation and communications provide direct benefits to society. While activities providing direct benefits may well influence or modify household and business economic behaviour, they are not considered regulatory activities. Indeed, government ownership and operations of such enterprises has traditionally been adopted in lieu of regulated private enterprise. In essence, government regulation for the most part attempts to modify or control economic behaviour but does not provide direct benefits in the process.

These basic characteristics of regulation tend to distinguish government regulatory activities from other instruments of government policy. There will, of course, exist a number of grey areas of policy which may be difficult to categorize. These need not be of major concern. The definition above provides a sufficiently distinctive and workable categorization to identify the large majority of regulatory policy instruments and provides a basis for the discussion and analysis of government regulation.

Forms of Regulation

The design of regulation to influence economic behaviour in production, distribution and consumption can take a variety of forms. These include regulation in the form of price controls to modify market conditions; business licences and charters to influence supply; the promotion of fair competition to influence prices and output; and, regulation in the form of standards and codes governing measurement, quality, content, and production conditions. The following examines these forms of regulation.

Price Regulation. One of the most common forms of regulation is the regulation of prices of goods and services, and in some cases prices of factors. This type of government regulation is most frequently found in industries characterized by monopoly or a high degree of imperfect competition and market concentration. Such industries have the power to manipulate prices and set them substantially higher than prices that would prevail if left to the forces of supply and demand. Utilities, including hydro-electric power, water supply, and telephone services and transportation services, have traditionally been viewed as natural monopolies and have come under this category of regulation. But, in addition to the highly monopolized industries, governments may occasionally intervene to control rising prices of services temporarily in short supply, such as rents when housing becomes scarce or the price of energy when that commodity comes under buying pressure. Furthermore, restrictions on price increases have been imposed through policies of wage and price controls applied as temporary measures to combat inflation.

In contrast to the imposition of price ceilings on goods and services to prevent them from rising, governments have also acted to establish price floors to prevent prices from falling below certain levels. Such price maintenance policies have most commonly been applied in the agriculture industry to avoid wide price fluctuations and subsequent fluctuations in farm income which frequently tend to occur in response to major fluctuations in the supply of agricultural products.

Licences and Charters. Businesses supplying goods and services require a licence, charter, or franchise from government in order to operate. Through licences, government can either permit or deny an individual the right to do business and can control the location of the business. In various activities restrictions are imposed on the number and types of entrants permitted into a particular industry such as banking, television, radio, and telephone. Along with the licences issued in some of these industries, conditions might be included specifying how the business is to be operated. Television stations, for example, are required in Canada to broadcast a specified amount of Canadian content. Regulations govern the ownership and the scope of operations of Canadian banks. Airlines and railways in Canada were at one time required to service specified areas. At the level of local government, in addition to a permit to operate, local zoning by-laws restrict the locations of various business establishments. Therefore, through licences, franchises and zoning, governments attempt to regulate the entry, exit, conditions of service, and even the location of a business.

Promotion of Competition. A major objective of government regulation is to promote fair competition in the market and prevent restrictive business practices such as collusion, price fixing, barriers to entry, and misleading advertising. The market system is basic to the economies of most Western democracies where free enterprise is emphasized. But an ideal functioning market economy requires competition as opposed to monopoly. Governments have assumed an obligation to monitor the operations of the market system and to introduce regulations to ensure fairness in competition. To this end, a variety of regulations can be found in anti-trust or anti-combines legislation prohibiting unfair business and marketing practices, and providing government with the authority to prevent and disband monopoly where it is deemed contrary to the public interest.

Standards. The establishment of standards is another very important form of government regulation which serves to protect the individual consumer, worker, and society. The standards may relate to the content and quality of products, the conditions of production, and various other aspects of economic activity. This is a form of regulation limiting choices particularly in the production and distribution processes. Consider some examples. There are engineering standards and building codes for the construction of buildings, bridges and various other engineered structures. Safety standards exist to protect workers on the job, particularly in reducing their exposure to hazardous products, noise, and dangerous equipment. There are safety standards for transportation and transportation vehicles. Quality and health standards are established for food products and drugs to prevent the production and marketing of unacceptably poor qualities of food products and health impairing drugs. Packaging and labelling standards and a standard set of weights and measures attempt to prevent the seller from exploiting the buyer. And, finally, governments attempt to establish standards for environmental protection, limiting pollutants being discharged into soil, air, and water.

These various forms of government regulation have recently been categorized into two groups, namely; economic regulation and social regulation.[2]

Economic and Social Regulation

Economic regulation is a term that has been used to describe the early type of government regulation, which of course continues to be applied, where regulations were concerned with industry practices involving pricing, marketing and competition. The regulations had a direct impact on industry structure and practices and were frequently aimed at specific industries or markets. From the characteristics of this type of regulation, it also became known as direct regulation and "old style" regulation.

Social regulation is the term which has been applied to describe that category of regulations which has become prominent in the last few decades and relates to the welfare of society. Regulations in this category tend to focus on the conditions under which goods and services are produced and distributed and on the attributes or physical properties of the products. They are primarily in the form of standards described above and relate to issues of safety, health, employment, the environment and a variety of social or welfare-related issues. The regulations for the most part are not directed at any one specific industry or market but tend to cut across industries. Pressure for these regulations generally originated from social groups including consumer interest groups, environmentalists, labour unions and others, and stem from social considerations related to improving the quality of life. This category of regulations has sometimes been referred to as the "new style" regulation or "new wave" regulation.

The concepts of both economic and social regulation are consistent with the definition of regulation presented in this work. Both are directed at modifying economic behaviour to achieve economic or social objectives and both relate to aspects of the economic activities of production, distribution, and consumption. For instance, when the government establishes safety standards for protecting workers, the need for these standards arise from dangers involved in the production process. The standards may force the producer to adopt changes in the production process and to introduce safer equipment or to reduce noise levels. This impacts on the production process and on the producer's choices, in other words, on the producer's economic behaviour.

Scope of Regulation

There are few economic activities which are not either directly or indirectly influenced by government regulations. These activities may range from regular, common-place activities where regulations might appear inconsequential to activities which are the mainstay of the economic structure. The regulations may

---

[2] These two categories of regulation are described in greater detail in Economic Council of Canada, *op. cit.*, pp. 44–45.

range from those which are viewed as minor irritants by those affected to those imposing major constraints and requiring considerable costs in terms of compliance.

It is impossible to measure accurately the scope of government regulations. Various proxies have been applied to attempt to do so but they are little more than general guides. One measure that has been applied is the proportion of gross national product that is affected by government regulation. It has been estimated that in excess of 25 percent of GNP in Canada and the United States is subject to some form of direct regulation of prices and production.[3] Direct regulation would include the regulation of public utilities, broadcasting, railroads, airlines, trucking, and agriculture. But, in addition to direct regulation, government also regulates indirectly. Practically all economic activity is conducted within a framework of general rules and laws since one of the objectives of government is to provide a framework for the orderly conduct of production, distribution, and consumption. It is not possible, however, to place any type of meaningful, quantitative measures on such indirect regulations.

The specific economic activities where government regulations may be found are much too numerous to list.[4] Some of the general areas, however, may be identified.

One area of activity that has traditionally been subject to regulation is transportation. Because of their importance for national unity and east-west relations in Canada, trans-Canada transportation facilities, such as railroads, air transport, and trucking, have been regulated from the beginning. Other modes of transportation subjected to some form of regulation include marine services, buslines, urban transit systems, and taxi services.

Communications is another field of activity that has been regulated from its inception. The communications spectrum is common property and a limited resource, and regulation has been justified to avoid congestion and abuse. In addition, regulation has been applied to communications to achieve economic, social, and cultural objectives. In the broadcasting area, radio and television, including cable and pay, are subjected to regulation. The telecommunication services of telephone and telegraph have also been quite closely regulated by the federal and provincial governments.

The regulation of the environment includes pollution control and the management of the nation's natural resources. Pollution control is a relatively new field of regulatory activity for governments but has reached wide-ranging proportions to cover practically all industry and consumer activities which may potentially damage the environment. Both the federal and provincial governments in Canada have become increasingly active in this area in the last two decades and a host of regulations concerning water, air, and land quality can be found in numerous

---

[3] *Ibid.*, p. 13.

[4] A list of the more significant areas of regulation in Canada can be found in Economic Council of Canada, *Ibid.*, p. 11.

government statutes. In addition to pollution, governments apply regulations as part of their policies to attempt to manage natural resources, such as energy, forests, minerals, wildlife and fisheries, and to manage land use, including parks, recreational uses and land use in urban centres.

The area of consumer protection relating to products and services is inundated with government regulations. These regulations govern the quality and content of products, and the conditions in which they are produced and sold, and include grading, labelling, weights and measures, advertising, and terms of sale. Regulations prohibit or restrict dangerous products including certain drugs, chemicals, and firearms. The quality of medical and health services and facilities are supervised, standards are established for buildings and related facilities, housing rentals are monitored, and monopoly elements in production and distribution are closely observed.

Financial markets and institutions, including banks, trust and insurance companies, credit unions, and the stock and bond markets, operate within a set of government regulations. Regulations also apply to pension and financial retirement plans.

In Canada, cultural activities have been subjected to government regulation and supervision with a view to protecting and fostering the Canadian identify. Coverage involves regulations on the ownership of broadcasting facilities and in particular, Canadian-content regulations in radio and television programming and in theatrical film. Publishing and advertising relating to publishing are also subjected to regulations.

Governments have traditionally been concerned with business practices and the establishment of a framework that will assure fair business operations. Consequently, provisions exist governing property, contracts, patents, copyright, incorporation, competition, bankruptcy, importing and exporting, and foreign investment and ownership. Other regulations can be found pertaining to worker occupation and safety, licensing and certification of professions and professional groups, gambling, labour organization and collective bargaining, and the production and consumption of alcoholic and tobacco products.

The scope of government regulation is extremely wide, infringing in varying degrees on almost all types of economic activities relating to production, distribution and consumption.

Growth of Regulation

Government regulations have existed ever since the first forms of government were established. Early forms of economic organization of society, being uncomplicated and simple, required correspondingly simple regulations. But, as countries grew and developed, fostered by changing technology and industrial development, economies become increasingly more complex, requiring increasing government involvement in monitoring and regulating economic activities.

Numerous attempts have been made to apply some quantitative measure to determine the growth of government regulation. These include the growth in the number of government regulatory statutes over time, the increase in the number of pages of statutory regulation, and the increase in the number of regulatory agencies and commissions. The Economic Council of Canada attempted to employ such measures in tracing the growth of regulation in Canada.[5] The Council reported that between 1870 and 1978 the number of federal statutes increased from 25 to 140 while the number of provincial statutes increased from 125 to 1608. The increase in the number of statutes was not uniform but tended to fluctuate from decade to decade, and has accelerated in recent decades. During the period 1940 to 1949, new federal and provincial statutes numbered 3 and 148 respectively. During the period 1970–78, the federal government passed 25 new statutes while provincial governments passed 262 new statutes. The Council attributed the recent explosion in government regulations to "new style" or "social regulation" in areas primarily consisting of consumer protection and information, health and safety, and protection of the environment. The growth rate in the passage of new regulations does not appear to have slowed in the 1980s. In 1987 the federal government announced its intention of introducing over 800 new regulations during that year. These consisted primarily of new or changed provisions to existing statutes and included rules governing the transportation of dangerous goods, regulations pertaining to nuclear energy, a multitude of changes in fisheries regulations, new rules governing environmental contamination, food labelling, smoking on commercial airlines, noise levels for airports, a new grading schedule for french fried potatoes, new standards for thickness in spaghetti sauce, and numerous other major and minor regulations.

The Regulators

Regulation in Canada is conducted through a wide variety of institutions including government ministerial or executive departments, boards, commissions, agencies, and tribunals. These institutions may be grouped into two categories; (1) government executive departments, and (2) statutory regulatory agencies (SRAs), which include the various commissions, boards, and agencies established by statutes. These two categories of regulatory bodies are found at both the federal and provincial government levels.

Government Departments

The government ministerial departments which are involved in regulatory activities are the ordinary executive departments of government. Each is controlled and directed by a Cabinet minister and is responsible for conducting the affairs of government within its particular jurisdiction. Executive departments are organized along functional lines. For example, government involvement in and administration of transportation activities is the responsibility of the Department of Transportation; agricultural activities fall under the jurisdiction of the Department of Agriculture; and, health and social services are the domain of the

---

[5] *Ibid.*, pp. 14–18.

Department of Health and Welfare. Each of these departments is involved in regulatory activity in varying degrees as part of their function of administering government programs. Some departments, however, were created primarily to perform regulatory functions. Examples include the federal Department of Consumer Affairs and its similar counterpart at the provincial level, which administer a variety of legislation dealing with consumer protection. The duties of the federal department include: the enforcement of regulations regarding packaging and labelling of products; advertising; the enforcement of hazardous product standards programs; the establishment of specifications for weights and measures; and, services to assist consumers to organize for collective actions and resolve complaints. Similarly, the federal Department of Environment is heavily involved in administering environmental protection and environmental conservation services. The Department is responsible for administering the Environmental Protection Act and its specific duties include monitoring and regulating use, discharge and disposal of toxic and hazardous chemicals and wastes. Environmental protection is shared with other Departments, such as the Department of Indian Affairs and Northern Development, which administers legislation for environmental management in the northern territories, particularly the protection of the northern environment from the impact of oil and mineral exploration. As in the case of all government administrative departments, the Cabinet minister in charge of the department has the ultimate responsibility for its activities. In turn, the minister and the Cabinet collectively are accountable to the House of Commons for the department's activities, including its regulatory activities. The personnel within the government departments responsible for managing daily affairs are career public servants or bureaucrats generally appointed through the public service selection process. They enjoy continuity of service and over time acquire considerable expertise on the programs and activities of their departments. Consequently, they are in a position to exercise a great amount of influence on the Departmental minister in the initiation and design of regulatory policies through the information and advice they provide.

Statutory Regulatory Agencies (SRAs)[6]

Statutory regulatory agencies are government commissions, boards, tribunals, etc. established by legislation for the purposes of regulation. They form a component of a large number of federally and provincially incorporated entities known as Crown agencies or Crown corporations. SRAs obtain their mandate and terms of reference from the legislation under which they are created. At the federal level, their financial control and accountability is governed by the Financial Administration Act. SRAs are responsible to the cabinet through the appropriate departmental minister, who also exercises financial control and direction over the

---

[6] A discussion of the various aspects of Statutory Regulatory Agencies in Canada is presented in Economic Council of Canada, *Ibid.*, Ch. 5.

agency. The budget of the agency is part of the budget of the department to which it is related.

Prominent among this group of regulatory agencies are the National Transportation Agency (NTA), formerly the Canadian Transport Commission (CTC), and the Canadian Radio-Television and Telecommunications Corporation (CRTC). The NTA obtains its mandate from the National Transportation Act and the Aeronautics Act. It is responsible for coordinating and regulating various aspects of land, water, and air transportation. In the area of air transport, it formulates air carrier regulations, including the licensing of air carriers, but shares regulatory functions with the Air Navigation Services Branch and the Aviation Regulation Branch of the Department of Transport which establish standards and procedures for air traffic control and ensure adequate safety standards.

The CRTC operates under the terms of the Broadcasting Act. Its primary functions involve the regulation (including rates) of federally incorporated telecommunications carriers and the regulation and supervision of radio and television systems and cable and pay television systems. The Department of Communications is also involved through its regulation of radio frequency spectrum. In 1987–88, of the Department's total budget of approximately $150 million, $25 million was provided for the CRTC. The senior personnel within an SRA are generally appointed by the Cabinet. They may be former public servants, former elected politicians or political party supporters who are rewarded for their service to the party. Appointees may also be selected from the business community on the basis of the expertise and experience they may bring to the agency.

One of the primary reasons for the creation of SRAs to administer regulations is to provide some distance between political considerations and the administration of regulations. SRAs are provided with a greater degree of political autonomy than are the ordinary executive departments of government. The degree of autonomy, however, varies among agencies. While some agencies require the approval of the appropriate minister for their decisions, others operate without this requirement and even exercise power to establish new regulations without ministerial approval but within the limits of the legislation under which they operate. Cabinet power to over-ride SRA decisions is provided in the legislation governing the SRA, and this over-ride power generally applies to agencies with broad mandates to develop and apply policy. Appeals to the Cabinet on SRA decisions are generally on issues of major policy. The Cabinet in turn may uphold the agency's decision, over-ride it, or refer the issue back to the agency with a directive for further examination and consideration. Right of appeal of SRA decisions to the courts acts as a further restraint on SRA autonomy.

A number of factors may determine the degree of autonomy that an SRA may possess. Generally, the autonomy of an SRA may vary directly with the length of appointment of its members. Members of an agency who are appointed for a lengthy, fixed period of time and who can only be removed for very serious breach of office may tend to act more independently than agencies whose members are appointed for a short term. SRAs will also have greater autonomy if appeals in their areas of jurisdiction are not a tradition or commonplace. A distinguishing feature between Canadian SRAs and those in the United States is that SRA decisions in Canada may be appealed to the Cabinet whereas in the United State this right of appeal does not exist. It is consequently contended that SRAs in the United States enjoy greater autonomy than their counterparts in Canada. The generality of the SRA's terms of reference contained in the enabling legislation will also affect the degree of autonomy. If the terms of reference tend to be broad, the agency may possess considerable latitude in interpreting the legislation and freedom to establish subordinate or new regulations without requiring the approval of the executive or the legislature.

An example of an SRA with a large degree of autonomy in its operations is the CRTC. It is composed of nine full-time members and ten part-time members appointed by the Govenor-in-Council. The full-time members are appointed for a relatively lengthy term of seven years. The CRTC's freedom of operations stems from its very broad terms of reference. It was established to implement the Broadcasting Act which contains numerous general clauses regarding goals and objectives for broadcasting in Canada. This provided the CRTC, given its day-to-day responsibility for regulating Canadian broadcasting, with a great deal of latitude in interpreting its mandate and wide powers to develop broadcasting policies and corresponding rules and guidelines. Furthermore, the CRTC has successfully resisted the Cabinet's attempts to rein in its powers. In the words of the Caplan-Savenageau Task Force on Broadcasting Policy (1988):

> While the federal government has pursued a succession of projects to obtain power of direction over the CRTC, the Commission has continued, as it is entitled, to operate independently, holding hearings on issues, deciding on policy, making regulations, and putting these decisions into effect, with varying degrees of informal consultation with the government and the Department of Communications.[7]

Regulation in Question

Within the last decade there appears to have developed within various sectors of society and business, a disillusionment with regulation and a trend toward deregulation. Nowhere has this been more evident than in the U.S., particularly after 1980 when President Reagan took office. To a lesser degree, a trend toward deregulation also developed in Canada. An attitude appears to have developed that the economies were over-regulated and that inefficiencies were being created by regulation that were proving to be excessively costly. The inefficiencies could be eliminated or reduced by substituting market elements for regulation. The assumption underlying this position was that the market system is a more

---

[7] Canada, *Report of the Task Force on Broadcasting Policy* (Ottawa: Supply and Services, Canada, 1986), p. 18.

efficient allocator of resources and a more efficient regulator of prices and output than are regulatory agencies.

Consequently, there have been movements in Canada and the U.S. to deregulate various traditionally regulated industries such as the airlines, trucking, and the telephone industry. In conjunction with the deregulation movement, there has also been a trend towards privatization of formerly government-owned enterprises in both North America and in Europe. Numerous industries that had been nationalized or that were government-created, particularly following the Second World War, have recently been sold by governments to private interests. This privatization movement has stemmed primarily from the same attitudes that initiated the deregulation process—a belief that productivity and efficiency would be enhanced in the industries involved.

Over the years there have existed numerous conservative groups, individuals, and businesses who have opposed the ever-increasing government encroachment in economic activities. But, interestingly enough, pressure for deregulation did not usually originate within the regulated industry. The telephone industry in Canada and the U.S. opposed the move by regulatory agencies to liberalize regulations and open the industry to competition. Frequently, the strongest supporters for continued regulation were the regulated firms and their employees who feared the adjustments and upheaval that could conceivably result. This lent credence to the charge that regulation benefitted the regulated and produced cartelization of the industry. The "old style" or "economic regulation" of prices and output consequently came under very careful scrutiny during the 1970s and 1980s with considerable pressure from consumer groups, as well as from potential competitors employing new technology, who wished to enter and compete with established firms in traditionally regulated industries.

Even in the area of social regulation, including the environment, health, and safety, continued and increasing regulation began to be seriously questioned. The prime concerns of the 1960s and early 1970s which led to numerous developments to reduce pollution, such as the pollutants from automobile emissions, appeared to subside in the early 1980s. In Canada, questions on the merits of the rapid escalation of regulation led the Economic Council of Canada to conduct a major investigation of regulation which produced a number of recommendations for the reform of the regulatory process. Proposals for reform on both sides of the Canada-U.S. border called for considerably closer scrutiny of the need for new regulations and the need for the continuation of existing regulations. A trend developed to apply benefit-cost analysis and cost-effectiveness analysis to evaluate existing and newly proposed regulations. While the need for continued regulation of various economic activities was recognized, the objective was to streamline the regulatory process, to cut some of the bureaucratic red tape which produced delays in decision making, and, where regulations are justified, to make them more effective. The issue of more efficient and effective regulation is covered in more detail in a later chapter.

2

THE "RAISON D'ÊTRE" OF REGULATION

The numerous attempts that have been made to explain the rationale of government regulation range from the relatively simple public interest theory to the development of complex models of economic behaviour and public choice. Economists have tried to develop and construct theories of government regulation that would explain why government regulates and that would permit predictions involving regulation. Frequently, the theories have not been confined to economics alone, but have drawn on aspects of politics, law, and administration. Unfortunately, while making contributions to the understanding of regulation, none of the various approaches have succeeded in the development of a universal or general theory. Such a theory would explain the reasons for government regulation, would apply to all situations, and would permit predictions regarding when and where government will apply regulation.

In essence, a general theory of government regulation does not exist. Some of the theories succeed in explaining government regulation in certain circumstances or observed situations, but fail to explain regulation or lack of it in other situations.[1]

The various approaches used in attempting to develop a theory of government regulation have focused on hypotheses regarding certain aspects of the market or special groups or components of the private sector and their behaviour. These have produced the market failure and public interest theories; the political-bureaucratic behaviour theories; and, the specialized private sector interests theories.

The explanation of regulation on the basis of failures of the market, and consequent need for government regulation to protect the interests of the public, has its origins in welfare economics and in the economics of the public sector. It employs the normative approach to economics by attempting to establish which activities should be regulated and to what degree. Implicit in the normative approach are value judgments that government should be involved, or that it would be good for society for government to be involved. The hypotheses that

---

[1] An overview of various theories of government regulation is presented in Harry M. Trebing, "Equity, Efficiency, and the Viability of Public Utility Regulation," *Applications of Economic Principles in Public Utility Industries*, eds, W. Sichel and T. Gies (University of Michigan, 1981); and, Christopher Green, *Canadian Industrial Organization and Policy*, 2nd ed. (Toronto: McGraw-Hill Ryerson Ltd, 1985), pp. 229–236.

have as their foundation the motives and behaviour of bureaucratic and political groups, and the interests of specialized components of the private sector, apply the positive approach to economics and economic modelling. They attempt to describe and explain observed phenomenon, a situation as it exists or as it is believed to exist. They concentrate on "what is" rather than on "what should be," and are based on judgments about existence for which reasons can ordinarily be given which are either empirical or "a priori." To a considerable extent, these positive theories draw upon developments in public choice theories and combine economics with studies of the political process. In the following, an attempt will be made to outline the essence of these hypotheses of the "raison d'être" of regulation.

Market Failures and the Public Interest

The focus on failures of the market economy to serve the public interest is one of the earliest attempts to explain regulation and has been referred to as the public interest theory of regulation. It is based on the assumption that government seeks to maximize social welfare. When the freely-operating market system fails to achieve efficiency of resource use and welfare maximization, the government assumes an obligation to correct or compensate for market failures and inefficiencies. Regulation is one of a number of policy instruments at the disposal of government to achieve this objective.[2]

Maximum efficiency in the use of resources is referred to as an optimum allocation of resources or as a *Pareto optimum*, named after the economist Wilfredo Pareto. Pareto established a number of technical efficiency conditions that had to be satisfied for the economy to achieve maximum efficiency in resource use. These included the following: prices are equal to marginal costs of production; firms make normal profits; factors such as labour are paid the value of their contributions to production; and, all factors seeking employment are employed. The ensuing state of economic efficiency, or Pareto optimality, has generally been described as one in which, given the availability of resources, the state of technology, and the distribution of income, it is not possible to make one person better off without making another person worse off.

Certain market conditions must be fulfilled if a freely-operating market system is to achieve Pareto efficiency and consequent welfare maximization. These include the existence of perfect competition, where prices and outputs are determined by the forces of supply and demand, the absence of externalities in production and consumption, and the divisibility of products and services so that they can be sold in the marketplace.

---

[2] Market failures and the need for government action to correct or compensate for these failures is discussed in most textbooks in public finance or public sector economics. See for example, R.A. Musgrave, Peggy Musgrave, and R.M. Bird, *Public Finance In Theory and Practice*, First Canadian Edition (Toronto: McGraw-Hill Ryerson Ltd., 1987), Ch. 1, 3, 4; or, R.W. Boadway and D. Wildasin, *Public Sector Economics*, 2nd ed. (Toronto: Little, Brown and Co., 1984), Ch. 3.

In perfect competition the forces of supply and demand determine what is produced, how much and in which manner goods and services are produced, and for whom goods and services are produced. The first two questions concern the use or allocation of resources, while the third question concerns the distribution of goods and services produced. Prices and quantities are automatically determined by the supply and demand forces operating as if guided by an "invisible hand." Perfect competition is characterized by a sufficiently large number of buyers and sellers, so that no one individual buyer or seller can influence prices. It is also characterized by perfect knowledge on the part of consumers and producers. Consumers have complete knowledge about the products and services available in the market, so they may spend their incomes with full knowledge of the attributes of goods and services on the market, making rational decisions to maximize their welfare in the consumption process. Producers are assumed to possess complete knowledge of the existing state of technology and the factors of production available enabling them to make rational decisions on the combinations of factors they employ in the production process so as to maximize profits. And, finally, it is assumed that factors of production are fully aware of employment opportunities and possess perfect mobility to take advantage of these opportunities.

While perfect competition is a necessary condition for the optimum allocation of resources, it is not a sufficient condition to ensure this optimum. In addition, there must be an absence of externalities in production and consumption, and goods and services must be divisible. Absence of externalities implies that all benefits of consumption accrue directly to the buyer as measured by prices, and that all costs are included in the costs of production of the firm and are covered by market prices. Goods and services must be divisible in order to be bought and sold in the market place. If a service does not have this characteristic, it will not be produced in the market even if there is a demand for the service.

Modern-day market economies fail to meet the above conditions for an efficient allocation of resources and welfare maximization. Imperfections of varying degrees exist in the market, including monopoly elements, lack of complete knowledge on the part of consumers and producers, and factor immobility. There are external costs, such as pollution, involved in many lines of production. Certain services such as national defense are in demand but they are not divisible and consequently will not be provided by private enterprise. Government, therefore, is required to interfere in economic activity and correct market imperfections, regulate monopoly, reduce external costs, and provide for public services which the market does not provide. The objective of government intervention is the public interest. In the process of reallocating the use of resources, the government supposedly moves the economy closer to the state of Pareto optimality and welfare maximization.

The public interest theory places emphasis on the protection of the individual consumer and society. The emphasis is on the provision of goods and services to the public as economically and efficiently as possible, with the assurance that the public is made aware of the attributes of these goods and services and is not misled or harmed in the consumption and production process. Furthermore, the public interest requires that the consumption and production process be conducted in an environment that provides for the development and provision of varied goods and services to meet changing consumer tastes and demands. An environment that provides for technological development can also be viewed as being in the public interest. In summary, regulatory actions to promote the public interest are those actions which create an economic climate that approximates, or that moves the economy toward, perfect competition.

The public interest theory can explain and justify a wide range of government regulatory activities. Regulation of monopoly industries, including prices, and promotion of competition is justified on the grounds that monopoly produces higher prices and smaller outputs than competition. The host of consumer protectionist policies—including standards for weights and measures, regulations on advertising, standards relating to food and drugs, and safety standards in the workplace—can all be justified in the public interest. On a more general level, it can certainly be argued that the control of industrial emissions, the use of chemicals, transportation of dangerous chemicals, regulation of nuclear energy, etc. is in the interests of society because of potential harmful externalities over which the market system provides inadequate and inefficient control.

Furthermore, the market system has a tendency to waste certain resources that fall into the category of "common property." These would include natural resources, such as fishing grounds, forests and minerals, and limited resources, such as the broadcasting spectrum. Because no one has exclusive property rights over these resources, as is the case of private property, there is a tendency to overuse, waste, and overcrowd. A case can be made for government regulating or managing the use of common property resources in the public interest to prevent waste and abuse. It could do so through the application of licences and quotas which ration and restrict use of the resources.

The initiative for government regulatory action to serve the public interest generally comes from the public and from policy-makers' perception of public wants. Public input comes via consumer-interest lobby groups, public opinion polls, and individual presentations and requests made to elected legislature representatives. Regulatory agencies may also give advance notice to the public of regulatory initiatives and provide opportunity for public response, including hearings on proposed regulatory policies to obtain public input.

The public interest theory has been widely criticized as being too general and even naive given the complexity of modern day economies and the operations of the political and bureaucratic processes. More specifically, there has been dissatisfaction over the emphasis the theory places on the regulation of monopoly and monopoly elements, and its stress on the importance of promoting competition. Some regulated industries do not fall into the category of monopoly. Indeed, government has imposed regulations which serve to restrict competition in the production and marketing of certain goods and services and which in essence create monopolistic and cartel-like situations.

Agricultural production is an example where regulations are imposed to restrict production and supply in an attempt to maintain prices above the levels of a free, competitive market. The justification for such regulation is to maintain stable agricultural prices and prevent cyclical fluctuations in farm incomes. While this may be deemed a desirable policy of income distribution, in the process the government interferes with the market mechanism and may move the economy away from the position of optimum resource allocation. The resultant artificially-high prices may cause inefficiencies and higher costs of production. If producers, not faced with open competition, are assured of profit levels or rates of return on their investments, it is argued that they will have few incentives to maintain maximum efficiency. While the agricultural sector benefits from stable prices and income levels, these benefits occur at the expense of consumers who are forced to pay the higher prices and consequently suffer losses in real incomes. The regulations reduce competition in the interests of the farmers, but if they result in a net decline in total social welfare they cannot be viewed as being in the public interest.

There has also been some doubt expressed over the capacity of regulatory agencies and commissions to regulate industry to correct market failures and to adequately promote the public interest. This explanation of regulation assumes that agencies possess the resources, personnel and expertise to identify market failures, determine the public interest and to regulate accordingly. In practice this may not always hold true, and indeed there have been numerous instances of an agency complaining of its lack of staff and budget to perform its regulatory functions adequately. The public interest theory of government correcting failures and inefficiencies in the market is based on the premise that government is itself efficient. It is not inconceivable that the inefficiencies in the market place will be displaced by the inefficiencies of government. Considerable empirical evidence is available illustrating inefficiencies in government enterprise and inefficiencies produced by regulatory government policies.

A further weakness of the public interest theory is based on an observation that regulatory agencies do not always appear to be acting in the best interests of the public, but rather appear to favour the industries which they are regulating. It has been argued that, frequently, regulatory decisions on industry pricing, entry, services, etc., can be observed to follow the requests and submissions of the regulated industry. Regulatory agencies are observed to act as pawns in the hands of the regulated. This contention and dissatisfaction with the public interest theory led to hypotheses of government regulation that have as their foundation the interests of producers and distributors.

Specialized Private Sector Interests

Attempts to explain government regulation based on specialized private sector interests have produced two theories; the *capture theory* and the *cartel theory*.

According to the capture theory of regulation, regulatory agencies which were created to regulate in the public interest eventually end up serving the interests of the entity or group that they regulate. In the cartel theory of regulation, on the other hand, it is contended that firms in the private sector seek regulation when they desire cartel-type benefits but find it too costly for them to form a cartel.

The Capture Theory

In the capture theory, regulatory agencies tend to weaken over time and gradually fall prey to the power of the firms or industry that they were originally established to regulate. The argument is made that regulatory agencies must frequently contend with large and powerful firms. These firms command large resources and expertise in their areas of operations. They frequently employ highly-organized and well-funded lobby and special interest groups with a high degree of expertise and are in a position to wield considerable public and political influence. Many regulatory agencies constantly complain about lack of adequate funding and insufficient staff to discharge their regulatory functions adequately. This makes them vulnerable to the expertise, evidence, and pressures that regulated firms can marshall in support of their requests and positions.

The capture theory was based on observations and perceptions that some regulated agencies appeared to promote the interests of, and made decisions to the benefit of, those whom they were supposed to regulate. For example, regulatory decisions restricting entry into an industry provide less competition in the industry and tend to enhance monopolistic power. This is at odds with the public interest. Similarly, regulatory decisions which maintain prices above the competitive level, or decisions which maintain industry profit levels which appear excessive, tend to be viewed as contrary to the public interest.

In the capture approach it is argued that, even if the original intent in creating a regulatory agency was to serve the public interest, unless that agency is strongly supported by government in the form of adequate funding and personnel for the agency to adequately discharge its duties, it can fall prey to the regulated. The probability of such an occurrence is particularly high if the agency is facing a strong and dominant industry. Canadian agencies such as the National Transport Agency and the Canadian Radio-Television and Telecommunications Commission, and American agencies such as the Federal Communications Commission and Environmental Protection Agency have frequently complained about inadequate resources to enable them to perform their duties effectively. These agencies are constantly faced with powerful representation from industry. A company such as Bell Canada or Canadian Pacific Railroad, requesting a rate or service charge, would generally come before an agency with well-supported arguments presented by a battery of lawyers, accountants and other experts. The agency might often find itself with insufficient resources and expertise to conduct a thorough investigation of its own into the issue in question and may be forced to rely on the information presented by the industry on which to base its decision. It is not surprising, then, that the consequent decision would likely be in favour of the industry. Lack of adequate resources cause many regulated agencies to react to industry initiatives rather than initiate investigations of their own, so that they remain passive in their regulatory roles.

Despite the evidence and arguments in support of the capture theory, it suffers from a number of weaknesses which are also based on observations. First, there is a contradiction in cases of regulatory decisions where it is readily apparent that the regulations are not in the best interests of a regulated firm or industry. Numerous regulatory decisions can be cited which have added to the costs of an industry, have curbed profits, or have reduced the monopoly power in an industry. For example, regulatory decisions in the late 1970s and 1980s to open to competition the telephone equipment manufacturing industry and the telephone service industry were vigorously opposed by the industries. The automobile industry, citing increased costs and inadequate technology, argued against the imposition of more stringent pollution control and safety standards, but these standards were subsequently imposed. During the period of their operations as regulated industries, the airline and railroad companies were obligated to operate unprofitable traffic routes and lines as part of their approved licences to operate. To the extent that such regulations contributed to higher operating costs and adversely affected profits, they were clearly not in the interests of the regulated companies.

A second weakness of the capture proposition is that it does not recognize the actions of consumer groups which have initiated or have been primary responsible for various regulations. Various consumer and citizens groups have led crusades which have contributed to the imposition of regulations and restraints on producers. The crusade of Ralph Nader and his group was a major factor in the imposition of higher automobile safety and pollution standards. The concern of the public over the safety of nuclear power plants, particularly following some serious mishaps at such plants, and the pressure the public brought to bear on politicians resulted in improved safety conditions for nuclear energy. Current concern over acid rain in the Great Lakes basin has led to the initiation of greater cooperative efforts by the Canadian and United States governments to attempt to curb sulphur dioxide emissions, particularly from mineral smelting plants and hydro-electric generating plants on both sides of the border. National and provincial and state governments have recently begun to strengthen pollution control legislation with more severe penalties imposed on environmental polluters. The public crusade against pollution will likely continue to force governments to act and impose more effective pollution control regulations.

Finally, the capture theory in many instances cannot adequately explain or precisely identify the captors in a multi-service or multi-product industrial sector. Some agencies regulate industrial sectors which provide various competing goods and services. Consider for example the National Transport Agency (formerly the Canadian Transport Commission), which is responsible for regulating the transportation sector. Transportation includes the airline, the railroad, and trucking industries—all of which are in competition with one another in the transport of freight. There is no evidence to suggest that any one group from these various means of transport has gained control of the Agency or has been favoured by it. A recent development in Canada in the transportation sector has been the deregulation of airlines, railroads, and trucking, with the intent of increasing competition within each mode of transportation as well as increasing competition between them. In this deregulation process there is no apparent evidence that the Transport Agency favoured any of the three industries. Nor is there evidence that the Agency catered to the large firms in these industries. In the airline industry, deregulation and increased competition was vigorously opposed by Air Canada, the largest of the airlines but was favoured by some of the smaller carriers. Similarly, in the trucking industry, the larger trucking firms did not believe that they had much to gain from a policy of reduced regulation and increased competition.

The Cartel Theory of Regulation

A cartel is formed when a group of firms come together for the purposes of gaining control of prices and output in their industry. The objective is to reduce competition and increase profits. A total volume of output is determined and production quotas are allocated to the member firms. One of the most successful cartels on the international scene has been the Organization of Petroleum Exporting Countries (OPEC). In a very short period in the early 1980s, OPEC succeeded in raising the price of oil from $4.00 per barrel to over $30.00 per barrel. Organizing a successful cartel, however, is not without problems. First, there is the legal question. In Canada and the U.S. cartels are contrary to anti-trust legislation and are, therefore, illegal. Second, there are costs involved in cartel organization. In addition to the costs of organizing to operate as a cartel, there is also the cost of free riders or firms who do not join the cartel but enjoy the benefits from higher prices and limited output. In general, the larger the number of firms in an industry, the more difficult it is to bring them all together to form a cartel.

This theory of cartels forms the basis of the cartel theory of regulation.[3] It was argued that a cartel and regulation produce similar results in the form of control over entry, production, and prices. According to the theory, industries will seek regulation when they desire the benefits of cartels but find that forming a cartel is too costly or is illegal. A largely competitive industry with numerous producers, such as agriculture, may seek regulation to maintain price and income levels because it is too costly to form a cartel. On the other hand, a monopoly or a tight oligopoly may seek regulation to protect their monopolistic positions. Such industries are already in a position to enjoy many of the benefits of a cartel and will wish to protect this position by barring new entrants and avoiding increased competition. Or conversely, governments may take the initiative to impose regu-

---

[3] George J. Stigler, "The Theory of Economic Regulation," *The Bell Journal of Economics and Management Science*, Spring 1971, Vol. 2, No. 1.

lation on a monopolistic, highly-concentrated industry because the government fears that the industry will exploit its cartel-type position at the expense of consumers. The cartel theory attempts to explain the observation that regulated industries seem to be at the extremes in the market spectrum—they are either highly competitive or monopolistic prior to regulation.

A problem with this theory is that it does not explain many cases of regulation and non-regulation. There are many oligopolistic industries which are not subject to regulation. While such oligopoly or monopoly industries as the airlines, railroads, and telecommunications have been traditionally regulated, numerous other oligopolistic industries such as automobiles, electrical appliances, textiles, and food processing are not subjected to price and output regulation. Similarly, there are many highly-competitive industries, including many small retail outlets, tool and die operations, etc., which are not regulated. Therefore, this theory does not adequately explain the existence or non-existence of regulation, nor does it enable us to predict accurately where regulation can be expected to be found.

Political-Bureaucratic Behaviour Theories

Numerous attempts have been made to explain regulation as emanating from the motivations, interests and behaviour observed in the political-administrative system. One approach concentrates on the political action of forming coalitions to maximize political support and gain elected office. Another approach attributes paternalistic or altruistic attitudes on the part of governments which lead them to replace market mechanisms with institutionalized-types of mechanisms to achieve income equity and stability objectives in the economy.

Political Coalition Formation

According to this approach, regulation stems from the coalition of various special interest groups which are manipulated by government to obtain their political support. Regulatory decisions are not unlike pork-barrel politics where government doles out special favours, concessions, and benefits to special groups and industries in return for their political support. Coalitions are consequently formed with these groups which are delicately balanced through favourable government regulations, as well as other policies and activities, to maximize support. Such regulations would include rate and pricing policies that would permit regulated industries a profit, yet not excessive profits that would earn government the wrath of consumers. Consequently, a policy of telephone rate-making could involve low, below-cost residential local rates but above-cost long-distance rates which permit the telephone company to make a profit for the two services. The low residential rates keep the mass of telephone users content, and an adequate profit will satisfy the telephone industry and its influential political lobby. Attempts to build coalitions of support would thus explain such regulatory policies as rate averaging and cross-subsidization of services.

Therefore, while the public interest theory explains regulation essentially as a means of curbing monopoly power, and the capture theory maintains that the regulated manipulate the regulators, the coalition-formation theory explains regulation as a process that seeks voter support by distributing benefits to the various constituencies or support groups of politicians and political parties. The initiative for regulation comes from politicians.

The coalition-building theory has its origins in public choice and political behaviour theories as developed by Anthony Downs, James Buchanan, Gordon Tullock, Sam Peltzman and others. It is essentially inherent in the more general framework of these political process theories.

Anthony Downs theorized that politicians are led by their own selfish motives, formulating policies and serving special interest and pressure groups in order to gain office.[4] In a world of imperfect knowledge, special well-financed interest groups can influence voters through persuasion and dissemination of information to support a cause. Politicians cater to these groups because they have the resources and capability to deliver votes, and the politicians' primary motive is to be elected to office. Buchanan and Tullock similarly argued that political parties form coalitions to win elections.[5] Through a system of log-rolling or vote trading, political parties attempt to build a coalition of minorities. Attempts are made to obtain support from groups by offering them certain programs or benefits in return for their support of other programs which may not benefit those same groups. Regulations can be a component of the mix of the various policy or program instruments at the politicians' disposal.

Peltzman hypothesized that basic to the regulatory process was the transfer of wealth in the form of regulated prices, entry restrictions, and other regulatory aspects.[6] Political support or votes are sought in return for these transfers. As in the case of a government policy that involves taxes and transfers, there are also gainers and losers in the implementation of regulations. To maximize votes and attempt to gain a majority, political parties attempt to maximize their gains and minimize their losses by selecting appropriate policies. The regulator will choose those transfers which produce the largest net political gain in the form of potential votes. Regulators seek a broad-based coalition of gainers. The earlier-cited example of the telephone industry, which was permitted to engage in cross-subsidization to enjoy profits and yet maintain low prices for local services for the mass of the public, would fit Peltzman's model.

The regulation theory based on building coalitions suffers from a number of weaknesses. First, the theory assumes that regulators possess the freedom to make arbitrary decisions. It does not recognize that regulatory decisions can be appealed to the courts by those disagreeing with the decisions or bearing subsequent costs. The availability of judicial review would suggest severe limitations

---

[4] A. Downs, *An Economic Theory of Democracy* (New York: Harper and Row, 1957).

[5] James Buchanan and Gordon Tullock, *The Calculus of Consent* (Ann Arbor: University of Michigan Press, 1962).

[6] S. Peltzman, "Toward a More General Theory of Regulation," *The Journal of Law and Economics*, Vol. XIX (2), August 1976.

to arbitrary decision making to attain political ends. Indeed, numerous cases can be found where the courts have overturned the decisions of regulatory agencies, such as the FCC in the United States in the area of telecommunications. A second shortcoming of the theory is the assumption that regulatory agencies and agents can be readily manipulated by politicians and governments in their self-interest. It fails to recognize that many regulatory agencies possess a considerable degree of autonomy and independence from the government legislature and executive. This is particularly true where agents are appointed for lengthy terms and can only be removed for just cause. These agents may not necessarily be motivated to enhance the political power and votes of political parties or individual politicians. They may assert their independence and act to foster the interests of society as they view these interests.

A third limitation of the coalition formation theory is the problem of identifying the gains and costs of alternative regulatory or political actions and of measuring these gains and costs. The theory implies some form of benefit-cost analysis applied to regulatory decision making. Various groups may be subjected to both gains and costs from a regulatory policy, and in order to determine the possible effects on their voting behaviour it would be necessary to assess if the net benefits to the group were positive or negative.

Income Redistribution and Stability

The equity and stability proposition attributes regulation to the government's desire to replace freely-operating markets with institutions to promote fairness in the distribution of income and to maintain income stability. This approach to regulation has its origin in the generally accepted goal of society, and consequent function of government, to achieve an equitable distribution of income and wealth in society.[7] An equitable distribution of income, however, remains a vague concept. Most people would agree that extremes in income distribution with a group of very wealthy and a group living in poverty should be avoided. Most would also likely agree that a goal of equal incomes is impractical and undesirable in a dynamic, free market system characterized by consumer and producer sovereignty and the maximization motive of households and business. An equitable or fair distribution of income, therefore, must remain a value judgment on the part of society and its government.

It is concluded that the market system, even when operating efficiently, generally produces too great a disparity between the wealthy and the poor, and leaves many members of society living in poverty. The market system may also produce widely fluctuating incomes in certain sectors of the economy. The government therefore assumes an obligation to redistribute and stabilize income, and as a minimum goal attempts to raise the incomes of the low-income groups to accept-

---

[7] An explanation and analysis of the government function to achieve an equitable distribution of income and wealth, along with criteria for equity and government policies, is contained in most textbooks on public sector economics. See, for example, Musgrave, Musgrave and Bird, *op.cit.*, Ch. 5.

able levels. While the tax and transfer system remains the major policy instrument for redistribution purposes, regulatory policies may also be applied to influence incomes or returns to factors of production. Consequently, markets are not replaced by regulatory institutions and agencies because the markets are inefficient. They may well satisfy the economic conditions for production and consumption efficiency, but in the process they may produce an unacceptable distribution of income along with income instability.

The result is government interference in the market to regulate and stabilize incomes and prices. Price ceilings are prices which are set below market prices and serve to redistribute income from producers to consumers. The government may establish minimum wage levels in an attempt to raise the income levels of unskilled workers. Rent regulation serves to keep rent prices at more affordable levels for low-income groups. Similar regulation of rates of other necessary services such as electricity, water, gas, etc. generally benefit lower-income groups more than the higher income groups. The control of entry into an industry or specific service by restricting the number of licences and franchises serves to regulate supply and maintain income and profit levels in that industry. This was the situation with airlines and the telephone industries when they were subject to regulation. Regulation of agricultural output through quotas, and regulation of prices through marketing boards, serves to maintain and stabilize farm incomes which may otherwise experience wide fluctuations if left to market forces.

Regulatory agencies which permit cross-subsidization can be said to be engaged in a form of redistribution of income. Profits are permitted in one segment of an industry and applied to cover losses in another segment. The results are similar to those of the tax and transfer process of income redistribution and for this reason the process has been called taxation by regulation. In the transportation industry, for example, prices are permitted which produce profits on routes with high-volume traffic, and these profits are expected to cover the losses on routes with low-volume traffic. Without such cross-subsidization, the losses on the low-volume traffic route would have to be covered by higher prices, thereby producing unequitable price differentiation or price discrimination on the two routes.

Regulation, therefore, reduces the uncertainties and the fluctuations of prices and output associated with the market and helps keep incomes more stable. It also is used to redistribute income, to help provide lower income groups with a pre-determined level of income, and to reduce poverty. The initiatives for regulation, according to this approach to regulation, stem from a form of paternalistic philosophy of government.

If indeed regulation rests on the government's desire to achieve a greater degree of equity and stability in the economy, then, as the economy becomes more complex and dynamic, government involvement in economic activity should escalate. Statistics on the growth of government do show a long-run trend to a larger government sector in the absolute and relative to the private sector. In recent years, however, there has been a levelling off of government growth, and even a trend toward retrenchment in a number of countries. The past decade has witnessed a privatization movement in a number of countries where government has sold its interests in government corporations and operations to the private sector. A trend toward deregulation of traditionally government regulated industries can also be observed over the last decade. The airlines, railroads, trucking, and various sectors of telecommunications have been released from government regulation. Deregulation has brought considerable instability in these industries as they attempt to adjust and operate in a more openly competitive environment. It has produced worker lay-offs, unstable profits, bankruptcies, and worker and company insecurity. These trends are completely contrary to the proposition that regulation originates from the government's desire to replace a volatile competitive market with institutional-type arrangements which produce increased equity and stability.

Furthermore, this theory offers no guidelines, principles, or criteria for equity. Fair prices and profits, and an equitable state of income and wealth distribution, essentially remain a value judgment on the part of government. Government presumably reflects the preference of society, and whatever government deems to be fair must presumably in the end be considered equitable.

Each of the various theories of regulation possesses some degree of validity in that each can be applied to some particular regulatory activity under certain circumstances. But there is no one theory that can explain regulation in all areas where regulation is observed and the manner in which it is applied. No general theory of government regulation exists that can be applied universally, can explain all regulation, and permits predictions about where regulation will be found. The usefulness of the aforementioned hypotheses lies in their contribution to a greater understanding of various aspects and issues of regulation and the rationale of regulation.

MARKET STRUCTURES AND REGULATION

Certain types of markets, such as monopolistic markets, tend to invite close government scrutiny of their operations, and in the interests of efficiency and the public good the government may determine that regulation is desirable. The following pages examine various market features which may invite regulation. These include the different types of market structures, the factors which give rise to these structures, and the consequent market practices and operations.

Types of Market Structures

In economic theory, four market models are generally recognized as representative of market structures. These four market models are: perfect competition, monopolistic competition, oligopoly, and pure monopoly. The market models are usually distinguished on the basis of the degree of competition, the number of firms in the market, and the degree of industry concentration in these markets. The number of firms and the degree of competition generally decline in a movement from one extreme of perfect competition to the other extreme of pure monopoly, while the degree of market concentration generally increases in such a movement.

Perfect Competition

Perfect competition describes a market situation where prices and output are determined automatically by the forces of supply and demand, and no one individual buyer or seller has any influence on prices and output. Perfect competition possesses four basic characteristics. First, the products are homogeneous. The product supplied by one seller is identical to the products supplied by any other seller and are, therefore, perfect substitutes for each other. Second, there exist a large number of buyers and sellers, each constituting so small a portion of the market that no buyer or seller can influence the prices of the products through their actions. Third, buyers and sellers possess complete knowledge of market conditions, including prices and availability of goods and services, and factors of production. Fourth, there is freedom of entry and exit in the market in the sense that producers and factors of production are completely mobile.

In this market, prices and output are determined by the interaction of supply and demand. Once the price is determined, each producer or firm in the market

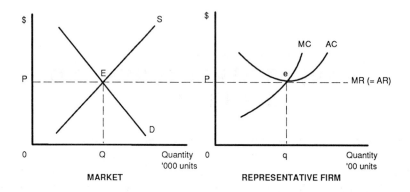

FIGURE 3–1: *The Market and the Firm in Perfect Competition in Equilibrium*

becomes a price taker, which means that the firm can produce and sell at that price without affecting the price. In such a situation the demand curve of the individual firm is perfectly elastic. In addition, the firms constituting the market or industry use resources at maximum efficiency, produce at least cost, and just make normal profits.

Perfect competition is illustrated in Figure 3-1. Diagram A presents the familiar supply and demand curves. The supply function, S, shows the aggregate output that will be supplied at various prices on the market by the firms constituting the industry. The demand function, D, illustrates the amounts that will be demanded at different prices by the buyers in the market. Market equilibrium is determined at the intersection of D and S at E, where price and output will be OP and OQ respectively, with output measured in thousands of units.

Diagram B shows a representative firm in the industry. The position and actions of this firm typify that of each of the firms that operate in this industry. This firm has marginal and average cost functions of MC and AC respectively. Since each firm is a price taker, the firms sell their outputs at the market-established price of OP. The price line Pe represents the firm's marginal and average revenue curve and is also the demand curve for the firm. Each firm may sell at price OP all that it is capable of producing. The marginal cost curve is the firm's short-run supply curve. Equilibrium for the firm is established where the firm's supply and demand curves intersect at e, the point where $price = MC = MR = AR = minimum\,AC$. The firm's output equals Oq, measured in hundreds of units. The aggregate of the output of all firms combined will be the industry output or OQ. The large number of competing firms will ensure that each firm only makes normal profits.

Normal profit is defined as a profit equal to the opportunity cost of the firm, or a return which is just sufficient for the firm to remain in the industry, and is included in the *AC* function. If excess profits or profits above normal profits existed, new firms would be attracted into the industry. The resulting increased output would cause *S* to shift to the right and consequently causes prices to fall. New entrants would continue to be attracted until all excess profits are competed away and firms are normally profitable once again. Similarly, inefficient firms with minimum costs above *OP* would have to sell their products at a loss. Unable to compete successfully, they would be forced to exit the industry. Consequently, open competition forces firms to operate at maximum efficiency, that is, to use the most productive techniques and technology to minimize costs, and to operate at their optimum scale or size.

The equilibrium conditions outlined above are the efficiency conditions for an optimum use of resources. Prices paid by consumers will be at their lowest possible level. Since prices represent the value or benefit of the product to the consumer, and since the marginal cost represents the added value or cost of resources used to produce a unit of the product, then at market equilibrium the marginal benefit to society from producing the last unit of the product is equal to the marginal cost to society to produce that product. Once equilibrium at *E* is attained, the welfare of society could not be improved by varying the output, and therefore social welfare is maximized at this point. The efficiency conditions represent a Pareto optimum in resource use.

In perfect competition, the efficiency conditions are automatically achieved through the market mechanism of supply and demand. The interaction of these forces determine how resources will be used and for what purpose, and prices act as a rationing device in the determination of the distribution of the goods and services produced. If efficiency in the use of resources is society's objective, given that certain other conditions are met, there is no need for government interference in this system and consequently no need for regulation.[1]

Unfortunately, the rigorous conditions required for the existence of perfectly competitive markets seldom are found in the real world. As outlined in an earlier chapter, imperfections and market failures abound. The value of studying perfect competition is that it serves as a standard or a norm to which the actual operations of markets in the real world may be compared and subsequently evaluated. If perfect competition is taken as the ideal type of market structure, the examination of other market structures will show how much they may deviate from this ideal.

---

[1] Perfect competition is a necessary but not a sufficient condition for an optimum allocation of resources. In addition to the efficiency or marginal conditions in production and consumption there must also be an absence of externalities, and all goods and services demanded by society must be divisible. Perfect competition will assure the attainment of the marginal conditions but does not ensure the latter conditions.

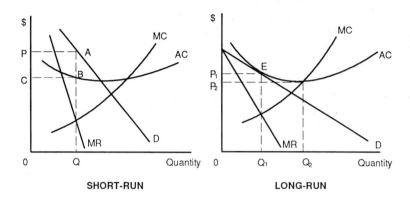

FIGURE 3–2:   *Monopolistic Competition. The Firm in Short-Run and Long-Run Equilibrium*

Monopolistic Competition

Monopolistic competition is a market situation characterized by a large number of buyers and sellers, relative ease of entry and exit into the market, and perfect or imperfect knowledge. Its primary distinguishing feature from perfect competition is product differentiation. Each firm in the industry produces a slightly differentiated product. The products are close but not perfect substitutes for each other. Differentiating features may consist of differences in product quality, packaging, location of the seller, or the reputation of the seller. Any feature attached to the product or seller which causes a consumer to prefer one product or seller over another represents product differentiation regardless of how closely identical the products are.

Product differentiation introduces an element of monopoly into the market. Firms no larger are price takers and need not charge identical prices. Each firm is faced with its own downward sloping demand curve. The elasticity of this demand curve is determined by the degree of substitutability of the products. The more closely substitutable the products, the greater the elasticity of the demand function, and the less freedom the seller possesses for manipulating price without major shifts in the firm's sales. In the short-run the firm may be in a position to make excess or monopoly profits, but in the long-run these profits are likely to be competed away through the entrance of new firms.

Figure 3–2 shows a representative firm in monopolistic competition in the short and the long run. In both cases the firm, because of product differentiation, is faced with a downward sloping demand curve *D*, which is also the firm's average revenue curve. The corresponding marginal revenue is *MR*. Given the average and marginal cost curves, the firm maximizes profits where the marginal cost of the output equals the marginal revenue ($MC = MR$). In the short-run, a firm can conceivably earn excess profits as shown when output is OQ. The price or average revenue exceeds average cost by AB at output OQ, which is the net revenue or excess profits per unit. The total excess or monopoly profit is shown as the area $CPAB$.

While firms may enjoy excess profits in the short-run, they are unlikely to do so in the long-run. Given ease of entry into the industry, new firms will be attracted by the excess profits. As new firms enter and begin to supply closely substitutable products they will take customers away from existing firms, thereby causing the demand curve for those firms to fall and shift to the left. New firms will continue to be attracted into the industry until all firms are just making normal profits. Conditions for long-run equilibrium are $MC = MR$ with the demand curve tangent to the AC curve, depicting normal profits. Faced with the new competition, the output and prices of existing firms will fall to OQ_1 and OP_1 respectively. New entrants will provide consumers with a greater choice of near-identical products, which will likely cause the demand curves of all firms to flatten out or become more elastic.

In comparison to perfect competition, monopolistic competition provides consumers with less standardization and therefore greater choice of products, but at a cost of excess capacity for each firm (Q_1Q_2) and higher prices since firms are no longer producing at the minimum point of their average cost curves.

Firms in monopolistic competition usually engage in non-price competition such as advertising and marketing. Through advertising, firms attempt to shift their demand functions to the right and increase sales and, hopefully, profits. Advertising, however, adds to costs of production and has the effect of increasing average costs. In the end, this type of non-price competition may only contribute to higher costs and higher prices in an industry with no firm obtaining any significant advantage over its competitors.

Monopolistic competition is commonplace in the economy. Examples include most small retail outlets in a community such as corner variety stores, drug stores, fast food outlets, gasoline stations, motels and hotels, beauty salons and barber shops, lawyer services, dental services, clothing and shoe stores, hardware stores, video tape rental outlets, etc. As in the case of perfect competition, each seller is relatively small and there are a sufficient number of sellers to ensure that competition will maintain prices very close to costs. There is generally little fear of price gauging and, therefore, little need for government regulation to prevent excessive prices. While price instability is not common, when it does occur it is frequently short-lived as in the case of price wars between gasoline stations in a community.

Oligopoly

An oligopoly is a market dominated by a few large interdependent firms producing nearly identical or differentiated products. In an oligopoly there may be various numbers of firms of various sizes, but the industry is highly concentrated in that a small number of firms account for most of the industry's output. These few firms are large enough to wield market power and influence prices. There may be varying degrees of product differentiation in that in some industries the products are practically homogeneous while in other industries consumers consider the products to be considerably different. Furthermore, the large firms are interdependent in the sense that they watch each other closely, and actions by one to gain an advantage over competitors will trigger reactions by the competitors. Oligopoly is generally characterized by intense competition and rivalry, although most of the competition usually takes the form of non-price competition. Another characteristic of an oligopoly industry is the existence of significant barriers to entry into the industry, either natural or artificial.

In most modern market-oriented economies, oligopolies account for a large proportion of the economy's output. Oligopolies can be found in major manufacturing and service industries such as automobiles, petroleum, major household appliances, steel, tobacco and cigarettes, liquor, automobile rentals, computers, photographic equipment and supplies, aircraft, chemicals, movies, insurance, soft drinks, and banking and financial services.

Oligopoly behaviour may take a variety of forms. Pricing may feature competitive prices, monopolistic prices, price rigidity, and price leadership. Other practices may include collusion, extensive promotion and advertising campaigns, and a variety of strategies by firms to gain advantages over their competitors. Given this diverse potential behaviour, it is not possible to construct one general theory of oligopoly as is the case of perfect competition or pure monopoly. Consequently, a number of models of oligopoly behaviour have been developed, each based on different behavioural assumptions or observations. These include models featuring price leadership, collusion, cartels, and sales maximization, and models applying game theory. In addition, a popular model found in microeconomic theory is the kinked demand curve model of oligopoly. Some of these models are outlined in the following pages.

The kinked-demand curve model focuses on the commonly observed feature of price rigidity and the absence of price competition in some oligopoly industries. It is based on the assumption that if one firm reduces the price of its product, rival firms, fearing loss of customers and their share of the market, will immediately react with a price reduction on their products. On the other hand, it is assumed that if a firm increases its price, rivals are not likely to follow. This situation is illustrated in Figure 3–3.

In the model, the demand curve of the firm is represented as the kinked curve D_1KD_2. This curve actually consists of portions of two different demand curves, namely D_1d_1 and d_2D_2. D_1d_1 is drawn as an ordinary demand curve showing the relationship between prices and quantity when all other variables are held constant, including actions by other firms. On the other hand, d_2D_2 is drawn as the demand curve the firm would face when other factors vary. Price is assumed to be established at OP or at the point of the kink, K, and output at OQ. If the firm

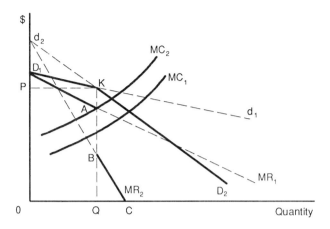

FIGURE 3–3:   *The Kinked-Demand Curve Model of Oligopoly*

reduces its price and rivals did not follow, it would slide down the portion of the demand curve Kd_1, rapidly increasing its sales at the expense of its rivals. But, given the keen competition in oligopoly, rival firms will immediately follow to avoid losing their share of the market. When all firms reduce prices, the initial price cutter finds that instead of following the fairly elastic Kd_1 portion of the demand curve D_1d_1, it will find itself on the inelastic demand curve KD_2, gaining little additional sales as prices drop. If on the other hand, a firm decided to increase price but rival firms do not follow, the firm will move along the elastic D_1K portion of the demand curve rapidly losing sales to its competitors. Had other firms followed as would be the practice in a situation of price leadership, the firm would have moved along the more inelastic portion Kd_2 of the demand curve d_2D_2. The expectation by all firms in the oligopoly that rivals will follow a price decrease but will not follow a price increase will serve to hold the price rigid at OP_1.

Even changes in costs of production may not cause prices and output to vary. This can be illustrated by introducing marginal cost and marginal revenue curves into the model. The marginal revenue curve corresponding to D_1d_1 is MR_1 and the marginal revenue curve corresponding to d_2D_2 is MR_2. However, the only relevant portions of MR_1 and MR_2 are those which correspond to D_1K and KD_2 portions of the demand curves. The marginal revenue curve D_1A corresponds to the demand curve D_1K, while BC corresponds to the demand curve KD_2. The resulting marginal revenue curve that corresponds to the kinked demand curve D_1KD_2 becomes D_1ABC, with a large gap at the point of the kink represented by

AB. If the marginal cost curve, MC_1, passes through this gap, the firm will produce output OQ and maximize profits. If marginal cost should increase to MC_2, intersecting the discontinuous marginal revenue curve at A or lower, the condition for maximizing profits, $MC = MR$, will not have changed and the firm will remain at output OQ and price OP. If, however, marginal cost increased to intersect MR_1 above A, firms will no longer be in a maximizing position. The result would likely be an increase in prices by all firms to establish a new kink along d_2K, and a new price which again would tend to remain rigid.

While the kinked-demand curve model is generally applied to explain price rigidity, the type of behaviour it depicts could also be applied to explain why in certain industries there is tendency to hold the "status quo" in products as opposed to frequent radical changes. Firms may fear to make sudden, drastic changes in their product lines because of uncertainty of consumer response, possible higher costs, and the reactions of competitors. If a firm drastically changes its product and the change meets consumer approval, rival firms will be quick to follow so that the increase in sales enjoyed by the first may be short-lived. In the process, however, the firm may have experienced large research, production, and advertising costs and if these are not offset by a permanent increase in demand, profits could fall. On the other hand, if consumers do not like the changed product, the firm in question could suffer a decline in demand, sales, and profits. In essence, the kinked-demand curve logic is that successful changes are followed and consequently produce only temporary advantages to the leader, and this can be applied to explain the tendency for gradual as opposed to radical changes in product lines from year to year in certain industries. This can be observed in the automobile industry where radical and costly model changes are uncommon, in the themes of motion pictures, in soft drink formulae, and in the products of competing fast food chains such as Macdonalds and Burger King.

Another model of oligopoly that may be applied to explain behaviour in certain industries is oligopoly characterized by price leadership. This is most commonly found in an industry dominated by a firm whose market power stems from its large size and substantial market share. The dominant firm tends to set the price and other firms in the industry follow. There is little fear by the dominant firm of losing a significant portion of its share of the market to competitors if they do not follow because these competitors are sufficiently small that they do not have the capacity to meet the demand. Prices need not be identical since there is product differentiation, but prices would tend to be within a certain range and move in the same direction. Examples of large firms capable of dominating an industry and exercising price leadership in Canada would include Northern Telecommunications, in the production of telecommunications equipment; International Nickel Co., in the production of nickel and copper; and, Steel Company of Canada, in the production of steel products. Price leaders in the United States which have exercised price leadership by virtue of their size include U.S. Steel in steel products, IBM in computers, AT&T in communications, and General Motors at one time in the automobile industry. With trade barriers continually falling, however, domestic companies are faced with increasing competition from foreign producers in a global market. This competition would appear to leave fewer opportunities for even the large, dominant firms in the domestic market to engage in price leadership.

In an industry where firms are about the same size, a firm may also be in a position to exercise price leadership by virtue of its relative efficiency. An efficient firm with lower costs of production than its competitors, and therefore lower prices, has some room to manoeuvre to increase price without fear of substantial loss of customers. Competitors may respond with increase of prices of their own to increase profit margins and still hold the relative price differential constant. On the other hand, the efficient firm is in a position to use predatory pricing to undercut its competitors and unless they can successfully reduce their costs they will be driven from the market. A price leader with a large market share is also in a position to use predatory pricing to drive out small competitors by lowering price below cost. The large firm will generally be capable of sustaining operating losses for a longer period than its small competitors. This type of predatory pricing to gain a market monopoly position has the potential of inviting government regulation or action to restore a competitive environment.

In addition to oligopoly behaviour depicted by the kinked-demand curve and price leadership, oligopoly may also be characterized by collusion where firms in the industry come together and arrange to control output and fix prices, with the objective of increasing their profits. There may be varying degrees of collusion ranging from the formal establishment of a powerful cartel to tacit collusion where firms through various signals tend to follow similar actions. Collusion is illegal in both Canada and the United States although tacit collusion is difficult to prove and consequently to prosecute under anti-trust laws. Various types of collusion are described later in the chapter.

Pure Monopoly

A pure monopoly is an industry in which there is only one supplier of a product or service for which there are no close substitutes. A monopoly firm is therefore the industry, and the demand curve for its product is the market demand curve. Since close substitutes are non-existent, the demand for the product of a pure monopolist will tend to be more inelastic than in the case of a firm in monopolistic competition or oligopoly. The monopoly will also be in a position to earn excess or monopoly profits as illustrated in Figure 3–4.

The monopolist will maximize profits where $MC = MR$, at output OQ and corresponding price OP. At OQ output, the price exceeds average cost by AB. Total excess profit is therefore the area $PABC$. This profit cannot be competed away because there are no close substitute products and therefore no competition in the industry. Indeed, the firm is in a position to set any price it desires. The effect of monopoly on economic efficiency is readily observable. Prices tend to be higher and quantity lower than would be the case if the firm operated in a

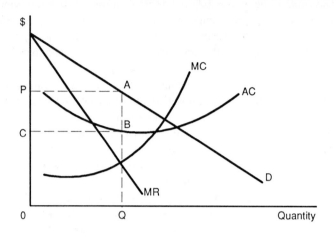

FIGURE 3–4:   *Pure Monopoly*

competitive market. The potential market power of a pure monopoly will invite close government scrutiny.

As with perfect competition, however, cases of pure monopoly are not very common. The few instances of industry approaching pure monopoly in Canada include the regional monopolies in telephone service. Bell Canada operates primarily without competition in providing local and long-distance telephone service in Ontario and Quebec, and provincial government-owned telephone systems enjoy a monopoly in certain other provinces. Various public utilities such as hydro-electric power, water supply, heating oil and gas, etc. can also be viewed as regional monopolies operating with little, if any, competition.

The majority of market structures in market-type economies lie somewhere between the two extremes of perfect competition and pure monopoly, exhibiting varying degrees of market imperfection and market concentration. The greater the imperfections and degree of concentration, the greater the potential for monopoly-type power to influence or control the market, including entry, output and prices. If economic efficiency and optimum resource allocation are desirable objectives and in the public interest, the greater the degree of monopoly power, the closer the government should scrutinize the practices of the industry to determine the need for corrective regulatory action. Appropriate corrective action may focus on modifying the behaviour of firms in an existing market or industry structure by regulating pricing policies and other practices. Alternatively, corrective action may take the form of attempting to change the market structure itself by focusing on the factors which gave rise to the specific market structure in question.

A number of factors or forces can be identified which determine the degree of competition, concentration, or monopolistic power in a market. The most significant factors are barriers to entry into a market. The more numerous and restrictive the barriers, the greater the potential for industry concentration and the exercise of monopoly power in any particular industry. Barriers to entry may be grouped into three categories. First are market or natural barriers which stem from the nature of the industry. Second are artificial barriers, which are restrictive competitive practices deliberately established by firms in the industry to discourage or prevent new entrants into the market and to eliminate weaker competitors. Finally, there may be legal barriers created by government. Each of these barriers may determine in varying degrees the number of firms, the degree of concentration, and the degree of competition in the market.

An objective of government regulation of markets or industry is to prevent and reduce barriers to entry where it is deemed desirable to enhance competition.

Market Barriers to Entry

There may be a number of elements inherent in a particular market which act to prevent new firms from easily entering that market. These so-called natural barriers are not created by the existing firms in the industry but rather stem from the nature of the product, the production process, the state of technology, or the availability of resources.

Entry may be prohibitive in an industry characterized by large economies of scale, where average and marginal costs of production decline as the size of the firm increases. One firm may be able to satisfy most or all of the demand near the low point of its long-run average cost. Small firms would not enjoy the low costs and therefore would be unable to compete and would be discouraged from entering the industry. This situation depicts the case of the natural monopoly which will be examined later in this chapter.

Closely associated with economies of scale are cost barriers. A new firm attempting to enter and compete successfully in a market may require huge investments in plant capacity in order to achieve the economies of large-scale production. Funds for such investments may be difficult to obtain. Even where extensive economies of scale are not present, an industry may be of the nature that any new entrant would face huge initial capital investments and start-up costs just to begin operations. Example of such industries include hydro-electric power, nuclear energy, railroad transportation, the automobile industry, pipelines, oil refineries, aerospace manufacturing, etc. The large initial capital requirements may effectively bar new firms from entering such industries.

Another effective barrier to entry is the control over the supply of necessary inputs by existing firms in an industry. The input may be a natural resource, such as high grade iron ore in the production of steel; or scarce and necessary technical skills such as those required in the development and manufacture of complex electronic equipment; or the ability to obtain readily large amounts of capital. Control by existing firms over a natural resource which is an essential ingredient of production will effectively bar new entrants from the industry. Similarly, firms possessing scarce, highly skilled technicians and state-of-the-art technology will have a clear competitive advantage over new firms attempting to enter and establish themselves in the industry. With respect to access to capital, well-established firms with a reputation of sound management and profitability and market-entrenched brand-name products will possess an advantage in capital markets over new firms with no track record of operations. They will have more ready access to capital for expansion, modernization, development of new products, etc. at lower rates of interest and, therefore, lower costs than new firms attempting to raise capital to establish production facilities and develop competitive products.

Product entrenchment can serve as a barrier to entry by creating difficulties for new firms to gain a foothold in the market with their products. If existing firms have established a reputation of superior products in the minds of consumers or they possess highly popular or familiar brand-name products, new entrants may face considerable difficulty in competing with these products and gaining a share of the market. This barrier may eventually be overcome by a new firm through extensive promotion and advertising of its products, but this would likely entail high costs.

These market barriers, as pointed out earlier, originate from the nature of the industry, usually from the production process, and vary among industries. They are generally high in the natural resource industries, such as mining, forestry, and oil and gas, and in certain capital-intensive manufacturing industries, such as automobiles and steel. They are frequently low in non-capital intensive industries including automobile parts, clothing, office supplies, and small retail and wholesale outlets. Government regulation to try to reduce these natural barriers and consequent industry concentration and monopoly elements may not be feasible or even desirable. Economies of scale, while potentially causing industry concentration and a high degree of monopoly power, do produce benefits in the form of reduced costs of production. In such instances, the objective of government scrutiny of the industry with a view to possible regulation would be to ensure that the benefits of economies of scale are passed to consumers in the form of reduced prices, and that the firm will not use its monopoly position to charge excessive prices to earn huge profits. Potential government involvement, therefore, would focus on the results (pricing practices, etc.) that these market barriers produce and attempt to modify these results as opposed to a focus on the barriers themselves. Government policies to reduce entry barriers are generally geared more to artificial barriers than natural barriers.

Artificial Entry Barriers and Restrictive Competitive Practices

Firms in an industry may deliberately resort to a number of restrictive practices which act as artificial barriers to prevent new firms from entering and becoming established in the industry. Firms may also employ restrictive practices designed to weed out competitors. Many such practices have been legislated illegal by government but, because proof of their existence may frequently be difficult, they may continue to be found in varying degrees. The most significant artificial barriers to entry involve collusion, predatory pricing, mergers, and franchise distribution.

Collusion

Collusion represents a situation in which the firms in an industry collaborate to gain some mutual advantage. Their objective is to control essential aspects of the market, including output, entry, and prices with the view of increasing profits. A variety of possible arrangements between firms represent collusion ranging from explicit, formal arrangements to very distant and informal connections. An extreme case of collusion is the creation of a cartel.

A cartel is a formal arrangement, either written or oral, between firms to control the price and total output of a product. The member firms agree not to compete with each other. Collectively they act as a pure monopoly. The total supply is restricted and remains fixed, and output quotas are established for each firm. The purpose of restricting supply is to increase price along with profits. The cartel provides the industry with potential power to prevent entry since new entrants may be barred from the cartel, and the cartel's control over price provides it with the opportunity to use predatory pricing to drive out new entrants before they can become established.

Cartels face administrative and legal difficulties. They are difficult to establish and to maintain over long periods. Each member must agree to accept a limited share of market sales and it may be difficult to obtain agreement on shares. Furthermore, there is a strong temptation for a firm to increase its profit by cheating and selling more than its allotted share. In view of their potential for market control and price gauging, both the Canadian and the U.S. governments have declared domestic cartels to be illegal.

Prime examples of cartel organizations are found in the international area where cartels have recently made headlines. The most familiar cartel has been the Organization of Petroleum Exporting Countries (OPEC). This cartel was formed by twelve, mostly Middle-East, oil producing countries in the early 1970s and succeeded in raising the price of crude petroleum from $4.00 per barrel in 1973 to over $30.00 per barrel by 1980. It produced huge profits for its member countries. OPEC was primarily an informal cartel in which target prices for different classes of petroleum, and quotas for member countries, were agreed at periodic meetings of the countries' representatives. Adherence to the established prices and quotas depended on the good will of member countries, as the organization lacked powers of enforcement and sanctions. The difficulty of maintaining an effective cartel over time has been demonstrated by OPEC. Faced with the development of new supplies of oil, particularly in the North Sea, and constant bickering among its members, OPEC has been on the verge of disintegration on numerous occasions. Its ability to control oil prices has steadily weakened and oil prices have declined substantially from their peak levels.

In 1972 Canada became a member of an international uranium cartel, along with France, Britain, South Africa and Australia. The cartel was established to prop up falling uranium prices, and succeeded in raising the price from $6.00 per lb. in 1971 to $40 per lb. by 1975.

In defence of cartels, industries have argued that they serve the public by providing price and output stability, reduce uncertainly for member firms, and avoid the cost of product promotion and advertising characteristic of competition. Opposition to cartels, of course, is directed at their monopoly powers, and potential excessive consumer prices and industry profits.

Where cartels are illegal, firms may attempt to reach more informal types of arrangements to control the market. These include the gathering of firms' representatives in back-room meetings at industry conventions, and similar behind-the-scene negotiations to restrict output, preserve market shares, and fix prices. Such arrangements are difficult to uncover and prosecute successfully under anti-combines or anti-trust laws. Firms may also engage in tacit or implicit collusion, which is even more difficult for government to control. Practices may include indirect signals between firms, such as a series of public statements emphasizing rising costs and the need to raise prices in the industry. Through such signals eventually a consensus may be reached on the actual amount of a price increase which all firms impose within a very short period of each other.

An industry dominated by a large firm may be characterized by price leadership, and in such cases it is very difficult to prove the existence of collusion. Practices within the industry may typify collusion without any deliberate collusion on the part of the firms. A price leader may increase prices citing increasing costs as the justification. Other firms may immediately follow, arguing that they are subjected to the same general cost conditions as the leading firm. On the other hand, should the dominant firm reduce prices, competitors who follow can argue that they are forced to also reduce prices in order to prevent loss of sales and their market shares. The firms in the industry may well have colluded to reduce prices to discourage new entrants, but this would be very difficult to prove.

Because collusion and price fixing are illegal in Canada and the U.S., firms and their executives in an industry usually take great care in their actions and associations so as not to be put in a position where it would appear that they were conspiring or making deals which could lead to charges of collusion. This was vividly illustrated by Lee Iaccoca in his autobiography. Iaccoca described that when he was an executive and later the president of Ford Motor Co., one of his neighbors in Detroit was the president of General Motors. Both took precautions not to be seen together or to socialize. When Iaccoca was fired by Ford, and was no longer involved with the automobile industry, the two neighbors began to associate with each other. Their socializing stopped and the two became strangers again the day Iaccoca was appointed as the president of Chrysler Corporation.[2]

Predatory Pricing

A firm in an industry may attempt to discourage other firms from entering the industry, or weaken competitors and force them out of the market, by applying temporary, selective price reductions. This is known as predatory pricing and may occur in a number of different situations. Where an industry features a few large firms and numerous smaller firms, the large firms may cut prices below costs so that all suffer losses. The larger firms, however, will generally possess the resources to sustain the losses for a longer period of time than the smaller firms. The latter will likely be forced into bankruptcy or be forced to merge with the larger firms. Such "shake-outs" are not uncommon, particularly in situations when numerous firms suddenly flock to an industry attracted by potential profits from new developments in that industry. This may be caused by a technological break-through resulting in new products and corresponding growing consumer demand. Large, well-established firms with huge resources, research facilities, marketing and distribution facilities have a distinct advantage over small, new entrants in such cases. An example is the desktop and home computer industry. As the market for small computers exploded in the 1980s, a large number of small firms attempted to become established in the industry, but were forced to compete with such giants as International Business Machines (IBM), to whom the home computer was but a small proportion of its business. While there has been no evidence of predatory price cutting by IBM, by virtue of its sheer size and the research and other resources at its disposal it has come to dominate the micro or desk-top computer industry and the IBM format has become fairly standard. A number of early upstarts quickly folded, although a few smaller, aggressive producers such as Apple and Commodore have managed to compete successfully and maintain a share of the market. IBM nevertheless would certainly have been in a position to apply predatory pricing to weed out competitors and prevent new competition from establishing in the industry.

Another situation of predatory pricing may take the form of selective price cutting on a regional base. For example, a large firm may sell a product nation-wide in the various geographical regions. It may enjoy a monopoly in some regions and competition from regional firms in others. The national firm is in a position to raise prices in the monopoly regions and to reduce prices in regions in which it faces competition. The firm may cut prices below costs in the competitive regions and subsidize the losses from monopoly profits in the non-competitive regions. Using such practices, the large firms can eliminate regional competition and also discourage new entrants. Similar predatory practices involving subsidization may be applied by a multi-product firm to prevent or eliminate competition from single-product firms.

---

[2] Lee Iacocca, *Iacocca: An Autobiography* (Toronto: Bantam Books, 1984), pp. 134–135.

In Canada, predatory pricing is a restrictive business practice prohibited by the Competition Act. Such practices, however, are difficult to police. It is often difficult for government to determine if prices were lowered by a firm in order to eliminate competition and to prevent entry, or whether prices were lowered by the firm simply to stay competitive.

Mergers

Mergers are a common practice and a major cause of market concentration. They also pose many problems for anti-competition enforcement and regulatory agencies. Three basic categories of mergers are vertical, horizontal, and con-glomerate mergers.

In a vertical merger, a number of firms merge or are absorbed to form one larger firm which controls the various stages of production, ranging from the production of raw materials, to the production of semi-finished goods, to the production of the finished product. For example, in the petroleum industry a firm, through mergers, could acquire interests in exploration, production of crude oil, refining petroleum, retailing gasoline, and the production of petroleum by-products such as plastics.

Horizontal mergers involve the merging of firms engaged in the same eco-nomic activity and usually in the same geographic market. Examples would include a taxi company buying out other taxi companies in a city, or a tool and die company buying up other tool and die companies in an area. The purchasing company might close some of the companies it purchased and expand its own production facilities to take advantage of any existing economies of scale.

In a conglomerate merger, firms producing different types of products and services amalgamate. For example, one holding company may acquire produc-tion and distribution interests in a variety of unrelated industries such as tobacco products, petroleum refining, beer and liquor production, transportation, commu-nications, etc.

Mergers have the potential of substantially reducing the number of firms and consequent competition in the industry and increasing the market power of the remaining firms. With increased market power comes the potential to establish barriers to entry and to limit competition.

During the latter part of the 1980s a tide of "merger mania" swept Canada, the United States and Europe. The period was characterized by numerous take-overs and buy-outs of small firms by larger firms, as well as of large firms by large firms. Horizontal mergers appeared to dominate, particularly in industries such as airlines, petroleum, mining, pipelines, and the food and beverage industries. The justification given for mergers in these areas was economies of scale and improved productivity. As well, some large conglomerates and multi-product firms began to spin off some of their peripheral activities and joint ventures with partners to achieve a greater degree of specialization in order to compete more effectively at the international level. In Europe, this trend in corporate strategy appears to have been triggered by the proposals for greater European economic integration by 1992, while in Canada it was argued that Canadian industries were preparing their corporate strategy to take advantage of and meet the challenge of Canada-United States free trade introduced in January, 1989.

Examples of recent mergers in Canada include the three significant merger proposals announced in early 1989. In the brewing industry, Molson Brewing Co. announced the acquisition of Carling O'Keefe Co. Combined, the two companies would control approximately 52 percent of the Canadian brewing market. In the airline industry, Pacific Western Airlines Corp., owner of Canadian Airlines, the second largest airline in Canada, acquired Wardair Ltd. the third largest airline. Imperial Oil Ltd. purchased Texaco Canada, increasing Imperial's share of the oil refining market to 28 percent of the Canadian total.

Marketing Franchises

Manufactured products such as automobiles, appliances, computer equipment, etc. are distributed and sold through franchised outlets. A distribution network may be very costly to establish and maintain. As a result, a potential new manufacturer may be discouraged from entering an industry because of lack of access to facilities for nationwide distribution, and therefore a potentially large market, and the manufacturer may not have sufficient resources to distribute its products. Under an exclusive distribution franchise, a distributor may agree to market the products of only one manufacturer, while the manufacturer in turn agrees that no one else in a particular area will be allowed to sell their product. Potential new producers are effectively barred from using the services of existing distributors, and consequently it becomes difficult and costly for them to enter the industry successfully. Fewer lines of marketed products imply less competition and increased market power of existing manufacturers and distributors to manipulate prices.

Legal Barriers

Restrictions on freedom of entry into industries may be deliberately created by government through their issue and control of licences, franchises, and permits to operate. Licences and permits for a particular activity may be restricted for a variety of reasons. The activity may involve the use of a scarce or limited resource, such as the broadcasting spectrum. Licences are restricted to avoid congestion of the broadcasting spectrum. Similarly, licences may restrict activity, such as hunting and fishing to certain periods of the year to preserve wildlife. Logging and lumbering activity is restricted to conserve forestry resources. The railroads, airlines, and trucking industries were all at one time protected by government from open entry and many public utilities have operated and continue to operate as government protected monopolies on the grounds that economies of scale prevailed in these industries. Urban planning dictates that the number and location of business establishments be governed by locally-issued licences and local zoning by-laws. The legal barriers are generally justified as serving the public interest and are a form of government regulation.

Government Policy and Artificial Barriers

In Canada, many restrictive competitive practices are prohibited under the Competition Act. Historically, these practices were governed by the Combines Investigation Act, which was first passed in 1889 and amended on numerous occasions over the years. The practices that were governed included collusive agreements, monopoly and mergers, price discrimination, predatory pricing, and misleading advertising. The Combines Investigation Act proved to be ineffective in preventing some of these practices. For example, under the jurisdiction of the Act the federal government did not obtain a single conviction in contested merger cases. The Act had placed the issue of mergers under the Criminal Code. Conviction required that it be proven beyond a reasonable doubt that the public had been adversely affected by the contested merger, which the government was unable to do in the mergers it contested.

In 1986, the federal government introduced the new Competition Act which placed the government's power to examine and curb mergers under civil law. A Bureau of Competition Policy was created as a combines watchdog to scrutinize and investigate proposed mergers and other potential competition-impeding actions by industry. Mergers which are found to be questionable are referred to a quasi-judicial Competition Tribunal for adjudication. The Tribunal has the authority to block or dissolve combinations, including mergers, acquisitions, or joint ventures, that are deemed to likely result in substantial lessening of competition in the market. In making a decision the Tribunal must determine if there are likely to be gains in efficiency that would exceed and offset the effects of reduced competition. The reduction in competition may be offset by economies of scale and increased productivity and consequent lower costs and prices. Not only would domestic consumers benefit, lower costs and prices would assist domestic firms to become more competitive in international markets and help domestic firms meet competition from foreign products in the domestic market, thereby boosting production and employment. Between 1986 and 1988 the Bureau investigated over 300 proposed mergers, blocking seven of them and forcing nine to be restructured.

The Act also contains provisions directed at firms or groups of firms deemed to have a dominant position in a given market. These provisions can potentially constrain firms in their decisions on pricing, promotion and distribution strategies. The Act prohibits all strategies designed to prevent the entry of new competitors, eliminate existing competitors, or restrict the degree of price competition in a market. Barred is the use of predatory pricing and other strategies for entry deterrence including buying up scarce resources to withhold them from competitors and forcing suppliers to refuse to sell to rival firms. The Act does permit, however, strategies that can be shown to derive from superior competitive performance. Firms demonstrating lower production costs or a superior product than their rivals are relatively free to pursue aggressive pricing and promotion strategies.

Penalties for violating the Act include fines, loss of licence, prohibiting orders limiting such practices in the future, and the break-up of a firm that has reached a dominant position through anti-competitive actions.

Contestable Markets: Freedom of Exit

A basic feature of the theory of perfect competition is mobility of resources, with a focus on freedom of entry of new firms into a market. In the literature on government regulation, entry into an industry has been a dominant issue. Much government regulation is geared to prohibit artificial barriers to entry which might lead to monopoly and monopoly practices. Even in an oligopolistic industry with a few large firms dominant, the industry will tend toward efficiency and toward cost-based pricing if the market is competitive or if there exists the threat of new entry into the market.

More recently, some attention in economic theory has been focused on the concept of contestable markets.[3] A market is considered to be contestable if there is relative ease of exit as well as ease of entry in the market. Freedom or ease of exit is defined as the ability to leave a market with little cost. This means that an entrepreneur or a firm that has invested capital to enter the industry can pull this capital out whenever desired. If a new entrant's initial investment in a market can be withdrawn or its assets can be readily resold without substantial loss, then the firm assumes little risk in entering the market. In such cases, an industry enjoying abnormal profits is vulnerable to "hit and run" tactics by potential new entrants. If the firms in an industry artificially maintain high market prices, and consequent high profits, outsiders can swoop in to capture the excess profits, and then retreat after prices drop and profits return to normal. This fear of a hit and run strategy, it is argued, will force existing firms in the industry to keep prices reasonably in line with their costs of production, and deter excessive profit-making.

An example of an industry exhibiting relative ease of entry and exit is the trucking industry. Even though the initial investment in trucks may be high, usually this investment may be recouped fairly quickly in the resale market for trucks. Trucks can be used in a variety of industries and therefore an active resale market can be expected. Ease of exit is assured in any industry which features assets that can be readily transferred from one industry to another or can be readily sold off without substantial loss.

It has been contended that greater attention should be given to the issue of freedom of exit than has been the case in the past. The government may introduce regulations to reduce or eliminate entry barriers, but entry of new firms and competition will not necessarily follow. New entrants will consider the risks involved, including the potential for failure. If an entrepreneur views the risk of failure to be high, with little hope for recouping the initial investment if the

---

[3] W.J. Baumol, J.C. Panzar and R.D. Willig, *Contestable Markets and the Theory of Industry Structure* (New York; Harcourt, Brace, Jovanovich, 1982).

entrepreneur is forced to withdraw from the industry, low entry barriers will likely be insufficient to entice the entrepreneur into the industry. Exit barriers must also be reduced. Since regulation basically offers little scope for lowering exit barriers, government could consider other policy instruments to reduce these exit barriers including generous deductions of losses for tax purposes.

Natural Monopoly

In economic theory, perfect competition is presented as the ideal market situation if the objective is economic efficiency or an optimum allocation of resources. In long-run equilibrium in this market all firms earn normal profits and operate at minimum average cost with price equal to marginal cost. Monopoly elements, on the other hand, lead to increased prices, excess capacity, and potential excess profits. It has, therefore, been argued that an objective of government regulatory policy should be to reduce monopoly elements and promote competition. While this is generally accepted, there exists an exception to the rule that, to achieve maximum efficiency and minimum prices, competition is preferred to monopoly. In the case of natural monopoly, greater economic efficiency with lower costs and prices can be achieved through monopoly than with competition.

Traditionally, natural monopoly has been defined as a industry where, due to economies of scale, one producer can meet the market demand and produce at lower costs than a number of competing firms. In this definition both supply and demand conditions are taken into consideration, with one firm capable of supplying enough to meet the market demand. The term "natural monopoly" originates from the fact that if a number of firms were competing in this industry, an inevitable outcome would be that one firm would come out on top. It is "natural" for one firm to make more efficient use of the resources than a number of small competing firms.

A basic characteristic of the traditionally defined natural monopoly is economies of scale or increasing returns to scale. The presence of economies of scale means that if all inputs in the production of a product are increased in a given proportion, the output will increase in a greater proportion. For example, if all inputs were increased by five percent, output would increase by a greater amount, lets say eight percent. The resulting increase in the output-input ratio reduces the unit costs of the product. Consider a simple example. Assume that 10 units each of labour and capital produce 100 units of output at a total cost of $800. The average cost per unit will be $8.00. Assume that labour and capital are doubled to 20 units each and output triples to 300 units. If the prices of units of labour and capital remain constant, total cost will double to $1600. But the average cost per unit of product will now be $1600/$300 = $6.40. Economies of scale are, therefore, characterized by decreasing long-run average costs of production.

Economies of scale can be attributed to a number of factors. These include specialization in the use of inputs, such as labour. As the scale of production is increased, there is greater opportunity for labour to become more highly special-

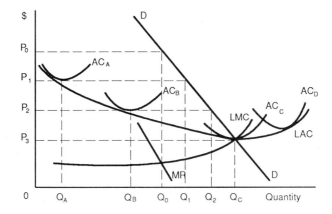

FIGURE 3–5: *Natural Monopoly*

ized and therefore more efficient. Certain techniques of production and certain equipment may become applicable to large-scale production whereas they may not be appropriate to production on a small scale. Some equipment and machinery may not be available in small units. Furthermore, large-scale production may offer increased opportunities for better organization of management and administration. Eventually, however, a firm may reach the point where economies of scale are exhausted, and further increases in size will lead to decreasing returns to scale and increased unit costs. This is likely to happen when the firm's size becomes so great that no further opportunity for specialization exists, and communications begin to break down resulting in managerial red tape, bottlenecks, delays in decision making and consequent increasing costs of production.

The model of natural monopoly is illustrated in Figure 3–5. Assume a given state of technology and a given market demand DD. Assume that four relatively small competing firms of equal size are supplying the market. Firm A is the representative firm with plant capacity to produce shown by the average cost curve AC_A. In equilibrium, this competitive industry of four firms would supply a total output of OQ_1, at price OP_1, with each firm making normal profits. Assume that economies of scale are realized as plant capacity is increased. Then two firms could conceivably supply the output to meet market demand, each firm with plant capacity and costs represented by AC_B. Each firm produces an amount equal to OQ_B for a market total of OQ_2 and market price OP_2. Further capacity expansion with continued economies of scale may lead to one large firm in the industry with average costs given by AC_C. Eventually, however, continued expansion produces decreasing returns to scale and increasing per unit costs as represented by average cost curve AC_D.

The expansion path of a firm exhibiting economies of scale is the envelope of the short-run cost curve representing varying plant size and is given by the long-run average cost curve LAC, and the corresponding long-run marginal cost curve LMC.

It has been contended that many public utilities are characterized by economies of scale and tend towards natural monopoly. These would include utilities such as telephone service, hydro-electric power, natural gas for home heating, and water supply, and may extend to services such as cable television. Some services which might exhibit economies on a smaller scale than others or be restricted to small geographical areas, have been termed regional monopolies.

While a natural monopoly industry is capable of producing at relatively low costs and prices, there is no assurance that it will. The industry faces no close substitutes or competition and is in a position to wield enormous market power. If the firm chose to maximize profits, its long-run equilibrium will be where $LMC = MR$ with output OQ_0 and price OP_0. Therefore, if natural monopoly is permitted to exist, the government must undertake to regulate the monopoly to ensure that it does not abuse its market power but rather acts in the public interest.

A great deal of controversy has surrounded the concept of natural monopoly. While the concept has been embodied for a considerable period of time in the standard theory of the firm or theory of markets, it is not without its critics. Questions have been raised about the actual existence of natural monopoly. There are problems in attempting to show conclusively, using empirical studies, the existence of economies of scale to the extent implied in natural monopoly. It has furthermore been contended that there is nothing natural about pure monopolies, and indeed where they exist they owe their status to man-made factors such as control over a scarce resource, a patent, a government licence, or government protection.

Economies of scale are difficult to verify empirically because they cannot be observed in isolation. It may be empirically shown that as a particular firm expanded and grew larger and larger its per unit costs declined. But, in addition to scale economies, other factors may have varied as the firm expanded and may have contributed to the decline in costs. One such factor is technological progress. Changing technology can lead to changes in the production process, the combination of factors used, more productive equipment and machinery, and changes in the output-input ratio. All can contribute to the reduction of per unit costs of production over time. If the impact of changing technology cannot be isolated, it is practically impossible to test for economies of scale.

Furthermore, new technology may enable a product to be produced efficiently on a small scale, so that a small firm may be able to produce just as efficiently as a large firm. In other words, under some given, constant technology an industry may exhibit economies of scale and tend towards a natural monopoly situation.

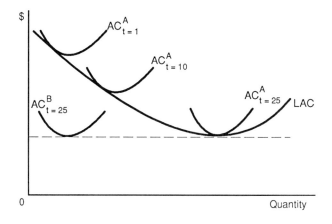

FIGURE 3–6: *Economies of Scale and Changing Technology*

But, just as the technology in question gave rise to the pure monopoly, changing technology can destroy the monopoly if it enables small firms to produce as efficiently as, and competitively with, the large monopoly.

The potential impact of changing technology over time is illustrated in Figure 3–6. Assume that over a twenty-five year period ($t = 25$) it is observed that average costs of Firm A declined from $AC^A_{t=1}$, to $AC^A_{t=25}$, following the long-run expansion path *LAC*. This decline may be attributed to economies of scale if technology is held constant and costs of factors have not declined. But technology does not remain constant. A dynamic economy is characterized by rapidly changing and improving technology. Consequently, a certain proportion of the low per unit costs represented by $AC^A_{t=25}$ may surely be attributed to technical progress. Furthermore, the technical changes may produce a situation represented by $AC^B_{t=25}$ in which a relatively small firm, Firm B, with capacity no greater than that possessed by Firm A in period $t = 1$, can now produce at low costs comparable to the costs of the large-scale Firm A. Assuming Firm A had enjoyed a natural monopoly position, this position will now be threatened by new entrants such as Firm B, applying the most modern technology.

The implications of changing technology for government regulation cannot be ignored. Numerous public utilities are viewed as natural monopolies, are protected from potential new entrants, and are regulated. But the conditions under which they were first designated as possessing economies of scale and therefore natural monopolies may be drastically altered over time by technology. With the new technology these industries might conceivably operate as efficiently in a competitive market, in which case competition could be substituted for monopoly and government regulation.

Another difficulty with the traditional concept of natural monopoly involves multiple products. Economies of scale, producing natural monopolies, imply one product or service, when in reality many modern-day large firms produce more than one product. The telephone industry, for example, produces a variety of communications equipment and provides a variety of communications services. With multiple products there is no longer a common unit of output. The firm's average cost curve reflects the average cost of producing the combination of the various products. But a small firm may be just as efficient in producing one of these products as the large firm. This was clearly demonstrated in the telephone industry in Canada and the U.S. The existing monopolies claimed economies of scale in both equipment and services and maintained that these economies gave the industries natural monopoly status. Yet, when the telephone equipment industry was opened to competition, small new manufacturing firms entered and by specializing in selective communications equipment they were able to compete successfully with the large existing monopolies.

Recognition of the problems that multi-production presented to the traditional natural monopoly concept based on economies of scale led to some attempts to redefine natural monopoly on the basis of economies of scope.[4] Certain equipment can be used for producing a variety of products, and contributes to a decreasing cost function when common costs of producing the several products are spread over the products. Baumol viewed an industry as a natural monopoly if a single firm was capable of producing the industry's output more efficiently than a combination of small firms. In this situation, the total costs of a multi-output firm for a given level and mix of output would be lower than the total costs if those same outputs were produced by a number of firms each producing one of the outputs.

This concept of natural monopoly, however, makes no reference to market size and demand or to the market power of the firm. The basic element in monopoly is market power and the ability to prevent entry into the market. Without this power there may exist the threat of firms entering with close substitutes and undermining the monopoly position of the multi-product firm. The new entrant may specialize in one of the line of products and take advantage of any existing economies of scale to manufacture the product as cheaply as the multi-product firm. Therefore, while a multi-product firm may enjoy economies of scope this does not necessarily provide the firm with the market power essential for monopoly status. If entry is not made prohibitive, the firm will not possess

---

[4] W.J. Baumol, "On the Proper Tests for Natural Monopoly in a Multi-Product Industry," *American Economic Review*, December 1977, pp. 809–822. See also, R.D. Willig, "Multi-Product Technology and Market Structure," *American Economic Review*, May 1979, pp. 346–351; and, K.D. Boyer, "Testing the Applicability of the Natural Monopoly Concept" in W. Sichel and T.G. Gies (eds), *Applications of Economic Principles in Public Utility Industries* (University of Michigan, 1981), Ch. 1.

absolute monopoly or market powers, and there will be potential for competition similar to the situation illustrated in Figure 3–6 where a small firm competes successfully with a large firm.

Other attempts have been made to redefine natural monopoly on the basis of unacceptable levels of market power by one firm. In such cases, government regulation would be required to ensure that these powers are not used to the detriment of the public interest. Questions are raised, however, regarding the definition of unacceptable levels of market power and how it would be recognized.

In summary, the concept of natural monopoly and the theory of natural monopoly remain in an unsatisfactory state. The traditional concept, based on economies of scale, continues to form part of the economics of market structures. While the concept remains useful in theoretically identifying a particular type of monopoly, its limitations must be recognized as a practical justification for maintaining regulated monopolies as opposed to promoting competition.

4

REGULATORY PRICING POLICIES

G overnments are actively involved in regulating prices or rates in certain industries. These are usually public utilities which are deemed to provide essential public goods and services. They are industries which also tend to oligopoly or monopoly structures. Some have been characterized as natural monopolies, some owe their monopoly positions to government protection, and others are government owned and operated. They include telephone services, hydro-electric power, urban water supply, natural gas supply, and areas in the transportation sector such as railways and airlines. Their position of, or tendency towards, monopoly and restricted competition creates potential for various monopoly pricing and operating practices. Government regulation has been judged necessary to prevent or restrict such practices.

An issue which must be addressed when government undertakes to regulate prices or rates of monopoly-type industries and public utilities is the determination of an appropriate pricing policy. A wide range of pricing policies is available for use by regulatory agencies. This chapter examines some of these pricing policies.[1]

Profit-Maximization Pricing

A regulatory agency responsible for regulating prices in a particular industry could conceivably permit that industry to operate as it normally would in the market. The firms in the industry, guided by the profit-maximization motive, would equate marginal cost with marginal revenue and set the price and output accordingly. In the unlikely case of perfect competition, all firms would produce at minimum average cost and just make normal profits. Where monopolistic and oligopolistic elements are present and each firm faces a downward sloping demand curve for its product, however, there may be considerable potential for a firm to set prices above costs and earn excess profits. This is particularly true in the case of pure or natural monopoly where no close substitutes exist and demand is inelastic. (Refer to Figure 3–4.) In such cases, profit-maximization pricing is neither economically efficient nor socially desirable. On the assump-

---

[1] These pricing policy models are part of standard microeconomic theory and can be found in various versions in most microeconomics textbooks.

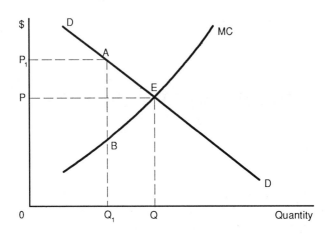

FIGURE 4–1: *Marginal Cost Pricing*

tion that regulatory agencies exist to regulate in the public interest, this pricing policy cannot be viewed as a practical option.

Marginal Cost Pricing

In a marginal cost pricing policy, the price is equated to marginal cost. As a general rule, marginal cost pricing results in an efficient allocation of resources for society. This is illustrated in Figure 4-1. In the model, the demand or average revenue curve DD and the marginal cost curves intersect at E. Price OP equals marginal cost QE with equilibrium output OQ. Marginal cost measures the addition to total cost of producing one additional unit of output. Price measures the marginal benefit or the addition to total benefit of consumers from the production and consumption of this additional unit. At an output less than OQ, for example OQ_1, the benefit of the marginal unit equals Q_1A while the addition to total cost in producing that unit equals Q_1B. At OQ_1 the net benefit to society from the marginal unit equals AB. Additional net benefits can be realized by expanding output, to Q. But beyond output OQ, the marginal cost exceeds price and results in a net loss of welfare to society. Total net benefit to society is maximized at output OQ where marginal cost equals price.

There are a number of problems, however, with marginal cost pricing which limit its use in practice. First, in certain situations marginal cost pricing may lead to an unsustainable industry. This will occur if the firm is a monopoly and is operating within the declining portion of its average cost curve where marginal cost is below average cost. As illustrated in Figure 4–2, demand intersects the MC curve below AC and results in a price OP and output OQ. The price is less

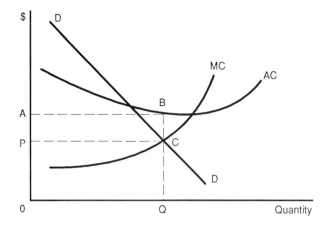

FIGURE 4–2: *Loss from Marginal Cost Pricing*

than the average cost, and produces a loss of *BC* per unit or a total loss of *PABC*. In this situation a regulatory policy of marginal cost pricing would force the firm to close unless the government agrees to cover the loss with a subsidy to the firm. The problem with a government subsidy, however, is that it would likely have to be financed by taxation. The taxpaying members of society would in effect be subsidizing the consumers of the product of this firm. This raises the question of equity or fairness in that consumers of this product are subsidized while other consumers do not receive such benefits. Furthermore, subsidies may produce inefficiencies. If the firm knows that its losses will be covered by a subsidy, there is little incentive for the firm to operate at maximum efficiency and minimize costs of production.

Instead of resulting in a loss for the firm, marginal cost pricing could produce the opposite effect and generate large profits. This situation would arise if the demand and marginal cost curves intersected well above the average cost curve. As with non-regulated firms, a government corporation income tax would reduce these excess profits. Alternatively, the regulatory agency could encourage the firm to increase output capacity and move the average and marginal cost curves to the right. This would be desirable if the firm is characterized by constant or increasing returns to scale as it would lead to increased output and a fall in price, and could potentially achieve the optimum condition where $P = MC = minimum\ AC$.

Still other problems may arise with marginal cost pricing. This policy assumes that the necessary information is available to determine the marginal costs of production. In practice, it may be difficult to determine marginal costs. Furthermore, the level of output and the marginal cost may frequently change in

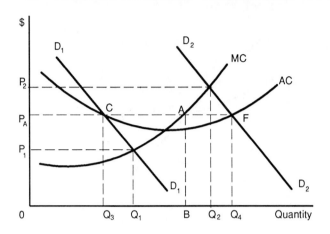

FIGURE 4–3:   *Long-run Incremental Cost Pricing*

response to fluctuations in demand. Demand for certain goods and services may fluctuate widely from period to period as in the case of changing seasonal demand. A marginal cost pricing policy would require the determination of marginal cost of production in each period, and a corresponding adjustment in price. This could produce a considerable degree of price instability.

A final difficulty with marginal cost pricing occurs when a firm produces several products, and some of its equipment or resources are used in the production of more than one product. In determining the marginal cost of each product, the common costs must be apportioned between the various products. This requires the development of some appropriate apportioning procedure by which the contribution of common resources to each product can be assessed.

These practical difficulties and limitations of marginal cost pricing have led to the development and use of a number of alternative pricing policies.

Long-Run Incremental Cost Pricing

In this pricing policy the marginal cost is averaged over a block of output and price is set equal to the average marginal cost. It is a policy designed to cope with periodic shifts in demand, and to eliminate the need to continually adjust price to equal marginal cost in any particular period. Figure 4–3 shows demand curves for two different periods. D_1D_1 may be the demand for the product in the winter season and D_2D_2 may be the demand in the summer. Marginal cost pricing with demand D_1D_1 establishes price and output OP_1 and OQ_1 respectively. The corresponding price and output with D_2D_2 is OP_2 and OQ_2. To avoid the need to change prices from period to period, the regulatory agency could

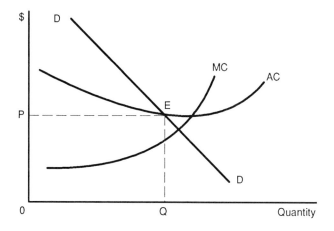

FIGURE 4–4: *Average Cost Pricing*

average the marginal costs over the block of output Q_1Q_2. Assume this average is AB. Price is then set equal to AB or OP_A. At this price, the amount produced and sold in Period 1 is OQ_3 and the amount sold in Period 2 is OQ_4. Total cost of production in the two periods is $OP_ACQ_3 + OP_AFQ_4$, the sum of which in this particular case is equal to total revenue. The average marginal cost could, of course, result in a price that might produce profits in both periods, or a loss in one period and a profit in the other.

Average Cost Pricing

In average cost pricing the price is equated to average cost, which includes normal profits. As illustrated in Figure 4–4, the price is determined at point E the intersection of the demand curve and the average cost curve of the firm. At price OP and output OQ, total cost equals total revenue and the firm just earns normal profits. This pricing policy avoids the problem of losses such as those created by marginal cost pricing in the case of a decreasing cost industry. Average cost pricing has also been referred to as full cost pricing.

When the firm is operating in the range of increasing average cost, average cost pricing leads to an output level greater than the optimal level in terms of social welfare maximization. Output will be carried to levels where marginal cost exceeds price, that is, where the costs to society of producing an additional unit exceed the benefits to society from that unit. Total net benefit to society will consequently be reduced. In deciding between a policy of marginal cost pricing and average cost pricing, the regulatory agency will have to consider the advantages and disadvantages and the problems associated with each policy.

Fully-distributed Cost Pricing

A multi-product firm may use particular assets and equipment to produce more than one product. The variable costs of producing each product may be determined, but if prices are set to equate the variable marginal or average costs, the costs common to the products will remain uncovered. There is a need to distribute or allocate the common costs of production to the various products.

One method of allocation is to distribute the common costs to the products in proportion to the incremental or marginal costs of each. Assume that a firm produces two products, A and B in which $MC_A = \$4.00$ and $MC_B = \$8.00$ and the common cost equals $6.00. If the common cost was allocated in proportion to the marginal costs, it would be allocated in a two to one ratio with $2.00 distributed to product A, and $4.00 distributed to product B. Incorporating these costs in a marginal cost pricing policy would produce a price of $6.00 for A and $12.00 for B. In effect, the common costs have been fully distributed among the products.

Benchmark Pricing

A situation may exist in which a firm produces a large number of products but the prices of only a few are regulated. Regulation of one of the products, for instance, employing a cost-based pricing policy would require the determination of the costs of producing that one particular product, including a portion of the common capital, marketing, and research costs. In practice, it is difficult to calculate marginal costs of production, and frequently the apportionment of common costs may be arbitrary and not adequately reflect the contribution of common facilities in the production of a particular product.

An alternative to cost-based pricing policies is benchmark pricing in which prices are set through the application of some established reference price. The benchmark price could be the average price charged in an earlier period, the prices of similar lines of products in the domestic market, the prices of similar products in the international market, or some combination of prices.

An example of benchmark pricing is found in the federal government regulation of patented medicines.[2] A patent granted by the government gives an inventor or developer of a new product the exclusive right to manufacture and market the product for a specific period of time. The grant of monopoly status is intended to encourage research and invention in goods and services, but at the same time monopoly creates potential for charging excessive prices for the potential products. In 1987 Parliament enacted amendments to the Patent Act to provide a greater degree of protection for consumers of pharmaceutical products.

---

[2] Canada, Patented Medicine Prices Review Board, *Bulletin*, Issue No. 1, July 1988; Issue No. 3, July 1989 (Ottawa), and *Statutes of Canada*, 35–36 Elizabeth II, Patent Act (Ottawa: Queen's Printer, 1987).

The amendments established the Patented Medicine Prices Review Board which was to safeguard against excessive prices for patented medicines that could result from the market power afforded patentees. The Board was authorized to review the prices of patented medicines in Canada and to protect consumer interests in cases where prices were found to be excessive. In this function, the Act empowers the Board to establish regulations for the disclosure of information on costs, prices, marketing, and other aspect of patented medicines. Where excessive prices are suspected, the Board initiates a hearing, and if it is determined that prices are indeed excessive, the Board could require the patentee to reduce the price of the medicine in question or the Board could remove the restrictions on the sale of the product that the patent provides.

A benchmark price is established as the criterion for determining whether the price of a patented medicine is excessive. The benchmark price may be historical or currently-determined. Historical benchmark prices are applied to patented medicines first marketed in Canada prior to the proclamation of the amendments to the Patent Act on December, 1987. They are the prices that prevailed at the time of proclamation, adjusted by the consumer price index (CPI). If the current price is greater than the CPI-adjusted price, the current price will be determined to be excessive.

Historical benchmark prices are not available in case of patented medicines first marketed after December, 1987. In the absence of historical prices, the Prices Review Board establishes a benchmark price based on international prices and what is known as the therapeutically-adjusted price of the patented medicine. The latter is the price of the medicine in question compared with the prices of other medicines in the same therapeutic class, that is, other medicines available in Canada which treat the same disease or symptoms. Prices are normally expressed as the price per kilogram of the active ingredient. Where a new product is introduced in which there is no existing therapeutic class in Canada, the Board relies primarily on the median international price as the benchmark. If neither international prices nor therapeutically-adjusted prices are available, the Board will make its decision on whether prices are excessive on the basis of the costs of producing and marketing the medicine. The Board will then request comprehensive cost information from the patentee, including product line costs and the procedures for allocating fixed and common costs among the various products. In general, however, the Board only uses a cost-based pricing policy in determining whether prices are excessive when benchmark prices cannot be established.

Price Discrimination

Price discrimination involves the sale by a firm of its product in two or more markets at different prices. These markets must be separated, however, with no possible resale between the markets by buyers. Resale between markets would lead to arbitrage and eventually prices in all of the markets would be equalized.

Markets may be separated by class of user, by the amount of the good or service used, and by the time factor in the use of the good or service. These

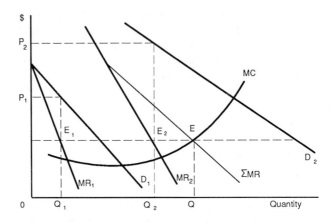

FIGURE 4–5:   *Price Discrimination to Maximize Net Revenue*

differences relating to buyers will produce different price elasticities of demand in the markets and make possible considerable discrepancies in prices.

Price discrimination may be applied by a regulatory agency for a variety of purposes. It may be applied to regulate and ration use of facilities, to enable a public utility or a firm to increase revenues, to attain greater efficiency, to achieve equity objectives and extend the use of facilities, and for conservation purposes. Methods of price discrimination, and rationale for this type of pricing policy, are examined below.

Price Discrimination to Maximize Net Revenues

Assume in Figure 4–5 that a firm produces a product for sale in two separate markets represented by demand curves D_1 and D_2. The optimum output of the firm is determined by equating the marginal cost of production with aggregate marginal revenue in the two markets. In this determination, the marginal revenues in Markets 1 and 2 are summed horizontally to derive ΣMR. Output is established were $MC = \Sigma MR$ at OQ. The marginal cost at output OQ equals QE. The amount sold in market 1 equals OQ_1 where $MC = MR_1$ and the amount sold in Market 2 equals OQ_2, where $MC = MR_2$, and $OQ_1 + OQ_2 = OQ$. Equilibrium in production and in each market is achieved when $MC = \Sigma MR = MR_1 = MR_2$ at points E, E_1 and E_2 respectively. Given the demand curves, price will be set at OP_1 in Market 1 and at OP_2 in Market 2 and the price difference equals P_1P_2.

That this is an optimum position can be shown by varying the amounts sold in the two markets. Assume that, given output OQ and marginal cost QE, sales are increased in Market 1, with a corresponding decrease in Market 2 causing

$MR_1 < MC$, and $MR_2 > MC$. This would not be a profit-maximization position, since total net revenues could be increased by curtailing sales in Market 1 where there is a marginal net loss, and increasing sales in Market 2 where marginal net revenue is positive.

Value of Service Pricing

This is a general concept implying that a seller charge what the market will bear. The service provided by a firm may be valued differently in two separate markets, which will be reflected by different price elasticities of demand. In a market characterized by a highly inelastic demand the product is important to the buyers and there are no close substitutes. In such a situation, a relatively high price may be charged with relatively little reduction in sales. On the other hand, in a market characterized by an elastic demand, there will be a number of close substitutes so that any attempt by the firm to raise prices to a high level will result in a drastic reduction in sales. A firm that has some indication of the price elasticities of demand in its markets can, therefore, charge a relatively high price in the inelastic market and a relatively low price in the elastic market.

This type of pricing is common in many regulated public utilities as well as in other industries. In the telephone industry, for example, if it is determined that telephone service is more important to business than it is to households, a higher price may be set for commercial use of telephone service then for residential use. Without telephone service, a firm might find it difficult and costly to operate, whereby telephone service is generally not considered absolutely essential to households. Pricing practices in the airline industry have also recognized differences in elasticities of demand for passenger services of different groups of travellers. Families travelling on vacation over a two or three week period usually have substitute means of travel at their disposal such as automobile, bus, and train. Business executives, on the other hand, are likely the travellers taking trips of one or two days duration and for whom time is important. Airline rates for travel of short duration can, therefore, be set higher without a major loss of potential passengers than rates for travel for longer duration, in recognition of the difficult price elasticities of demand for the two groups of travellers.

Value of service pricing need not follow any particular formula or precise rule but may simply be based on a seller's perception of the price elasticities in the various markets, and may be set on a trial and error basis. One attempt, however, to establish a formula for establishing prices in markets with different price elasticities of demand is inverse elasticity pricing or Ramsey pricing.

Inverse Elasticity Pricing Rule or Ramsey Pricing

This pricing rule originated with the work of economist and mathematician Frank Ramsey in 1927. Ramsey's work related to issues in taxation and the question of imposing taxes on goods and services with different price elasticities of demand so as to minimize the net welfare loss to society from taxation. As applied to pricing and the regulation of prices, the Ramsey criteria dictates that, when a good is sold in separated markets, the greater the inelasticity of demand in a market, the higher the relative price.

More specifically, the rule is generally viewed as applicable in an industry where marginal cost pricing leads to an operating loss. It may be recognized by a regulating agency that price will have to be set above marginal cost to permit a firm to break even. But how much higher than marginal cost should the price be set, and if the firm is selling in more than one market what should be the relative prices in each market? According to the inverse elasticity pricing rule, where prices must be set above marginal cost to permit a firm to break even, the relative retail mark-up of price to marginal cost should be inversely related to the product's own price elasticity of demand. In other words, the smaller the coefficient of price elasticity of demand (i.e. the more inelastic the demand), the greater the mark-up and therefore the divergence of price from marginal cost.

The inverse elasticity pricing rule is related to a Ramsey number which is the price mark-up multiplied by the coefficient of price elasticity, and is shown

$$R = \frac{P - MC}{P} \, e$$

where R = Ramsey Number
    P = Price
    MC = Marginal cost of production
    e = coefficient of price elasticity of demand

Where a firm sells its product in more than one market and the markets are not interdependent, optimal pricing requires that the Ramsey number be the same in all markets. Given the marginal cost of production and the sale of the product in two markets, Market 1 and Market 2 with prices P_1 and P_2 and coefficients of price elasticity e_1 and e_2, then

$$R = \frac{P_1 - MC}{P_1} \, e_1 = \frac{P_2 - MC}{P_2} \, e_2$$

It follows that

$$\frac{\dfrac{P_1 - MC}{P_1}}{\dfrac{P_2 - MC}{P_2}} = \frac{e_2}{e_1}$$

In other words, the ratio of the price markup in the two markets is equal to the inverse of the coefficients of the price elasticities of demand of the two markets.

Consider a numerical example where $MC = \$4.00$, $P_1 = \$5.00$, $e_1 = .5$, and $e_2 = 1.5$. What should be the level of P_2? Solving for P_2 in the above equation yields $P_2 = \$4.28$. The mark-up in Market 1 as a percentage of the retail price in that market is 20 percent, or three times greater than the mark-up in Market 2,

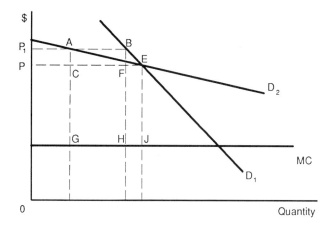

FIGURE 4–6: *Price Discrimination, Elasticity and Welfare*

which is approximately 6.5 percent. This corresponds to the inverse of the price elasticities where the coefficient of elasticity in Market 2 is three times as great as the coefficient of elasticity in Market 1. In this example the Ramsey number equals .1 in each market.

Applying price discrimination to two markets using Ramsey pricing enables a firm to increase prices to break even and at the same time minimize the net loss of welfare to society from the price increases. This is illustrated in Figure 4–6 where two segments of demand curves D_1 and D_2 intersect at E and price is assumed to be OP.[3] If demand is the relatively inelastic demand curve D_1, an increase in price to OP_1 results in a loss of consumers surplus of PP_1BE. Net revenue to the seller, however, will increase by the amount PP_1BF minus $FEJH$. The portion of net revenue gain, PP_1BF, offsets a portion of consumers' surplus loss equal to PP_1BF, leaving a net loss of consumers' surplus of BEF. This combines with revenue loss for a total net loss to society equal to $BEJH$.

With the relatively elastic demand curve D_2, the loss of consumers' surplus from the price increase is PP_1AE. The net gain in revenue to the seller is $PP_1AC - CEJG$. The net reduction in welfare to society is the area $AEJG$. This is much greater than the loss of $BEJH$ incurred under the inelastic demand curve D_1. The total net loss in welfare to society could be reduced by increasing the price in the inelastic market D_1 above OP_1 and reducing the price in the elastic

---

[3] This analysis is based on W.J. Baumol and D. Bradford, "Optimal Departures From Marginal Cost Pricing," *American Economic Review*, Vol. LX, No. 3, June, 1970, pp. 265–283.

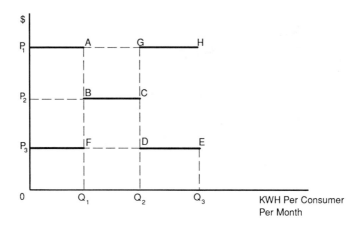

FIGURE 4–7:   *Block Pricing of Hydro Electric Power*

market D_2 below OP_1. This loss to society would be minimized when the aggregate reduction in net revenue and consumers' surplus in Market 1 is equal to that in Market 2.

Block Pricing

Another form of price discrimination involves the sale of a good or service in blocks. This form of pricing is commonly used by public utilities such as electricity, gas, and water supply. Figure 4–7 illustrates two forms of block pricing of hydro-electric power. Declining block pricing is represented by price OP_1 for OQ_1 kilowatt hours per month; price OP_2 for the amount Q_1Q_2; and, price OP_3 for the amount Q_2Q_3, and is illustrated by the steps P_1ABCDE. Under this system, the more electricity used by a consumer per month, the lower is the price for additional amounts or blocks. This system is designed to encourage consumption and would be applied if the hydro utility had excess capacity and energy was abundant. The opposite is an inverted block pricing policy, illustrated by the steps OP_3FBCGH. Prices rise as additional blocks are consumed. This pricing scheme is designed to discourage consumption and promote conservation of hydro-electric energy.

Ontario Hydro, which provides electricity in the Province of Ontario employs a declining block pricing policy. Recent residential by-monthly rates amounted to 6.15 cents per kwh for the first 500 kwh, and 4.02 cents per kwh for amounts exceeding 500 kwh.

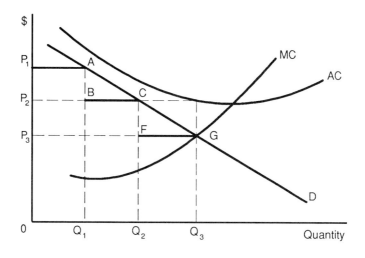

FIGURE 4–8: *Block Pricing to Cover Operating Losses*

Union Gas Ltd. also employs a declining block pricing system for its supply of natural gas for commercial and household use. Recent Union Gas rates for residential customers included a monthly fixed charge of $6.25 plus 20.2 cents per cubic meter for the first 1400 cubic meters consumed per month; 17.5 cents per cubic meter for the next 4600 cubic meters; 16.75 cents for the next 124,000 cubic meters; 16.58 cents for the next 270,000 cubic meters; and, 16.25 cents for consumption exceeding 400,000 cubic meters per month.

A strong case can be made for employing block pricing in a public utility experiencing long-run declining costs. Earlier it was shown how marginal cost pricing could result in a loss to the firm when demand intersects marginal cost below the average cost. This loss could be covered by employing a system of declining block pricing. A price above average cost could be charged for the first block of units consumed, with marginal cost pricing for the remaining block of units. The average price for the total amount consumed could be sufficient to cover the average cost of producing the total output. Similarly, as illustrated in Figure 4–8, a policy of block pricing could permit an otherwise unprofitable or untenable utility to break even and continue in operation. In Figure 4–8, average cost is shown to be everywhere above the demand curve. No single price for the output of this utility would be sufficient to cover the average cost of production. Multiple pricing over blocks of output, however, could conceivably produce an average price that would cover the average cost. For output OQ_3 in the model, the firm would charge price OP_1 for the block OQ_1; price OP_2 for block Q_1Q_2; and, price OP_3 or marginal cost price for the remaining block Q_2Q_3. The average

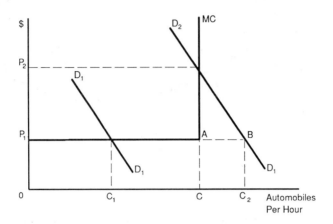

FIGURE 4–9:   *Peak-Load Pricing: A Traffic Bridge*

price or revenue would equal total revenue $OP_1AQ_1 + Q_1BCQ_2 + Q_2FGQ_3$ divided by output OQ_3. Assuming the average price equalled OP_2, it would be sufficient to cover the average cost of producing output OQ_3, enabling the firm to break even and continue in operation.

Peak-Load Pricing

Facilities such as public utilities may have fixed or limited capacity in the short run. Demand for services may vary from period to period and may in some periods exceed the firm's capacity to supply sufficient services to meet the demand. In such instances, regulatory agencies may use prices to regulate the use of the facility and to ration the facility during periods of peak or excessive demand. Such a pricing policy is known as peak-load pricing and is illustrated in Figure 4–9.

Assume that the facility is a traffic bridge with a maximum capacity of handling OC automobiles per hour. Assume further that the marginal cost of handling traffic up to the point of capacity is constant as represented by the line P_1A. Once capacity OC is reached, the bridge cannot accommodate any additional automobiles in the short run at any cost and therefore the marginal cost curve becomes vertical. Assume that D_1D_1 represents the demand by automobile drivers in the non-rush hour of traffic or the off-peak period, while D_2D_2 represents demand in the hour of maximum demand or the peak period. Applying a policy of marginal cost pricing in the off-peak period results in price or a toll of OP_1 per automobile, with OC_1 number of automobiles using the bridge. At this price during the peak-period, however, OC_2 number of drivers will wish to use the bridge. The amount demanded exceeds capacity by CC_2. This excess demand will likely lead to traffic congestion, delays, inconvenience to the drivers, and will increase the potential for automobile accidents. The solution to this problem of excess demand in the peak-period is to increase the toll to OP_2, where D_2D_2 intersects the *MC* curve in its vertical section, and the amount demanded equals the capacity of the bridge. The increased price acts to ration the limited capacity of the bridge and to eliminate the excess demand. As the price rises some automobile drivers who are not prepared to pay the higher prices will either find alternative facilities or if they have flexibility will switch to some other hour to cross the bridge.

Pricing and Cross-Subsidization

It is not uncommon in the regulation of public utilities, where a utility provides multi-services or services in various areas, for the regulatory agency to permit prices for some services or is some areas to be set well above costs while other prices are kept below costs. Profits in the former are then applied to cover losses in the latter. This is known as cross-subsidization of services.

Cross-subsidization has been applied extensively in the provision of telephone services. Regulatory agencies have permitted the telephone company to charge prices in excess of costs for long-distance service. But, in an attempt to keep local telephone rates sufficiently low to enable all households to afford local telephone service, local telephone service has traditionally been priced below the costs incurred in providing local service. The excess profits from long-distance service were then applied to cover the losses incurred in providing local service. A similar type of cross-subsidization has been employed in the provision of urban and rural telephone service. The high volume of telephone use within and between large urban areas results in relatively low average costs of telephone service per user and consequently this would enable the telephone company to charge urban users relatively low rates. On the other hand, in the sparsely-populated rural areas the average cost of providing telephone service is much greater than in urban areas. If the objective of a regulatory agency is universal telephone service at uniform prices, the price of the service in rural areas should not exceed prices in urban areas. Cross-subsidization permits a uniform rate which in the urban areas exceeds average cost but is below average cost in the rural areas. The profits earned in urban areas are used to cover the losses incurred in the rural areas.

Rate of Return Regulation

In conjunction with the regulation of prices of specific goods and services sold by firms, regulatory agencies frequently regulate to limit the overall earnings of the firms to a specified rate of return on investment. Indeed, a regulatory agency may focus on the overall rate of return of a multi-product industry and grant the firms in the industry considerable flexibility in establishing the price or rate structure for the goods and services produced and sold.

In essence, the rate of return is the net revenue or profit a firm receives on its investment. Total revenues must be sufficient to cover costs of production plus a profit. The profit, measured as a percentage of investment, is viewed as the rate of return. The formula relating revenues, costs, and profits is:

$$TR = OC + CD + (V - AD)_r$$

where TR = total revenue
OC = operating costs
CD = current depreciation
V = value of capital assets
AD = accumulated depreciation
r = rate of return

Isolating r gives the rate of return equation as:

$$r = \frac{TR - (OC + CD)}{(V - AD)}$$

where $(V - AD)$ is the rate base.

The elements that must be determined in this equation are costs, the rate base, and a fair rate of return. The measurement of these elements frequently poses problems for regulating agencies. Consider each of these elements, their composition, and some of the difficulties involved in determining their values.

Operating Costs

These are the costs incurred in the every-day operation of the firm. They include wages and salaries, expenses on materials and supplies, fuel, electricity, advertising, and services (such as telephone and postage), and taxes. These costs are not difficult for a regulatory agency to determinate, since firms must establish rigorous accounting systems for financial management purposes, for reporting to shareholders, and for taxation purposes. But, while the calculation of costs pose no difficulty, the regulatory agency may question whether certain cost items should be included in the calculation of the rate of return. Regulators may be required to form judgments on whether certain expenses are excessive or even necessary. For example, many regulated public utilities are monopolies and it may be questionable whether these utilities require extensive advertising to promote sales, since the utilities' services are frequently essential to consumers and few, if any, substitutes may exist. The regulators may also examine closely the salaries of a utility's executives and their expense accounts to determine if they are reasonable. This was illustrated in a recent CRTC examination of a rate increase application submitted of the British Columbia Telephone Co. (BC Tel). The CRTC's examination of the application included a review of salary increases paid to BC Tel executives, office expenses, and advertising expenses. It was revealed that BC Tel paid its executives salary increases in excess of the rate of inflation, and various office expenses were not adequately explained. The result was that the CRTC reduced BC Tel's office expenses by $4 million for the purposes of calculating its rate of return. In addition, one million dollars was shaved from BC Tel's advertising expenses on the grounds that the amount of advertising was excessive and conferred no obvious benefits to the subscribers of BC Tel.

Rate Base

The rate base is undoubtedly the most difficult element to calculate in rate of return computation. A method must be determined for valuating capital assets. In addition, a depreciation method must be designated along with appropriate depreciation rates for various classes of assets.

Capital generally consists of investment in plant and equipment and would include all physical assets such as buildings, machinery, vehicles, tools, etc. Various methods can be used for calculating the value of these capital assets in computing the rate base. Capital assets may be valued on the basis of purchase price, reproduction cost, replacement cost, or some mix of the three. Purchase price is the original cost of the assets. Reproduction cost represents the price of the original equipment adjusted by an inflation factor, and is the cost of replacing this equipment at current prices. Replacement cost is the estimated expense of replacing the existing equipment with equipment representing the most up-to-date technology and at current prices. An additional valuation method might consist of a combination of two or more of the above methods to obtain what is frequently referred to as a fair value for the assets.

The method chosen for the valuation of assets will have an effect on the rate base. Valuation on the basis of original cost produces a smaller rate base than valuation on the basis of replacement cost using current prices and modern technology. The larger the rate base, the larger the amount of total revenue required to attain a given rate of return.

The value of capital assets of a firm will be reduced over time by accumulated depreciation. Assets such as plant and equipment wear out during the production process or tend to become obsolete as changing technology results in new and more efficient machinery and tools and more efficient production processes. Depreciation reflects the physical deterioration and the obsolescence of capital assets over time.

In the rate of return equation, depreciation during the current production period is the cost of using capital assets during the productive process and is treated as a current operating cost. The accumulated depreciation reflects the aggregate cost of using existing capital and is a measure of the total reduced value of the assets. Therefore, while current depreciation of capital assets is added to current operating costs, accumulated depreciation is deducted from the value of the assets and has the effect of continually eroding the capital stock or the rate base in the rate of return formula.

Numerous depreciation methods exist but the two most commonly applied in business are the straight-line method and the diminishing balances method. The straight line method calls for a constant fraction of the cost of the asset to be deducted each year. For example, if an asset is valued at $1000 and the depreciation rate is set at one-fifth or 20 percent, then $200 will be subtracted from the value of the asset each year. Over a five year period, the entire asset will have been depreciated or written off. In the diminishing or declining balances method, a certain fraction or percentage rate is applied to the undepreciated balance of the asset each year. In the above example in year one, 20 percent or $200 will be deducted leaving a balance of $800. In year two, 20 percent of the $800 balance will be deducted, and so on. If the asset has been deemed to have a life-span of five years, then in the final year the straight line method is applied and the remaining balance is depreciated in its entirety. The essential difference between these two methods of depreciation is that the straightline method permits an even reduction in value over the life-time of the asset whereas the diminishing balances method permits a larger absolute reduction in the early years of an asset's life. If the life-time of the asset is declared the same under each method and the same depreciation rate is applied under each method, the straight-line method produces a faster decline in asset value and therefore the rate base than does the diminishing balances method.

Traditionally, regulatory agencies have been rather conservative in establishing depreciation rates. High rates of depreciation quickly erode the rate base and at the same time add substantial increases to operating costs. High rates consequently exert upward pressure on prices of the products being produced if a given rate of return is to be maintained. Increased prices result from the need to increase total revenue to cover the higher operating costs. This is illustrated in the following numerical example. Given the formula

$$r = \frac{TR - (OC + CD)}{V - AD}$$

assume that $TR = \$3400$, $OC = \$1800$, $CD = \$200$, $V = \$8000$ and $AD = \$1000$ (includes the $200 CD).

In this example,

$$r = \frac{3400 - (1800 + 200)}{8000 - 1000} = 20\%$$

Assume current depreciation is raised from $200 to $600. Then

$$r = \frac{3400 - (1800 + 600)}{8000 - 1400} = 15\%$$

In order to maintain $r = 20\%$, prices will have to be increased to raise total revenue from $3400 to $3720.

Fair Rate of Return

In the application of a policy of rate of return it is the responsibility of a regulatory agency to establish a fair rate of return for the industry being regulated. A fair rate of return is generally viewed as a rate necessary to attract capital into the industry. This rate should approximate the opportunity cost of capital, that is, the rate that capital would earn in alternative uses. An investor with available funds has a number of investment alternatives including the purchase of government securities, corporate bonds, mortgages, real estate, or corporate stocks of varying degrees of risk. Returns on these investments take the form of interest, dividends, rent, or capital appreciation and consequent capital gains. A regulated industry, even a public utility, must compete with these alternative uses for funds in the capital market. If its rate of return is low relative to the amounts capital earns in other uses, the utility may find it very difficult to raise the required capital to finance expansion and modernization of its facilities. If on the other hand, the regulated facility is permitted an excessive rate of return, there will be a tendency for the utility to over-capitalize and use capital inefficiently.

The regulatory agency must determine a rate which will be sufficient to attract capital into the regulated utility. Generally, the factors taken into account in its determination will include the average rate of interest on long-term government and corporate bonds, the degree of risk associated with an investment in the utility relative to other investments, and the general economic health of the utility including the performance of its publicly traded shares and its share price-earnings ratio.

A regulatory agency such as the CRTC, in determining appropriate rates of return for Bell Canada and BC Tel, generally relies on counsel and evidence from investment analysts and capital market analysts at open hearings on applications for rate increases. An examination of the rates of return in the telephone industry shows that, when interest rates in the economy were high, the rate of return permitted was correspondingly high. As rates of interest fell, the permitted rate of return was correspondingly reduced to a level considered by the CRTC as reasonable and sufficient for the telephone companies to raise their projected capital requirements.

Adjustments in the permitted rate of return of a utility will normally require adjustments in the prices of its output. In effect, in periods when the CRTC has reduced the maximum level of rate of return for the telephone companies, they in turn have been forced to reduce prices of telephone services in order not to exceed the maximum rate allowed.

Implications In Rate of Return Regulation

There are a number of well-recognized limitations in the application of rate of return regulatory policy. These include the effects of rate of return regulation on the operating efficiency of an industry, the effects on factor combinations, and potential problems with rate structures.

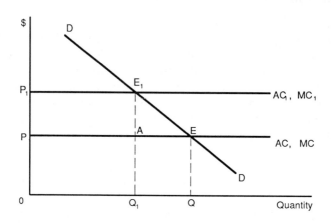

FIGURE 4–10: *X-Inefficiency in Production*

Efficiency

It has been contended that rate of return regulation leads to technical or X-inefficiency, which represents the wasteful use of resources. The regulation guarantees a firm a specified rate of return on its assets. In such a situation it is argued that there is no incentive for the firm to try to keep costs of production as low as possible or to maintain operative efficiency. This is readily apparent from the formula

$$r = \frac{TR - (OC + CD)}{V - AD}$$

If costs represented by OC increase, then prices will have to be increased in order to increase total revenue and to maintain a specified r. If the firm is assured of r regardless of OC, it is argued that the firm will have no incentive to keep costs down, to take a strong position when bargaining with labour unions in wage negotiations, to make use of the latest technological cost saving innovations, to streamline administrative procedures, or to introduce any other cost-cutting initiatives. This could result in a level of costs above the minimum level possible, higher prices, and a lower quantity of production, as illustrated in Figure 4-10.

Faced with demand curve DD and constant average and marginal costs, AC and MC respectively, a firm operating at maximum efficiency and applying a policy of marginal or average cost pricing would produce quantity OQ at price OP. However, if the firm lacked incentives to minimize costs, its cost curves could conceivably be AC_1 and MC_1, with corresponding quantity OQ_1 and price

OP_1. The inefficiency per unit equals E_1A and the corresponding increase in price and reduction in quantity produces a loss of consumers' surplus equal to PP_1E_1E. The total waste of resources in producing OQ_1 at an average cost of Q_1E_1, which could be produced at an average cost of Q_1A if maximum productive efficiency was achieved, is represented by the area PP_1E_1A. This is the value of resources which could have been used in producing more of the output in question or which could have been used elsewhere but because of the inefficiency are not available for other uses.

Over-capitalization

Rate of return regulation may result in an excess use of capital relative to other factors of production. This is frequently called the rate base effect of rate of return regulation. It is also referred to as the Averch-Johnson effect (A-J effect) after the two economists who developed the concept.[4] Over-capitalization or the A-J effect may result because rate of return focuses on one factor or input which is capital. It is a rate of return on capital. If the rate of return allowed by a regulatory agency exceeds the opportunity cost of capital, the effect is similar to a subsidy paid to capital. The price of capital will be viewed as being lower than it actually is, and lower relative to the price of labour. The firm will consequently begin to substitute capital for labour. If the labour-capital ratio had been optimum prior to substitution, the effect will be a departure from the optimum factor combination and the use of excessive capital relative to labour. The result will be an inefficient mix of resources or factors of production. The A-J effect is illustrated in Figure 4-11.

Given prices of labour and capital, and a budget for production, the optimum combination of inputs or capital-labour ratio will be determined at point E, where the budget line AB is tangent to isoquant I. Now assume that the rate of return allowed on capital exceeds the actual cost of capital in the market, that is, it exceeds its opportunity cost. The firm will view the cost of capital to be less than the actual cost. In other words, if the opportunity cost of capital is r, and the rate of return permitted is higher as represented by s, the firm will consider the excess as a form of subsidy and view the cost of capital as $r - (s - r) = c$. If $r = 10$ percent, and $s = 12$ percent, then c will be 8 percent. The lower price of capital will be represented by a shift in the budget line to AC, reflecting the changes in the relative prices of capital and labour. At the relative prices represented by AC, the combination of labour and capital used to produce the output represented by isoquant I is E_1, where FG, a line parallel to AC is tangent to isoquant I. The capital-labour ratio will have been increased from the efficient ratio, $\dfrac{OK}{KE}$ to an

[4] H. Averch and L. Johnson, "Behavior of the Firm under Regulatory Constraint," *American Economic Review*, Vol. 52, Dec. 1962, pp. 1053–1069. The Averch-Johnson effect is also discussed in most micro-economics textbooks.

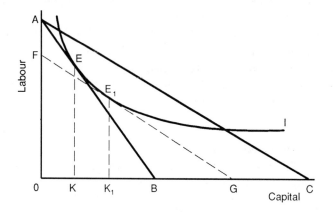

FIGURE 4–11: *Over-capitalization in Production: The Averch-Johnson Effect*

inefficient ratio $\dfrac{OK_1}{K_1E_1}$. The excess of capital used in the production of the given output represented by I is KK_1.

The potential for over-capitalization is also apparent in an examination of the rate of return formula

$$r = \frac{TR - (OC + CD)}{V - AD}$$

If a specified r is set by a regulatory agency, an increase in the rate base $V - AD$ will require an increase in TR in order to maintain the specified r. By increasing its capital assets, V, the firm will succeed in increasing its rate base, requiring an increase in prices and corresponding total revenue if r is to be maintained. This assumes, of course, that an increase in output does not result from the higher level of capital stock or from increased efficiency of capital which could produce an increase in revenues without raising prices.

Rate Structures

Concentration by a regulatory agency on rate of return to the neglect of regulating specific rates of various services provided by the regulated firm may lead to a variety of possible rate structures. A firm may be tempted to charge excessively high prices for the services it provides in lucrative markets, markets with inelastic demand, or non-competitive markets, but at the same time follow a policy of predatory pricing in the more competitive markets. High profits in the former could be applied to subsidize losses in the latter. In essence, a firm left free to determine its rate structure, but operating within the rate of return limit, could apply a considerable degree of arbitrariness in setting specific prices and be highly discriminating in its pricing policies. To prevent undue or unjustifiable price discrimination, a regulatory agency may be required to regulate rate structures as well as the overall rate of return, or as a minimum, establish guidelines or limits in the form of price ceilings and floors for the various services provided by the firm.

Rate of return regulation has been widely practiced in the regulation of public utilities and other regulated industries despite these limitations. Concern over the effect of rate of return regulation on efficiency, however, has recently caused some movement to find a replacement for this regulatory policy. An alternative method of regulating public utilities currently being considered in some quarters, particularly the regulation of telephone services in the United States, is a system of price caps.

The Price Cap System

The price cap system of regulating rates focuses on the establishment of price ceilings for the services of a multi-service regulated industry.[5] Instead of setting a rate of return, the regulatory agency would establish price ceilings above which prices could not be raised. To prevent and to protect customers and competitors from sharp fluctuations in prices, or predatory pricing if the opportunity arose, a price floor would also be established below which prices could not go. The firm would be free to set its prices within this established range or band without the approval of the regulator. The price ranges would be periodically reviewed to determine if changes are warranted.

The objective of the price cap system is to encourage cost efficiency and innovation by the regulated industry. Under such a system, a firm could increase its profits by reducing costs. It is expected that the potential of higher profits would provide an incentive to improve operating efficiency and employ the optimum combination of factors and the most modern technology. In essence, price caps are viewed as a means of avoiding the problem of x-inefficiency caused by rate of return regulation, where profits are fixed and a firm cannot increase them, even through cost reductions. A price cap system would also eliminate any tendency toward over-capitalization associated with rate of return regulation, since a firm would desire to maximize efficiency and employ the optimum capital-labour ratio or input combination in production.

---

[5] In 1988 the Federal Communications Commission in the United States proposed a price cap plan for telecommunications carriers. The background and details of this proposal are presented in Federal Communications Commission, *In the Matter of Policy and Rules Concerning Rates for Dominant Carriers*, Cc Docket No. 87–313, Released May 23, 1988, Washington, D.C.

5

REGULATION FOR PRICE AND INCOME MAINTENANCE

In addition to regulating prices and rates of return of monopoly-type public utility industries to achieve a more efficient allocation of resources, governments have also been involved in regulating prices, outputs, wages, and rents in other sectors of the economy. In these latter cases, the justifications for government regulation include the deemed need to stabilize prices and markets, and to maintain or increase income levels to achieve greater equity in the distribution of income. While regulation for more efficient resource allocation is mostly aimed at specific industries, regulation for stabilization and equity purposes has ranged from industry-specific regulation to cross-industry and economy-wide regulation. It has been applied to prices and outputs in goods and services industries and to prices of factors of production.

Prominent among the specific industries that have experienced government price and output regulation for stabilization, conservation, and equity purposes are agriculture, energy, fisheries, forestry, and housing. Governments have attempted to stabilize prices and incomes in agriculture by establishing price floors and output quotas for farm produce. Price ceilings on rental housing attempt to prevent landlords from arbitrarily charging high rents, causing hardships for low-income tenants. Fishing and timber-cutting licences and quotas are designed as conservation measures. Price controls on oil and gas have been used to encourage exploration and encourage more conservative use by consumers and industry. Minimum wage levels have been legislated as part of anti-poverty programs and to achieve greater equity in the distribution of income.

Regulation of prices and incomes on a more general, economy-wide basis is distinguished from regulation of specific industries in terms of objectives. The objective of economy-wide or multi-sector regulation of prices is to control inflation and stabilize the general price level, as opposed to price regulation to achieve economic efficiency or equity. It is generally used to supplement anti-inflationary fiscal policy involving government expenditure and tax policies, and monetary policy directed at interest rates and the money supply.

This chapter outlines and examines in both theory and practice some price and output regulatory policies designed to achieve price and income stability, and to reduce inequities in income distribution. A common regulatory pricing policy has been the application of price ceilings and price floors. A theoretical analysis of price ceilings and floors is presented, followed by a discussion of

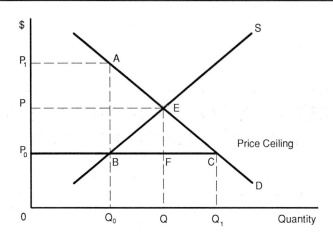

FIGURE 5–1:   *Price Ceiling*

their application in Canada. Market and income stabilization has also been pursued through the regulation of supply. Output quotas have been common in agriculture, forestry, and the fishing industry. Government agencies administering these policies include price stabilization boards and commissions and marketing boards.

Price Ceilings

In certain instances the equilibrium market price of a particular commodity or service determined by the competitive forces of supply and demand may be deemed to be excessively high. The criteria or standard generally used to determine if the price is excessive is fairness or equity in terms of the relationship of the price level to income levels and income distribution. A high price of a commodity or service lowers the real income of consumers purchasing the commodity. This may place a considerable burden on consumers if they are low-income groups and spend a large proportion of their incomes on the commodity or service in question. In the interest of equity for these groups, the government may intervene in such markets and impose a price ceiling. A price ceiling is an established maximum price that sellers cannot exceed. This price is generally set below the price that would prevail in a freely-operating market.

The concept of a price ceiling and its effects are illustrated in Figure 5–1. Market equilibrium is determined by the forces of supply and demand at E, with price OP and quantity OQ. A price ceiling is set at price OP_0, below the market price. The price ceiling has the desired effect outlined earlier of keeping the price low, but it also produces some undesirable effects. At the lower price OP_0, the amount demanded is OQ_1, but only an amount of OQ_0 will be supplied. There is an excess demand, or a shortage of the commodity equal to Q_0Q_1 or BC. Suppliers will not produce more than OQ_0 at price OP_0 because for any amount greater than OQ_0, the unit cost of production exceeds price and producers will incur a loss. Therefore, while consumers who are able to purchase the commodity benefit in the form of lower prices, less is being provided than would be the case if the market was left to seek its own equilibrium. Price ceilings interfere with the working of the price mechanism in allocating resources, causing fewer resources to be channelled into an industry than would otherwise be the case. Where severe shortages are created, price ceilings may have to be accompanied by other policies including rationing of the scarce commodity, or the payment of subsidies to producers to increase output. Rationing consists of placing limits on the amount each consumer may purchase so that the quantity OQ_0 is equitably distributed among consumers. If a policy of supply subsidization is applied to increase output to the market equilibrium level OQ, a subsidy of P_0P per unit or P_0PEF in total would have to be paid to producers. This amount would be just enough to cover production losses incurred in producing and selling OQ at price OP_0.

Another potential problem with price ceilings is the creation of a black market. A black market is one in which a commodity is illegally sold at a price above the established price ceiling. People purchase the commodity at the established price and turn around and sell it at a higher price, making profits in the process. In Figure 5–1, the amount OQ_0 could be sold at a price of OP_1 in a black market. Potential black market profits for $O\ Q_0$ output are represented by the area P_0P_1AB.

Rent Controls

Rent control programs governing the prices that tenants pay for rented houses and apartments are essentially price ceilings. Controls may take the form of a freeze on rents preventing any rent increases, or limits on the amount that rents are permitted to increase annually. Governments have frequently applied rent controls in a period of rising demand when excess demand over supply for housing has placed upward pressure on rents. A large number of those who rent houses and apartment are low-income families who cannot afford to purchase homes. Higher rents would reduce the real income of these groups by forcing them to allocate a larger proportion of their budgets for rent with a smaller portion left for other goods and services.

Unfortunately, if the rising rents were caused by a shortage of rental units, rent controls will have the effect of perpetuating the shortage. Assume in Figure 5–1 that quantity measures housing rental units and that initially the supply and demand curves intersected to establish equilibrium at B, with market price and quantity OP_0 and OQ_0 respectively. Assume that the demand curve now shifts to intersect the supply curve at E. The supply of rental units in the very short run remains fixed or inelastic since it takes time to construct new units. In the absence of controls, prices would increase to OP_1. Over time, however, market forces would channel additional resources into the housing market to increase rental units by Q_0Q and reduce price to equilibrium at OP. But, if the price is frozen at OP_0 in the form of a price ceiling, the number of rental units will also remain fixed at OQ_0. Existing tenants enjoy the benefits of stable rents, but at a cost reflected in other prospective tenants unable to find adequate housing facilities. This problem will likely persist unless government introduces subsidies for apartment and house construction or itself builds homes and apartments to rent at subsidized prices.

Despite the theoretical analysis and considerable empirical evidence of the adverse impact on the rental housing market of rent controls, governments have persisted in periodically applying rent control policies. Most provinces in Canada imposed some type of rent control throughout the 1970s and into the 1980 decade. A moving price ceiling was most frequently applied with annual rent increases generally limited to the inflation rate. In other cases, no ceilings were imposed, but rent increases were subject to review by a provincial rent review board or commission. During the period of rent controls in Ontario, some variations in policy were attempted including the exemption of high-priced rental units which were beyond the means of low-income groups and where controls could have no significance for these groups. This policy in effect established a dual market for rental units; a controlled market and an uncontrolled market.

In the Canadian provinces the justifications most commonly advanced for rent controls included: to prevent rent gauging in periods of temporary housing shortages; to make available affordable housing and avoid financial hardships for low-income groups; and, to avoid increasing disparities in income distribution between high and low-income groups on the premise that landlords who control housing capital tend to be high income groups and renters are low- and middle-income groups. [1] They have also been justified as part of a general anti-inflationary policy. Some have argued that rent controls have been imposed for political reasons. Rent controls appear to bring immediate and visible benefits to a fairly large group of potential voters, with no direct public cost, and governments are continuously weighing policies for their vote-gain and vote-loss potential.

Price Floors

A price floor is the opposite of a price ceiling. It is an established minimum price below which sellers cannot sell a good or service. The price floor is set

---

[1] An analysis of rent controls in Toronto led to the conclusion that the program was an "extremely inefficient and inequitable method of income redistribution," and produced reduced investment in new construction, and other inefficiency costs. See George Fallis and Lawrence B. Smith, "Rent Control In Toronto: Tenant Rationing and Tenant Benefits," *Canadian Public Policy*, Sept. 1985, pp. 543–550.

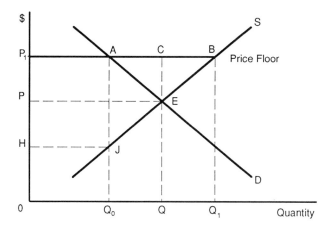

FIGURE 5–2: *Price Floor*

above the price that would prevail in a freely-operating market. The basic concept of a price floor is illustrated in Figure 5–2. In perfect competition the freely-operating forces of supply and demand will determine equilibrium at E, with price OP and quantity OQ. Assume a price floor is set at OP_1. At this price the amount OQ_0 will be demanded, but OQ_1 will be supplied, for an excess supply, or surplus, equal to Q_0Q_1 or AB. The obvious problem with a price floor is that producers will be unable to sell the total output that they produce.

Price floors have been most commonly applied in the agricultural industry in an attempt to maintain stability in the prices of agricultural goods and in farm income. The agricultural industry is susceptible to wide fluctuations in output and prices. Output of farm crops is highly affected by weather conditions. In favourable weather conditions, crop yields and therefore market supply will be high. Demand, however, tends to be relatively stable. The increase in supply causes prices to fall, and if demand is inelastic, farm incomes will also fall despite the increase in yields. In poor weather conditions, supply will fall causing prices of farm crops to rise. Weather conditions likewise affect farm livestock food supplies and therefore the supply and price of meat and dairy produce. There is a tendency for farmers to overproduce when prices are high and to depress prices in the process. As prices fall and profit margins are squeezed, farm production is scaled back and this forces prices back up again. The result is a perpetual cycle of large outputs causing low prices causing reduced outputs which in turn cause prices to rise once again. The fluctuating prices bring fluctuating incomes, aggravating the uncertainties which are inherent in the agricultural industry and discouraging farmers from continued operation. In an attempt to provide some stability in the agriculture industry, the federal and provincial governments have intervened extensively in agriculture with a wide variety of policies including price floors, subsidies, quotas, insurance, storage and transportation assistance, and marketing assistance. A brief analysis is presented in the following pages of regulation policies for agriculture prices and incomes involving price floors. These include price support programs, deficiency payments, and output restrictions.

In a basic price support program the government establishes a price floor such as OP_1 in Figure 5–2. The government guarantees this price to farmers, but in order to maintain it the government must purchase Q_0Q_1 in the marketplace. The cost to the government of this purchase is Q_0ABQ_1. Farm receipts will equal the revenue from market sales or OP_1AQ_0 plus the government expenditure, for a total income of OP_1BQ_1. The government may apply a number of alternatives to the surplus it has purchased. This surplus could be stored and returned for market sale in some future period when farm output falls below OQ_0. The government could also use the surplus produce as a form of foreign aid to underdeveloped and agriculturally-poor countries, either free of charge or at some price range below OP_1. While farmers benefit from this program, there is a cost to other members of society. First, as consumers they have less produce available and at higher prices for a loss of consumers surplus of PP_1AE in comparison to the market equilibrium situation. Second, as taxpayers they will likely have to finance the purchase and storage of the surplus produce, or finance the difference between the price paid to farmers by government for the surplus and the amount that government receives if it attempts to sell the surplus in international markets at lower prices.

The main difficulty of the above-outlined price support program is the generation of surplus produce. This could be avoided by permitting the market to determine price and output at OP and OQ respectively. The government would then, through a program of deficiency payments or subsidies, establish a price floor OP_1 and pay farmers the difference between OP_1 and the market price OP for output OQ. The total cost to the government of this program would be PP_1CE. Consumers are required to pay only the market price, although as taxpayers they will likely be required to bear the financial burden of the deficiency payment.

A third policy designed to maintain a price floor involves output restrictions. In Figure 5–2, the price floor OP_1 can be maintained by limiting total output to OQ_0. The per unit cost of producing OQ_0 is HO, and a price OP_1 yields a monopoly profit of HP_1 per unit. This policy does not require any direct government payments to farmers and therefore no financial burden on taxpayers. A burden does exist, however, in that the price is higher and the quantity available to consumers is lower than would be the case in a competitive market. In addition to establishing a quota for total output, quotas would also have to be established for each producer in the market with close supervision to ensure that no one producer exceeds their quota. This poses another problem of determining equitable allocations of quotas among the producers.

Marketing Boards

Programs involving price floors and supply regulation have been widely used in Canadian agriculture and have been administered by federal and provincial authorized marketing boards.[2] They have been applied to such agricultural products as grain, fruit, eggs, poultry, hogs and dairy products. A marketing board consists of a group of producers formed under the authority of government for the purpose of marketing their product. Once established, all producers of the product in question are subject to its regulations. The marketing board is basically a regulatory agency. Its functions and powers range from the simple sales promotion of products to the control of most aspects of production and distribution of specific products.

The Agricultural Stabilization Board is responsible for administering the federal Agricultural Stabilization Act. The Act provides a guaranteed price of 90 percent of a moving five-year average price for cattle, hogs, lambs, wool, milk, corn, barley and other grain crops. Another important agency is the Canadian Wheat Board, a regulatory and marketing agency formed in 1935 to market Canadian grain. It has the authority to buy, sell, and store grain produced in the Prairie Provinces. Farmers deliver grain to grain elevators under a quota system established by the Board. An initial price is established by the Board at the beginning of the crop year and the farmer receives this initial price when the farmer's grain is delivered to the elevator. The Board is responsible for marketing the grain, after which a final payment is made to the producer depending on the price at which the Board is able to sell the grain in the domestic and international markets.

While the regulation of quality standards and marketing of milk are provincial responsibilities, the federal Canadian Dairy Commission has the authority to assist dairy producers to obtain a fair return for their products. The Commission consists of three members appointed by the government and is advised by a committee of nine members representing dairy producers and processors. The Commission is responsible for supply management and coordinates a national market sharing system for milk. A quota for milk production is determined for each province and quotas are in turn established for each producer. Producers receive an established price per hectolitre (100 litres) of their quotas, but receive a much lower price for any surplus milk they deliver. The Commission administers direct subsidies to dairy farmers for milk and cream production. The subsidy ensures the farmer a stable and adequate price over cost, and maintains stable prices of milk for consumers. The price floor for industrial milk was set at

---

[2] For an outline and evaluation of marketing boards in Canada, see Economic Council of Canada, *Reforming Regulation* 1981 (Ottawa: Supply and Services, 1981), Ch. 6.

$47.00 per hectolitre for 1987–88 and the subsidy was slightly above $6.00 per hectolitre.

Price floors which are essentially support prices were also established for butter and for skim milk powder. With respect to the latter two products, after wholesalers and retailers have purchased the amounts they require, the Commission purchases the remainder. Most of the skim milk powder is not needed in Canada and is exported, but at a price which results in a loss. A levy on milk producers is used to finance the export sales and to offset the export losses.

The Canadian Egg Marketing Agency (CEMA), established in 1972, performs a similar function in the egg-production industry as does the Canadian Dairy Commission. CEMA and its provincial regulatory counterparts establish quotas for total egg production and allocate quotas among producers. Limits are placed on the number of egg-laying chickens a producer may possess, with production size varying considerably among producers. CEMA and the provincial regulatory agencies set prices according to a formula incorporating costs of production within each region. Restrictions were also placed on egg imports.

The objective of the federal and provincial price and supply regulatory marketing boards such as the Canadian Dairy Commission and CEMA has been to achieve increased and stable incomes and fair rates of return for producers, together with price stability for consumers. The Economic Council of Canada in its 1981 report on regulation concluded that these objectives had to a large degree been achieved, but not without a major transfer of income from consumers to producers and not without inefficiencies in the use of resources. It was estimated that for 1980 the transfers to the dairy industry averaged approximately $100 per Canadian family.[3] It was further estimated that the operations of CEMA added an average of $15,000 to the income of registered egg producers in Canada.[4] With regard to inefficiency, both CEMA and the Canadian Dairy Commission have been accused of mismanagement that led to the overproduction and waste of eggs and milk powder.

Marketing boards possessing wide price and supply regulatory powers perform a function similar to that of a cartel. The operations of agricultural marketing boards lend support to Stigler's economic theory of regulation which states that producers, wishing the benefits of a cartel but unable to organize as such, seek government regulation. These supply regulators generally set prices above the equilibrium price that would otherwise prevail in the market. Prices are typically set on the basis of costs of production and deemed fair rates of return. This type of price setting permits the survival of less efficient firms which otherwise would not survive in a competitive, unrestricted market, and offers no incentives for producers to maintain maximum efficiency.

The equity and effectiveness of the quota system has also been questioned on the grounds that it has not distributed farm income to those farmers most in need,

---

[3] *Ibid.*, p. 63.

[4] *Ibid.*, p. 64.

who are typically the small farmers. Quotas for total production are determined on the basis of projected demand and sales. With respect to the individual producers, the largest producers receive the largest shares. Furthermore, if quotas are permitted to be bought and sold among individual producers, large producers have the opportunity to become larger. It has been contended that, since the rewards are based on output, the cartel operations of marketing boards benefit the largest producers the most, and leave small producers with major income problems.[5]

Minimum Wage Regulation

Another form of price floor is the establishment of a general minimum wage level in the labour market. In the occupations and industries where the minimum wage applies, an employer cannot hire a worker below this wage. For most employment in Canada the minimum wage is below the actual market wage being paid, and it only has an effect in those labour markets where the wage would otherwise be below the wage floor established. This is usually in the unskilled labour market and in low-paying occupations and industries.

Minimum wage levels have been used as part of government income redistribution and anti-poverty programs. The federal government and all of the provinces have legislated minimum wage levels, which are periodically increased to take into account economy-wide increases in salaries and wages and rising prices. The objective of these programs has been to increase income levels of low-income groups. Various economic factors determine income levels and the distribution of income, including opportunities for acquiring an education, training and skills, and these combine with social and cultural factors. Some workers suffer from low incomes because of unemployment. Others lack the necessary skills and training to fill high-wage jobs and are restricted to low productivity and unskilled employment at correspondingly low wages. These latter "working poor" are gainfully employed but at wages which barely provide them and their families with a subsistence standard of living. The establishment of a wage floor is designed to increase the standards of living of this group of workers.

Minimum wage policies have been subjected to a considerable amount of controversy. Some contend that they lead to an increase in unemployment. This can be illustrated in Figure 5–2. Assume quantity of labour is measured on the horizontal axis and wages are measured on the vertical axis. In a relatively competitive market in a certain occupation, the wage level and the amount of labour employed will be determined at OP and OQ respectively. If the government establishes a wage floor of OP_1, an amount of labour OQ_0 will be employed while OQ_1 will seek employment at that wage. The wage floor has the effect of pricing workers out of the market and reducing employment by Q_0Q. Employers have argued that in certain industries there exist various menial tasks

---

[5] *Ibid.*, p. 65.

that do not required skilled labour, but the low productivity of this labour or the value added to the product only justifies correspondingly low wages. Employers claim they would be prepared to hire low-productivity workers for these menial tasks at a correspondingly low wage, but cannot afford to hire them at the established, higher minimum wage. Workers willing to work at these tasks are instead relegated to the ranks of the unemployed. Therefore, while the minimum wage does lead to higher wages and incomes for those who are able to retain their jobs, it reduces the number of potential jobs available for other workers, particularly young workers who are just entering the labour market and have not had an opportunity to acquire the necessary skills.

Anti-Inflation Price and Wage Regulation

In periods of rapidly rising prices, fed by shortages or rising costs, governments have resorted to the application of price ceilings on a very broad level, covering practically all sectors of the consumer and factor markets. Such a policy of price and wage controls has commonly been referred to as an incomes policy. For the most part governments have been reluctant to employ this policy because of numerous difficulties associated with it. On the few occasions that governments have resorted to wage and price controls, they have used them as a supplement to traditional fiscal and monetary measures and then in periods when the latter have been deemed ineffective in curbing inflation, or when it has been deemed inappropriate to apply stronger fiscal and monetary policies.

Price and wage controls may be applied in varying degrees of severity. They may range from voluntary wage-price guidelines to a wage and price freeze with the application of strong sanctions for non-compliance. Voluntary wage-price guidelines are generally viewed to be ineffective as they rely on the voluntary cooperation of both business and labour and this cooperation will not always be forthcoming. A program of extensive mandatory controls on the other hand requires an elaborate monitoring and administrative mechanism to avoid inequities from creeping into the system.

Two basic problems with wage-price controls is that they interfere with the operations of the market as an allocator of resources, and unless rigorously and widely applied, can contribute to income inequities. The first problem has been discussed and illustrated in the previous section. Price ceilings on goods and services and on factors of production can lead to the supply of smaller amounts than would be supplied without controls, and invariably to shortages. With respect to the second problem, if income inequities are to be avoided, all forms of income and prices must be subject to the controls and very closely monitored. Incomes include salaries, wages, rent, dividends, interest, and profits. If certain incomes are excluded from the controls, or are permitted to rise relatively more than others, or rise because they are not detected, then those with the flexible incomes gain an advantage in terms of the level of their relative incomes over those whose incomes are tightly controlled. Similarly, if some prices are permitted to rise more rapidly than others, the consumers of products subject to the more rapidly rising prices will suffer relatively more in terms of reduced real income.

The following pages examine in some detail the Canadian government's experience with wage-price controls to illustrate how such a program may be administered, and to identify some of the regulatory issues associated with wage-price controls and the difficulties of determining the effectiveness of controls.

A very rigorous policy of wage-price controls was imposed by the Canadian government during World War II. At the outbreak of the war in 1939 the diversion of productive factors and materials to the war effort caused shortages of consumer goods and services and the shortages began to place an upward pressure on consumer prices. Between 1939 and late 1941 the consumer price index (CPI) increased by 18 percent. The Canadian government's answer to this inflation was a wage and price freeze affecting the entire industry base and economy. A universal price ceiling was established with the four-week period from September 15 to October 11, 1941 designated as the base period. Sellers were prohibited from selling any goods or services at prices in excess of the prices in effect during the base period. Wages and salaries were likewise stabilized. Responsibility for the administration of this program was placed in the hands of a Wartime Price and Trade Board. The public was urged to restrain consumer demand. In instances of upward pressure in production costs, such as attributed to the rising costs of imports used in production, subsidies were paid to the producer to cover cost increases and keep prices down. With shortages of various commodities, a system of consumer rationing was introduced in an attempt to achieve some equity in the distribution of scarce goods. Basic goods and a number of items such as gasoline, tires, and farm equipment were subject to the ration. The effectiveness of this wartime price regulation program is reflected in the fact that the CPI increased by less than three percent between the time of its imposition in 1941 and the end of the war in 1945.

The first postwar experiment with wage and price regulation began in 1969[6] with a program of voluntary wage and price guidelines administered by a Prices and Incomes Commission. The guideline for annual wage increases was set at 6 percent. The guideline for prices was that increases were to be less than the amount needed to cover all increases in costs. In February, 1970, the commission succeeded in bringing together approximately 250 business and professional representatives to a conference on price restraints and obtained a commitment from them to follow the price guidelines it recommended. Organized labour, however, refused to attend the conference or to cooperate with the commission. Labour in general argued that a wage ceiling would hold the "status quo" on income distribution or relative income shares and that this was inequitable, as wages had considerable catching up to do on profits and other forms of income.

---

[6] The information on Canada's wage-price control programs contained in this section is taken from J.C. Strick *Canadian Public Finance*, 3rd ed. (Toronto: Holt, Rinehart and Winston, 1985), pp. 185–188.

Labour also refused to accept wage controls on the grounds that other forms of income, such as rents, profits, and interest, were not subject to controls.

During the early months of 1970, the Prices and Incomes Commission did manage to persuade various industries to agree to a moratorium on price increases, and a number of announced and intended price increases were postponed. Without the cooperation of labour, however, the commission's task was extremely difficult, for it was apparent that business would not be prepared to maintain a freeze on prices for any length of time if labour costs continued to rise. By late 1970, business declared that it no longer could cooperate with the commission and, in December, the government announced that it was abandoning its program of voluntary price restraints.

The rate of inflation decreased during 1970 but it is difficult to determine to what extent the work of the commission contributed to this moderation. The rate of economic growth declined in 1970 and aggregate demand levelled off; these factors could be expected to have some moderating influence. The CPI increased from 127.9 in December 1969 to 130.5 by July 1970 before it stabilized. In October 1970 a major food price war broke out among the major grocery chains resulting in a three-point decline in the food price index. Food is a major component in the basket of goods used to determine price changes, and the reduction in food prices reduced the CPI to 129.8 by December 1970. Therefore, one can only speculate on the degree of price increases in 1970 if aggregate demand had not become depressed, or if the decline in the food prices had not occurred.

Canada's second postwar experiment in wage and price regulation began in 1975. With prices increasing at an annual rate of approximately 11 percent and wage settlements averaging 16 percent to 18 percent per year, the government introduced a three-year anti-inflation program of mandatory wage and price controls. Wages were controlled directly. Prices were controlled by a complex system of monitoring corporation profit margins. In addition, a list was established of some 500 companies which were required to give advance notice of planned price increases. Dividends, the incomes of professionals, and the federal public service were also covered under the controls program. Agreements were entered into with eight provinces whereby the regulations were applied to provincial public service employees.

Inflation rate targets were set at 8 percent, 6 percent, and 4 percent for the first, second, and third years, respectively. Wage guidelines were based on the inflation target factor plus a productivity and experience adjustment factor, with a maximum annual increase of $2,400. For the year 1976, the guideline could vary between 8 percent and 12 percent and would decline for each of the subsequent years, although provisions were included to permit additional flexibility if necessary to maintain historic relationships between income groups.

Three administrative bodies were established to administer the program: an Anti-Inflation Board to establish guidelines, to review wage settlements and income increases, and to monitor prices and profits; an Administrator to investigate contraventions of the guidelines and to enforce compliance where neces-

Table 5-1: Anti-Inflation Board and Wages:
Summary of Effective Rates of Increase in Compensation and Relationship
to Wage Guidelines by Program Years

Period	No. of Employees (000s)	Average Effective Increase[a] (%)	Average Guideline (%)
Immediate Pre-program	183	12.5	10.6
First Program Year 1975–1976[b]	3,019	9.3	9.7
Second Program Year 1976–1977[b]	3,406	7.3	7.6
Third Program Year 1977–1978[c]	471	5.2	5.6
All Program Years	7,079	8.2	8.4

[a] Weighted average of settlements within guidelines and after board decisions.

[b] October of one year to October of the following year.

[c] October 1977 to February 1978. Employee groups began to be freed from the guidelines in early 1978.

SOURCE: Department of Finance, *Economic Review*, April, 1978 (Ottawa: 1978), p. 36.

sary; and, an Anti-Inflation Appeal Tribunal to consider appeals on the rulings of the Administrator.

During the first program year (October 14, 1975 to October 13, 1976), compensation plans covering approximately 3 million employees in the public and private sectors were submitted to the Anti-Inflation Board. Plans covering over one-third of these employees contained increases beyond the guidelines and required a decision by the Board. Some compensation increases approved early in the program were in excess of the guidelines, primarily to maintain historical relationships. As the program continued, compensation plans showed a continued deceleration in the rate of wage increases being sought and being approved (see Table 5–1). During the second program year, for example, approximately 70 percent of employees were seeking increases within or below the guidelines, while the remaining 30 percent sought increases averaging 1.8 percent above the guidelines. The effective rate of increase in the average of settlements was reduced steadily in each year of the program. It is estimated that the average wage roll-back by the Anti-Inflation Board was 2.0 percent in the first year and 1.2

percent in the second year. The increase in first-year wage settlements of large bargaining units was reduced from 21.1 percent in 1975 to 8.0 percent in 1977, and, by the end of the second quarter of 1978, the first-year wage settlement in collective agreements of bargaining units of 500 or more employees had fallen to 6.6 percent.

The wage and price controls were gradually phased out during 1978 and expired at the end of the year. During the regulation period, the increase in the CPI moderated from 10.9 percent in 1974 to 7.5 percent in 1976 and then began gradually to move upward to 8.9 percent by 1978. While the inflation rate target set for 1976 (8 percent) was surpassed, the targets for the second and third years were not achieved.

As a means of controlling inflation, the wage and price regulation program is extremely difficult to evaluate for its effectiveness, because one does not know what would have occurred in the absence of the program.[7] As was the case in 1970, part of the improvement in the rate of change in the CPI reflects factors beyond the direct control of the program. During the first year of the Canadian experiment, unemployment increased and international inflation abated to a degree, which may have had a moderating impact on the rate of inflation in Canada. Then there were other variables, such as food prices, which increased by only 2.7 percent in 1976 compared with an increase of 12.9 percent a year earlier. This helped to moderate the increase in the CPI and yet food at the producer level was exempt from the controls of the anti-inflation program. While the food component tended to be a moderating factor in 1976, it became a contributing factor to inflation in 1977 and 1978 when rising food prices refuelled inflation. Fear was expressed that, with aggregate inflation again on the rise, inflationary expectations would also be raised, which in the post-control period could lead to higher wage and salary demands and to a renewed wage and price spiral. This did indeed occur as the average negotiated wage settlement, which had declined considerably between 1975 and 1978, began to increase in 1979 and continued to rise into 1982 along with consumer prices.

Fearing a renewed surge in the wage and price spiral, the government again turned to wage restraints. In 1982, the government introduced the "6 and 5" pay restraint policy for the federal public sector and expressed hope that the other levels of government and the private sector would follow Ottawa's example. Some provinces had already announced measures to limit pay increases of some categories of public sector employees and others were quick to introduce restraint programs similar to the federal program.

The momentum of rising wage settlements and earnings began to break in 1982 and continued to decline into 1983. Numerous factors combined with the 6

---

[7] A number of studies have attempted to analyze the impact of the 1975–78 anti-inflation program on wages and prices using various data and economic models, and most come to the conclusion that the program did keep prices and wages below the level they would likely have attained without the controls. See David A. Wilton, "On Evaluation of Wage and Price Controls In Canada," *Canadian Public Policy*, June, 1984, pp. 167–176.

and 5 program to contribute to the decline, including a high rate of unemployment, a serious recession, and a moderation in international inflationary forces. Since 1984 the Canadian economy has experienced relatively stable prices, with the annual inflation rate fluctuating at rates below 5 percent, and the government found no need to continue with any program of price or wage restraint.

6

ECONOMIC IMPACT OF REGULATION

Government regulation results in both benefits and costs to society and the economy and its components of consumers, producers, and distributors. While the benefits of regulation have received considerable attention in the economic literature, particularly in the literature on theories of regulation and on the reasons and justifications for regulation, the cost side of regulation has to a large extent been neglected. Only in recent years has more attention been devoted to attempts to explore and quantify the costs of regulation. Since various justifications and inherent benefits of government regulation were covered in an earlier chapter, this section will be devoted primarily to an examination of the costs of regulation, with only a brief review of benefits.

Benefits of Regulation

As outlined earlier, there are a variety of reasons for government regulation in the economy. They range from a general obligation of government to regulate economic activity in the public interest to regulation for the benefit of a particular industry. Specific benefits to an industry are readily quantifiable in the form of secure profits or rates of return and, barring competition, reasonably stable outputs. Benefits of regulation to society in general or to individual groups or members are, however, difficult to quantify even though they may be readily recognizable.[1] The difficulty of measuring the beneficial impacts of regulation on the economy and society stems from the fact that benefits frequently take the form of costs prevented or avoided. If regulation prevents a particular event or activity from actually happening, then that event has not entered the market, and therefore the market does place a value on the event. For example, the benefit of environmental pollution control is recognized but remains largely intangible. Pollution control prevents the deterioration of air, water, and land quality. The benefits include the reduction of hazards to the health of humans and wildlife and the maintenance of a more pleasant environment. It is extremely difficult to attempt to determine the extent that pollution would otherwise have damaged the quality of life, shortened life spans, etc., and even more difficult to quantify such

---

[1] Some of the difficulties of measuring the benefits of regulation, particularly social regulation, are discussed in Economic Council of Canada *Responsible Regulation* (Ottawa: Canadian Government Publishing Centre, 1979), Ch. 3. See also Robert E. Litman and W.D. Nordhaus, *Reforming Federal Regulations* (New Haven: Yale University Press, 1982), Ch. 2.

benefits. What value is to placed on a more healthy society, extended life, reduced birth defects that might be attributable to pollution, and other such benefits?

A similar problem is encountered attempting to determine and quantify the benefits of food and drug regulations. The regulations are designed to reduce the possibility of harmful foods and drugs entering the market. To the extent that such items are barred from the market, their potential adverse effects on the health of humans are avoided. But it would be very difficult if next to impossible to determine the degree or amount of harmful products that regulations ban from the market. Some such products might actually be produced, but if they do not meet health safety standards they are not permitted on the market. Other potential products may be discouraged and never enter the development or production stage because of the rigorous standards and testing procedures to which they would be subjected. Consequently, the costs so avoided may be substantial but it is not possible to measure them.

In addition, certain benefits in terms of costs avoided may not accrue or be observable until sometime in the future. The classic example is exposure to products such as asbestos and various chemicals whose adverse effects on health may be a very slow process and may not be evident for years in the future.

Consequently, while many benefits of regulation may be immediate, tangible, and quantifiable, there are numerous benefits which are not immediate, are intangible, and non-quantifiable. They are recognizable, but their impact on the economy and society cannot be easily measured.

Costs of Regulation

During the last two decades increased attention has been devoted to the costs of government regulation to the economy, including attempts to identify and measure these costs.[2] No doubt the attention directed to this issue by economists such as W.L. Weidenbaum and others in the late 1970s influenced the Reagan Administration in the United States in its policies on deregulation and on reforming regulation during the early 1980s. In Canada, at about the same time, concern was also growing over the potential costs of regulation. This issue was addressed by the Economic Council of Canada as part of a comprehensive study conducted by the Council of government regulation[3]. The Council categorized the costs of regulation as direct administrative costs, compliance costs, political activity

---

[2] See, Murray L. Weidenbaum, "The High Cost of Government Regulation," *Challenge* Nov-Dec. 1979, pp. 32–39; Murray L. Weidenbaum, *The Future of Business Regulation* (New York: American Management Associations, 1980); Economic Council, *op. cit.*; and, Litman and Norhaus, *op. cit.*

[3] Economic Council of Canada, *Responsible Regulation: An Interim Report* (Ottawa: Canadian Government Publishing Centre, 1979); and, *Reforming Regulation, 1981* (Ottawa: Canadian Government Publishing Centre, 1981).

costs, induced costs, and costs that might arise from changes in industry structure.

Direct Administrative Costs

Direct administrative costs are the costs of administration incurred by regulatory agencies. They are generally the most readily identifiable and measurable, but form the smallest portion of the total costs of regulation.

Some estimates have placed these costs at the federal level of government in Canada to less than two percent of total government expenditures.[4] In 1986 a federal government study determined that the cost of administering federal regulatory and regulatory-related programs to be $2.7 billion for that year[5] which, given total federal budgetary expenditures of $111 billion in the fiscal year 1985–86, amounted to 2.4 percent of government expenditures.

Compliance Costs

Compliance costs are the costs incurred by industry in complying with government regulations. They may range from the nuisance of completing government forms to huge capital investments made necessary to meet regulation requirements. While these costs are incurred primarily by the private sector, the public sector crown corporations are not exempt from regulations and may also incur compliance costs. To the extent that these costs cause increases in of the operating costs of corporations, they are reflected in increased consumer prices.

The major costs of compliance with regulations are incurred in meeting the requirements in areas of public health and safety, working conditions and safety in the workplace, the environment, and specific requirements in specific industries. In addition to capital costs that may be incurred, there is the cost of the paperwork involved in maintaining records, the cost of employing legal counsel and other experts to interpret and advise on the regulations, and the cost of extensive testing of newly proposed or developed products to determine if they meet regulatory requirements.

Consider for example, the costs incurred by the automobile industry to comply with automobile safety regulations between 1968 and 1978. This was the period when consumer groups were very active in campaigning against the lack of safety features in the automobile, particularly the group headed by automobile safety crusader Ralph Nader in the United States. During this period, regulations were passed making mandatory such features as seat belts, increased bumper strength, improved side door strength, head restraints, reductions in flammable materials, improved brake and fuel systems, and higher standards for reducing

---

[4] *Op. cit. Responsible Regulation*, p. 34.

[5] Canada, Task Force on Program Review, *Introduction To The Process of Program Review* (Ottawa: Supply and Services, 1986), p. 28.

exhaust emissions, including the catalytic converter. It was estimated by Weidenbaum that these requirements added approximately $665 to the retail price of an automobile and over $7 billion dollars in costs to the industry over this ten year period.[6]

In the area of pollution control, the estimated compliance costs of recently strengthened pollution control regulations are indicative of the very high costs that may be required to restrict environmental pollution. Ontario Hydro, an alleged heavy air polluter from its hydro-generating stations, has estimated that it would cost over one-half a billion dollars for Ontario Hydro to install scrubbers, which are pollution reduction devices. Similarly, the nickel and copper smelting industry has estimated costs of roughly one-half a billion dollars on pollution control devices to reduce substantially pollutant emissions which are a major cause of acid rain and have a destructive impact on the environment.

Weidenbaum estimated, on the basis of his own as well as other studies, that for every dollar of administrative costs, the private sector incurred $20 in compliance costs. This twenty to one ratio of compliance to administrative costs was determined on the basis of the costs that were quantifiable. In the United States, Weidenbaum in 1979 estimated administrative costs to be $4.8 billion and compliance costs to be $97.9 billion.[7] In Canada, it was estimated in 1986 that the hidden costs to taxpayers and consumers of federal government regulations amounted to approximately $30 billion per year.[8]

Weidenbaum's estimates of compliance costs have been strongly criticized. As the Economic Council of Canada observed, it is extremely difficult to make even a rough estimate of compliance costs. While some empirical evidence may be gathered on the impact of certain specific regulations on specific firms, it is practically impossible to derive data on the total costs borne by firms and individuals on an economy-wide basis.

Political Activity Costs

These are costs associated with the initiation and passage of regulatory legislation. They include the costs incurred by government in reaching its decision to introduce particular regulations and by the legislature and its committees in reviewing and eventually incorporating the regulations in statutes. During this political process, additional costs may be incurred by industry and consumer groups and individuals who are likely to be affected by the regulations, whether positively or negatively. Industry usually retains legal counsel and other experts to make representations to government on regulatory matters and on contem-

---

[6] Murray L. Weidenbaum, *The Future of Business Regulation* (New York: American Management Associations, 1980), p. 13.

[7] *Ibid.*, p. 23.

[8] Task Force, *op. cit.*, p. 28.

plated regulatory policies. Various industries make their positions known through strong lobby groups which attempt to influence elected politicians and government officials. In addition, there are the costs involved in court challenges to regulations and their interpretation in particular cases.

Some estimates have determined these various political activity costs to equal approximately ten percent of compliance costs.[9] It has also been estimated that business executives may spend up to one-third of their time dealing with government and regulation related issues.[10]

Induced Costs of Regulation

Regulations may produce a variety of induced costs on the economy in the form of adverse effects on innovation, capital formation, production, efficiency, employment, and industry structures.

(i) Innovation. Regulations may retard innovation by reducing technological research and development in the area of new products and new production processes. Instead of scientific research to develop new technology, new products, new processes, etc. industry is forced to engage in what Weidenbaum has called defensive research.[11] As regulations proliferate and become more rigorous, industry becomes obligated to apply an increasing portion of their research funds and facilities to develop the technology needed to meet regulatory requirements. Less is available for the development of new technology that might improve productivity, reduce costs, and lead to the development of a wider range of new products and services. Furthermore, regulation may result in a longer time span between the development and the actual marketing of products which may discourage the development of new products or make them more expensive. The greater the number of tests to which a new product is subjected and the longer the period between the idea for a new product and its marketability, the less the incentive to develop new products.

Regulation may retard technological development and innovation in other ways as well. Consider the case of a regulated industry which tends towards monopoly and owes its monopoly position partly to the fact that government bars new entry. Some public utilities, and the telephone industry as it operated in the past, are good examples. Bell Canada was a government regulated and protected monopoly in both telephone services and equipment. Competition in the industry was non-existent. Given this situation, there was little incentive for Bell Canada to devote resources to research and technological development and to develop new products and services. Consumers were obliged to use the services and products provided by Bell since no substitutes were permitted. New innovations in the telecommunications industry could therefore be expected to develop much

---

[9] Murray L. Weidenbaum, "The High cost of Government Regulation," *Challenge*, Nov/Dec. 1979, p. 38.

[10] Murray L. Weidenbaum, *"The Future of Business Regulation, op. cit.,* pp. 36–37.

[11] Weidenbaum, *Challenge, op. cit.*

slower than if the industry had been subjected to the competitive forces of the market.

(ii) Capital Formation and Productivity. Regulations which cause industry to divert financial resources to meet government-mandated safety and environmental standards leave the industry with fewer financial resources for investment for productivity improvement and for new plant, equipment, and machinery. The consequent reduced rate of capital accumulation may result in a reduced rate of long-run economic growth. Regulation which results in the creation of non-production capital (i.e. capital not used to expand capacity) tends to reduce the output-capital ratio, since a lower output is generated by any given increase in capital stock. Estimates of the effects of regulation on productivity growth vary widely. There tends to be some agreement that in the U.S., after averaging an annual growth rate of 2.5 percent during the period 1948-1973, productivity fell to .5 percent annually, and of this reduction, approximately .25 to .4 percentage points can be attributed to regulation. The general conclusion from the various studies was that regulation was a fairly significant factor in the poorer productivity performance of the U.S. economy during the 1970s.[12]

(iii) Employment. Minimum-wage legislation has been included in government policies to redistribute income and to increase income levels of lower income groups. All provincial governments in Canada have legislated minimum wage levels, but as discussed in the previous chapter, minimum wage policies have stirred considerable controversy. Some have contended that minimum wages lead to unemployment, particularly among the young and the unskilled members of the labour force. Mandatory minimum wages, it is contended, price these workers out of the labour market. There may be numerous menial tasks for which a potential employer may be prepared to hire workers at relatively low wages. But, if the employer is forced to pay a wage substantially higher than the productivity required for these tasks, then these potential positions are simply not created or remain unfilled. The result is a higher level of unemployment than otherwise and a increased drain on the government's and society's resources as these unemployed workers become dependent on the rest of society.

(iv) Efficiency. The impact of regulation on economic efficiency may take a variety of forms. First, as explained earlier, direct regulation of industry on the basis of rate of return may lead to technical or X-inefficiency because the industry is left with little incentive to maintain maximum efficiency and minimize costs of production. Second, rate of return regulation may lead to a non-optimum mix of factors of production, producing over-capitalization or the Averch-Johnson effect. This effect was also analyzed in an earlier section. Third, regulation may result in long delays in the establishment of new industries. The Economic Council of Canada has pointed out that this is particularly likely in the establish-

---

[12] Robert E. Litman and W.D. Nordhaus, *Reforming Federal Regulation* (New Haven: Yale University Press, 1982), Ch. 2.

ment of industry in new geographical frontiers, such as the Canadian Arctic region, where the effects of industry such as oil and gas exploration and production on the ecology remains uncertain.[13] Delays will also likely be found in the establishment of industries which plan to produce new products, particularly chemicals, where there is uncertainly of the effects of the production process on the health of workers. The Council has identified a number of cases which typify the kinds of delays that can occur.[14] In one case the Steel Company of Canada (Stelco) applied to develop an industrial park on the banks of Lake Erie. Stelco was required to obtain the approval of seven different federal and provincial government agencies. In another cited case, Dow Chemical Corporation proposed the construction of a deep-water chemical shipping terminal on the west coast. Dow was required to obtain approval from five government agencies including the Departments of Fisheries and Environment, and the federal Harbours Board. An extreme example of the complexities that regulatory approval may produce was the Standard Oil Company proposal to construct a pipeline from Texas to California. The company was required to obtain 712 permits from a host of federal, state, and local agencies. The difficulties and delays in obtaining these necessary permits caused Standard Oil eventually to abandon the proposed project. And, in another case, former President of the United States, Jimmy Carter, whose family was in the peanut-growing and processing business in Georgia, once complained that it took the Food and Drug Administration twelve years and one hundred thousand pages of testimony to decide the percentage of peanuts that went into the composition of peanut butter.

A fourth factor that may impact on economic efficiency by producing delays and uncertainty relates to jurisdictional disputes and conflicting regulations. In a number of regulatory areas, federal and provincial regulatory agencies exercise joint jurisdiction. An example is environmental protection. It is not uncommon for jurisdictional disputes to arise between the two, leaving the affected industry in the middle with considerable uncertainty and costly delays. Disputes have arisen between the federal government and the coastal provinces over the regulatory jurisdiction of off-shore oil and gas exploration and off-shore fisheries. Similarly, disputes have occurred between Ottawa and Alberta over energy prices, causing some oil exploration companies to move to more favourable regions. The overlap and duplication of responsibilities may lead to conflicting regulations, as each level of government may have it own priorities and goals. Contradictory goals produce uncertainty for regulated industries because they receive conflicting directives or indicators from the agencies regarding their operations. For instance, during the period of energy shortages and rising prices in the late 1970s, consumers and industry were urged to conserve energy. At the same time in both Canada and the U.S., the emission standards for automobiles were raised in the interests of pollution control, causing a reduction in the num-

---

[13] Economic Council of Canada, *Reforming Regulation, 1981*, Ch. 11.

[14] *Ibid.*

ber of kilometres per litre of gasoline that automobiles travelled. Similarly, in the U.S., at the same time that the Department of Energy was urging industry to convert from oil to coal to conserve the consumption of oil, the Environmental Protection Agency was urging plants to convert from coal to oil to reduce air pollution.

Industry Structure

Regulations which force firms to incur high compliance costs may cause difficulties for small firms to remain in operation. To the extent that higher costs force small firms to leave, the industry will become more highly concentrated and more monopolistic. There does not, however, appear to be conclusive evidence that compliance costs have had this effect. The more significant compliance costs appear to have been incurred by oligopolistic-type industries, characterized by relatively few large firms, which to date do not appear to have been overly burdened by compliance costs. These include the automobile industry, nuclear energy, mining and smelting, iron and steel, oil and gas, and the petro-chemical industry.

The Economic Council of Canada in its examination of regulation conducted a survey of business enterprises to determine how they tend to view regulation and the costs that regulation may force the enterprises to incur.[15] It was discovered that costs incurred by firms tend to vary considerably depending on the type of industry and the size of the firm. In the survey, two groups of firms were identified; large corporate enterprises and small business. The large corporations, as expected, reported the most costly effects of regulation. The costs reported were primarily in terms of efficiency, innovation, expansion of operations, and the development and marketing of new products. The main irritant to small business of government regulations was the paperwork involved in maintaining records and filing the required reports to regulatory agencies. Most firms in the survey reported that their problems with regulation were not with the regulations themselves. Firms tended to understand the necessity and purpose of the regulations to which they were subjected. Their major complaints concerned the regulatory process and the inefficiencies in the process. These inefficiencies, with their delays and bureaucratic red tape, tended to add to the costs incurred by business in complying with regulations. Businessmen argued that there was a need to reform the regulatory process and the operations of regulatory agencies to make regulation more efficient.

Extreme caution must be observed when viewing this complex issue of the costs of government regulation. The very high estimates of the various costs might lead to a questioning of the desirability of many regulations and demands for reduced regulation. It must be remembered, however, that there is another side to regulation. The costs of regulation should not be considered in vacuum. Regulations are introduced for a purpose and certain benefits are expected. A

---

[15] *Ibid.*

major component of the benefits derived from regulations are costs prevented. So while the cost for the economy may be large in absolute dollar terms, the costs must be examined within the context of, and relative to, the benefits received. Indeed, an objective evaluation of government regulation is most appropriately conducted applying a form of benefit-cost analysis. This was one of the significant features of the recommendations for regulatory reform examined in the following chapter.

7

REGULATORY REFORM

The decade of the 1970s witnessed increasing concerns over the growth and extent of regulation and other government involvement in the economies of most Western countries. Among the driving forces of these concerns was technological change, which had a direct effect on the structure of industry and caused questions to be raised over the necessity of continued regulation of various industries. There was also an increasing awareness of the costs to the economy of regulation and inefficiencies in the regulatory process. Questions relating to regulatory costs and the need for regulations continued to be raised into the 1980s, and caused governments to examine regulation more closely with a view to making it more efficient and effective. This examination of regulations and the regulatory process led to varying degrees of regulatory reform and a trend to retrenchment of regulations and to deregulation. Combined with this movement of regulatory reform and deregulation was a movement by governments to begin privatizing government enterprises in a variety of areas.

Regulatory reform, deregulation, and privatization during this period can be observed in Canada, the United States, Europe, and Japan. In Canada, for example, the movement towards deregulation of the airline industry and promotion of competition eventually led to the privatization of government-owned Air Canada. The trucking industry, historically a regulated industry, was deregulated. The telecommunications equipment industry and specialized telecommunications services industries were deregulated and thrown open to competition. In areas of economic activity where a continuation of regulation was considered to be necessary and desirable, strong pressures were brought to bear on government and regulatory agencies to reform and improve the regulatory process to reduce inefficiencies, bureaucratic delays and administrative red tape, and to examine more carefully and systematically the need for introducing new regulations as well as the need for continuing existing regulations.

Deficiencies in the Regulatory Process

The growing concerns over the adverse effects of regulation on the economy produced a number of studies of regulation in Canada. These included studies by Parliamentary committees, by the Economic Council of Canada, and by the Federal Task Force on Program Review. The studies exposed the shortcomings of the regulatory process and put forward numerous recommendations for change.

The Economic Council of Canada in its extensive examination of regulation in the late 1970s and early 1980s focused on the general process of regulation; regulation in specific industries such as transportation, telecommunications, agriculture and fisheries; regulation to safeguard the environment; and, regulation of occupations, health and safety.[1]

Among the numerous deficiencies of regulation highlighted by the Economic Council were those relating to the process of introducing new regulations and monitoring existing regulations. The deficiencies enumerated by the Council included: inadequate information and notice provided to, and inadequate consultation with, affected individuals and groups in the development of proposals for new regulations; failure to assess the costs and benefits of newly proposed regulations; failure to re-evaluate existing regulations in any systematic manner; and, inadequate coordination of regulatory policy and regulations.[2]

The Council recommended three major initiatives for reducing these inadequacies and improving the regulatory process.[3] First, the Council recommended that federal and provincial governments provide advance notice of their intentions to initiate major new regulations and permit interested and affected parties an opportunity to examine and comment on the proposals. It was suggested that the government give a two-month notice of its intent to create a new regulation and this notice be published and widely distributed. Following this period, the government would publish a draft of the proposed regulation along with an analytical statement of its possible effects. A three-month study and comment period would follow, and on the basis of the information, comments and analysis produced by outside parties, the government would either proceed with, withdraw or change the proposed regulation. If this process was followed, it was argued, the government would avoid rushing into new regulations without adequately considering all aspects of the proposed regulation. Those parties adversely affected would likely draw attention to the potential costs that the regulation might produce, and regulators could weigh these costs against potential benefits. The additional information provided during this period of advance notice and consultation would enable governments to assess more accurately the desirability of proposed regulations before introducing the legislation.

The Economic Council proposed that public interest groups and interveners be encouraged to participate in the debate on the regulatory proposals. It was recognized that the public interest might not be very well represented in such

---

[1] The recommendations of the Economic Council of Canada for improving the general regulatory process are contained in Economic Council of Canada, *Responsible Regulation* (Ottawa: Canadian Government Publishing Centre, 1979), Ch. 6 and 7. Recommendations regarding the regulation of specific industries are contained in Economic Council of Canada, *Reforming Regulation, 1981* (Ottawa: Canadian Government Publishing Centre, 1981).

[2] *Responsible Regulation, op. cit.*, pp. 69–70.

[3] *Ibid.*, pp. 70–72.

debates because of the time and cost involved in organizing groups to represent general public opinion. Individuals as well might be discouraged by the personal cost involved in appearing at regulatory agency hearings to present their views. The Council believed that such public participation was desirable to balance the views of special interest groups and the views of strong, well-financed industry lobby groups. In an attempt to encourage public participation, the Council recommended that the government or its regulatory agencies help fund the costs incurred by public interest groups and individual interveners in the debate on proposed regulations.[4]

Second, the Economic Council recommended that all major new regulatory proposals be subjected to a form of benefit-cost analysis.[5] Benefit-cost analysis involves the identification and measurement of all benefits and costs of a proposal. If benefits exceed costs, or the benefit-cost ratio is greater than one, then the proposal would produce a net benefit to society and is considered justifiable on economic grounds. Benefit-cost analysis enables decision makers to determine if a government project (in this case a regulatory proposal) is justifiable, serves to identify marginally valid proposals, and serves to weed out undesirable or non-economic proposals where costs to society may greatly exceed benefits. The main limitation in the application of benefit-cost analysis is the problem of measurement. Many benefits and costs might be readily identifiable, but they may be intangible in that they do not enter market transactions and are difficult to price or to value. As mentioned earlier, numerous benefits take the form of costs prevented and are very difficult to measure. Despite its limitations, however, it can be argued that benefit-cost analysis would result in a greater amount of information on potential social and economic costs and benefits and enable the government to make a more objective decision. Even a process of identifying the various benefits and costs involved would be a useful exercise because it would help to focus on the issues involved in a regulatory decision. Some have proposed the preparation of a formal regulatory budget, which would consist of a budget or statement of the potential costs and benefits of every proposed regulation, including a comparison of the regulations. Individual regulatory proposals would, consequently, not be considered in isolation but would be compared with

---

[4] *Ibid.*, p. 82.

[5] For an outline and discussion of the principles and mechanism of benefit-cost analysis, see for example, E. Stokey and R. Zeckhauser, *A Primer For Policy Analysis* (New York: W.W. Norton & Co., 1978), Ch. 9; R. Sugden and A. Williams, *The Principles of Practical Cost-Benefit Analysis* (Oxford: Oxford University Press, 1978). For an outline of the application of benefit-cost analysis to regulation, see Murray L. Weidenbaum, *The Future of Business Regulation* (New York: American Management Associations, 1980), pp. 62–67; and, Douglas Needham, *The Economics and Politics of Regulation* (Toronto: Little, Brown, & Co., 1983), Ch. 3.

each other in terms of benefits and costs, as well as compared with other policy instruments designed to achieve similar objectives. The fact that the regulatory proposals have been costed and included in the budget would necessitate the involvement, review, and approval of both the cabinet and legislative committees. The regulatory budget would, therefore, ensure that both branches of government have considered the regulatory proposals before allocating and appropriating the required resources for their implementation.[6] Indeed, as part of regulatory reform some have called for a greater role for parliamentary committees in the regulatory process.[7] Parliament bears the ultimate responsibility for regulatory legislation and should be in possession of as much information as possible on the costs and effects of proposed regulations before enacting the legislation. A detailed analysis of relevant benefits and costs would avoid the introduction of new regulations which may appear desirable on the surface but where an in-depth analysis might show them to produce excessive costs to the economy or some of its components relative to the benefits attained.

Another form of economic analysis that may be used by government to analyze regulatory proposals is the application of measures of effectiveness. In this process, government determines an objective and considers various alternative means, including regulation, of achieving the objective. Measures of effectiveness assist the government to determine the alternative most effective in achieving the objective. For example, assume that an objective of government is to raise the income level of the lower-income groups of society. One possible method is to apply a minimum-wage regulatory policy. Alternatives might include the increased use of transfer payments, retraining of unskilled workers enabling them to find better-paying jobs, or various job-creation programs. Measures of effectiveness may be developed and applied to help determine the alternative most effective in achieving the stated objective of raising income levels.

The third recommendation of the Economic Council for improving the regulatory process was for governments to evaluate periodically existing regulations and operations of regulatory agencies.[8] Regulations introduced in an earlier period may have outlived their usefulness and the only way to determine whether such is indeed the case is through a periodic re-examination of these regulations. Periodic re-assessment would also be useful to determine whether the regulations have been effective in achieving their objectives, and would serve to identify possible conflicting regulations. One method proposed to ensure the periodic assessment of regulations is the application of sunset laws. These are provisions attached to regulatory legislation that would terminate the legislation after a specified period of time. Such provisions systematically force the regulatory

---

[6] A discussion of the regulatory budget and its purpose is contained in Robert E. Litan and William D. Nordhaus, *Reforming Federal Regulation* (New Haven: Yale University Press, 1983), Ch. 6.

[7] Economic Council of Canada, *Responsible Regulation, op. cit.*, pp. 80–81.

[8] *Ibid.*, 71–72.

agency and the legislature to review the regulations prior to the expiration date. Consequently, the fact that regulations are contained in legislation would no longer be justification for their continuation. They would have to be reviewed and would be re-legislated only if their continuation is justifiable.

In addition to the above recommendations for improving the general management of government regulation, the Economic Council of Canada made numerous proposals for the reform of regulation in various specific areas of government regulatory activity. The recommendations were designed both to streamline the regulatory process and where possible to reduce the extent of regulation in specific regulated industries. The areas examined included: trains, trucks, taxicabs and airlines in the transportation industry; telecommunications; agriculture; fisheries; pollution; and, occupational health and safety.[9] In the area of rail transportation, the Council made several recommendations designed to streamline the regulatory process and reduce administrative delays. These included giving the then regulatory agency, the Canadian Transport Commission, greater freedom in responding to rate grievances and to change the appeal procedures of the Commission to expedite the settlement of grievances. In the airline industry, the Council proposed that restrictions on entry into the industry be relaxed to permit greater competition in the industry and that the Transport Commission relax its regulation of fares, leaving fares to be more freely determined by competition and market forces. Increased competition and relaxed regulation was also recommended for the telecommunications industry. In the area of agriculture, the Council strongly cautioned against the establishment of additional agricultural marketing boards with power to control output and prices and with influence over imports. It was recommended that the output quota system be restructured to permit increased output and to allow increased application of market forces to clear the expanded production. It was suggested that governments examine alternative policies to help solve the problems of low income and income instability in the farming industry. Furthermore, the government was advised to review the membership of its agricultural regulatory agencies and boards to ensure an adequate balance of representatives from agricultural producers, consumers, and processors. Similar proposals were directed to the fisheries industry, including the gradual elimination of subsidies and other concessions to the industry.

Environmental control was of major concern to the Council. It proposed a number of changes to the regulatory process to strengthen and make more effective the regulations protecting the environment. These included more rigorous regulations dealing with the storage, transport, and treatment of hazardous waste products; increased cooperation between the governments of Canada and the U.S. to reduce pollution of the Great Lakes; and, increased use of financial incentives to encourage pollution control.

---

[9] *Ibid.* For a list of the recommendations of the Economic Council, see pages 143–147.

Regulations designed to assure workplace health and safety were found to be defective. The Council recommended that governments allocate more resources to this area of regulation, including improved staffing qualifications for regulatory personnel and increased compensation for the staff, along with an increase in the number of inspectors and inspections. It was further recommended that enforcement procedures be strengthened, and that the legislation and regulations pertaining to occupational health and safety be consolidated under one administrative department.

Government Actions on Regulatory Reform

Among the government's early initiatives to institute some reform in the regulatory process was the establishment of an Office of Regulatory Reform. Following the Economic Council's recommendation, this Office was given the mandate to publish regulatory agendas of Departments, outlining proposed new regulations and inviting public input. Further action was initiated in 1984 when the government announced an Agenda for Economic Renewal, a key component of which was the reform of regulation. Government policy, as outlined in the Agenda, was to "redefine the role of government so that it provides a better framework for growth and job-creation and less of an obstacle to change and innovation."[10]

A Task Force on Program Review was established under the chairmanship of the Deputy Prime Minister, Mr. Erik Nielsen, to review federal government programs with a view to provide better service to the public with greater efficiency. Within this context, the Task Force conducted a comprehensive and intensive review of government regulations, the regulatory process, and of regulatory agencies. In its report in 1986, the Task Force stated that "Canada is both over-regulated and badly regulated."[11] In the view of the Task Force, there was too much regulation relative to the public's capacity to absorb it and relative to the availability of resources to implement and enforce it. The public had too little access to, and involvement in, the development and review of regulation and Parliament did not have adequate control over the regulatory system. The Task Force concluded that the cumulative effect of regulation at the three levels of government in Canada constituted a major impediment to economic growth, initiative, enterprise, and personal freedom. Many of the recommendations of the Task Force for reforming and improving regulation were similar to those proposed earlier by the Economic Council of Canada.

On the basis of the regulatory review by the Task Force, the Federal Government in 1986 announced its Regulatory Reform Strategy, outlining federal regu-

[10] Canada, Office of Privatization and Regulatory Affairs, *Regulatory Reform: Making It Work* (Ottawa: 1988), p. 7.

[11] Canada, *Management of Government: Regulatory Programs*, A Study Team Report to the Task Force on Program Review (Ottawa: Supply and Services Canada, 1986), p. 17.

latory reform policy and reform guidelines. In introducing the Reform Strategy in Parliament, Mr. Nielsen emphasized that it represented

> the government's intention to stem the growth of regulation, especially economic regulation, and wherever possible to get the existing regulatory burden off the backs of productive Canadians ... yet it also confirms our intention to protect the public through the use of regulation wherever it is the best and most economical instrument for doing so.[12]

The two fundamental themes of the Strategy were: (1) reforms in the regulatory process to provide better regulation and avoid indiscriminate regulatory activity, and (2) reforms to existing regulations to improve their efficiency and effectiveness.[13] The program of reform would not necessarily mean the massive reduction of regulations; indeed, the government specifically rejected systematic across-the-board deregulation. Instead, the government would attempt to "regulate smarter" through greater efficiency, greater accountability, and greater sensitivity to those affected by federal regulations.

The framework for regulatory reform was set out in ten guiding principles. These included: the recognition of the vital role of an efficient marketplace and the recognition that regulation should not impede the efficient operation of the market; the continued use of regulation to achieve social and economic objectives; limit as much as possible the overall rate of growth and proliferation of new regulations; an evaluation of social and economic costs and benefits of new regulations and a clear indication that benefits exceed costs before proceeding with new regulatory proposals; greater control and review of regulation by Parliament; increased public access and participation in the regulatory process; a streamlined system that would reduce costs, uncertainties and delays; greater cooperation with the provincial governments on regulatory matters; and, the establishment of a new Ministry for Regulatory Affairs responsible for coordinating and managing the government's regulatory policy and reform strategy.[14]

At the same time the government announced the adoption of a Citizens' Code of Regulatory Fairness. The Code was based on the premise that citizens are entitled to be informed of the government's policy and criteria for exercising regulatory power, so that they have a basis for judging the regulatory performance of government and in a sense regulate the regulators. Some 15 specifications were outlined in the Code, committing the government to openness, fairness, efficiency, and accountability. The specifications in the Code included a commitment that regulations would be characterized by minimum interference with individual freedoms; that government would encourage and facilitate a full opportunity for consultation and participation by citizens; that early notice of regulatory initiatives would be provided; that once regulations were in place the

---

[12] Canada, House of Commons, *Debates*, Vol. VII, Feb 13, 1986, p. 10783.

[13] *Regulatory Reform: Making It Work, op. cit.*, p. 1.

[14] *Ibid.*, pp. 65–66.

government would clearly communicate what the regulatory requirements were; that the regulations would be securely founded in law; that officials responsible for developing and enforcing regulations would be held accountable for their actions; and, that government would not use regulation unless a problem clearly existed, that government intervention was justified, and that regulation was the most appropriate policy to apply. In addition, the Citizen's Code provided that benefit-cost analysis be applied to new regulations; and, that government avoid introducing regulations to control supply, price, entry and exit in competitive markets unless "overriding national interests are at stake." [15]

Among its actions in implementing its new regulatory reform strategy the government introduced several innovations.[16] First, the government implemented an annual regulatory planning and priority-setting exercise, the results of which are to be published in an annual Federal Regulatory Plan.[17] In this process, departments are required to submit for Cabinet approval in the fall of each year an outline of their proposed regulatory initiatives for the coming year. The information must contain, for each proposed initiative, the title of the proposal, a description of the purpose and content of the proposal and how it will be accomplished, the statutory authority or law on which the proposal is based, a statement on the anticipated impact of the proposal on society and the economy, the anticipated date of the final notice for the pre-publication of the draft proposed in the *Canada Gazette* (which must be at least thirty days before the proposal becomes final), and the name and telephone number of the official who can be contacted for additional information on the proposal. The objective of this Regulatory Plan is to provide advance notice of the government's intentions to introduce new regulations and to provide full opportunity for those affected to react before the proposals come into effect. The public and business are therefore provided with an opportunity to participate in the regulatory decision making process. The 1987 Regulatory Plan described 822 regulatory proposals from 25 federal departments and agencies. The 1988 plan contained 954 entries. All of these entries are required to be reviewed by the Cabinet before being authorized for publication in the annual *Regulatory Plan*.

The second innovation in the government's regulatory reform plan was the implementation of a regulatory impact analysis exercise to accompany all proposed regulations. This exercise emphasizes the application by regulatory agencies of benefit-cost analysis to regulatory proposals where appropriate, or other analysis designed to provide more and better information to decision makers. The result of this analysis appears in summary form in the annually-published *Federal Regulatory Plan* as a regulatory impact analysis statement (RIAS) mentioned above. The inclusion of the RIAS in the *Regulatory Plan* is designed to

---

[15] *Ibid.*, pp. 67–68.

[16] *Ibid.* For an outline of these innovations, see pp. 11–14.

[17] See, for example, Canada, Office of Privatization and Regulatory Affairs, *Federal Regulatory Plan*, 1988 (Ottawa: Canadian Government Publishing Centre, 1987).

provide the public or affected parties with a basis for comment, inquiry, or challenge to the regulation.

A third component of the government's regulatory action program was a commitment to reduce the length of the regulatory approval process from an average of nine months prior to 1984 to an average of three months. The objective of reducing the past lengthy delays was to reduce the confusion and uncertainty of those affected by the proposed regulations.

The final innovation was the introduction of a program of systematic review and evaluation of all regulatory programs over a continuing seven-year cycle. This periodic re-assessment would serve to identify regulations that may be becoming obsolete, determine the effectiveness of regulations and keep them current or up-to-date.

The government announced in 1988 that its program of regulatory reform initiated in 1986 was making good progress. In that year a new Ministry called the Office of Privatization and Regulatory Affairs was created to oversee and coordinate the regulatory reform program, and to ensure that those affected by regulations had an opportunity to respond to proposed regulations before they came into effect. Since 1986, federal departments and agencies have engaged in extensive examinations and reforms of their regulatory programs, including the development of closer cooperation between agencies which shared regulatory jurisdictions in an attempt to harmonize activities and to reduce the degree of duplication. The government claimed that the paperwork involved in regulation had been substantially reduced, that regulatory programs had been made more effective and responsive, and that regulation no longer represented a hidden layer of government—making rules without adequate public input. The further claim was made that "Canada now has one of the most effective regulatory oversight systems in the world." [18]

Approach to Regulatory Reform in the United States

Introducing the regulatory reform program in Canada in 1986, a spokesman for the federal government stated that it was the government's intention to get the regulatory burden off the backs of productive Canadians. This statement appeared to be an echo of an earlier promise in 1980 by the President of the United States, Ronald Reagan, to reduce the role of government in the economy, including regulation, and to restore the principles of free enterprise to the economy. To achieve this objective, the President had established the Office of Information and Regulatory Affairs and charged it with the responsibility of reviewing and approving all new regulatory proposals. Regulatory agencies were required to give advance notice of sixty days of their intent to propose new regulations, and all new regulations were required to be justified by applying benefit-cost analysis. At the same time, the President appointed a Task Force on Regulatory Relief, chaired by the Vice-President. The function of the Task Force was to oversee the

[18] *Regulatory Reform: Making it Work, op. cit.*, p. 9.

Administration's deregulation program. This program included: the appointment of regulators who supported regulatory reform and deregulation; the reduction of the budgets of regulatory agencies; a proposal to Congress to attach "sunset laws" to new regulatory legislation; proposals to streamline the regulatory process by reducing unnecessary paperwork and administrative delays; and, the encouragement and continuation of the deregulation movement that had begun in such long-standing regulated industries as airlines, railroads, and telecommunications. The Administration also clearly identified areas where it was deemed that regulations were impeding economic efficiency and productivity and, therefore, should be relaxed. A number of agencies and regulations were targeted in this "regulatory hit-list." The Environmental Protection Agency was to be encouraged to relax some of its pollution standards. The Occupational Safety and Health Administration was to be encouraged to relax its standards for increased occupational safety, which required large investments in safer machinery and equipment. Alternative methods to improve safety were to be considered. The Energy Department was instructed to re-examine the effects on the environment of increased conversion of industry from oil to coal with a view to relaxing requirements and facilitating conversion. The Nuclear Energy Commission was encouraged to revise the licensing procedure to promote wider use of nuclear-generated electrical power.

The degree of success of this program has been a subject of considerable debate. By 1983, the Task Force on Regulatory Relief estimated that its success in reducing bureaucratic red tape and delays, the application of benefit-cost analysis which slowed the introduction of new regulations, and the relaxation of various regulatory requirements would save American consumers and business approximately $150 billion over a ten-year period. Critics of the program, however, charged that the program had consisted primarily of non-enforcement of existing regulations rather than regulatory reform. Employment in regulatory agencies had been reduced by 15 percent from 1980 to 1986 and the budgets of some agencies had been reduced, while those of others were held relatively constant. The result was a weakening of regulatory agencies' capacity to enforce regulations. Furthermore, environmentalists and consumer protection groups charged that the financial savings were being made primarily at the expense of the environment and consumer protection, and that the current savings from the relaxation of regulation standards would be more than offset by the future damage caused by increased pollution and dangers to health and safety. Toward the end of the Reagan Administration, the crusade for increased deregulation and relaxation of regulatory requirements appeared to moderate, particularly in the areas of environmental protection, and occupational and consumer health and safety. Congress and state governments began to express increasing support for the need to reduce pollution and maintain health and safety standards.

This program of regulatory reform and deregulation in the United States appears to have taken a somewhat different direction from that attempted in Canada. While the Canadian government and the provinces did pursue a program of economic deregulation and privatization during the 1980s, and attempted to streamline the regulatory process and regulate smarter, there is little evidence of relaxation of regulatory standards in the area of social regulation, such as environmental protection and worker and consumer health and safety. In fact, the federal government and many provinces strengthened their environmental protection laws, and the Canadian government expressed increasing concern with the need for international cooperation and action to reduce pollution causing acid rain and depleting the earth's ozone protective shield. Government actions in Canada regarding regulation that drew the most attention were those pertaining to the deregulation of traditionally regulated industries and the revision of the Combines Investigation Act, which formed part of the regulatory reform program.

The most prominent areas of deregulation in Canada have been transportation and telecommunications. In the transportation industry, certain segments, such as trucking, the railroads, and the airlines, had a long history of regulation of rates, services, and entry. The telephone industry had been regulated almost from its inception, and was a government-protected monopoly. These industries experienced major changes in structure during the latter part of the 1970s and 1980s as the government embarked on its program of deregulation.

The underlying assumption of the deregulation program was that the market system and competition is a more efficient allocator of resources and more effective regulator of prices and output than are regulatory agencies. Greater reliance on competition and market forces, however, assumes that fair competition will be the norm in an industry. Governments, therefore, have an obligation to ensure fair competition and prevent restrictive competitive practices if reliance is to be placed on market forces.

The federal government finally managed to replace its outdated and ineffective Anti-Combines Act with the Competition Act in 1986. The Act removed federal powers over mergers and monopolies from criminal law, thereby improving the federal governments' ability to respond effectively to issues of mergers and other anti-competitive practices. Some areas of deregulation in Canada, and the application of the new Competition Act, are examined in the following chapters.

PART TWO

CASE STUDIES IN GOVERNMENT REGULATION IN CANADA

THE AIR CARRIER INDUSTRY

In the last decade the Canadian transportation industry has witnessed major retrenchment in government involvement in transportation activities together with significant structural changes. The air carrier and railway components of the industry have traditionally operated as highly-regulated, monopolistic enterprises. They owed their monopolistic positions to government control of entry into the industry, and in return were subjected to government control of their fares, routes, and other aspects of their operations. Government regulation was a substitute for competition in the industry.

In the last decade, however, airlines, railways, and trucking have in varying degrees been freed of government regulatory control and have been left to operate in a more open, competitive market. A movement in the late 1970s toward deregulation culminated in 1987 with the passage of the new National Transportation Act, which deals with the economic regulation of air, rail, and water transport, and the passage of the Motor Vehicle Transport Act, which covers the regulation of truck transportation.

This chapter focuses on the air carrier industry in Canada. Beginning with a brief historical background of transport regulation, the chapter proceeds to a description and analysis of the regulation of the airlines industry and its operation under regulation. This is followed by an analysis of deregulation of the industry and its current structure and operation. The air carrier industry provides an excellent case study of the operation of an industry under regulation compared with its operation as a deregulated industry.

Background to Transportation Regulation

Transportation is important to the development and operation of an economy, particularly a country as geographically large and diversified as Canada. Transportation serves to bring the various regions together both economically and socially, and has been used in Canada as an instrument of national policy. It was recognized early in the economic development of Canada that a strong network of transportation would be required, particularly an East-West network, to tie the regions together and to resist the more natural North-South pull on the North American continent. The cornerstone of Canada's National Policy of 1879 was the construction of a transcontinental railway, the Canadian Pacific Railway, which was constructed only after considerable government involvement and financial assistance. Government policy in transportation continued to follow this direction with significant direct funding for construction of roads, rail lines, canals and harbours, including such major projects as the Trans-Canada Highway and the St. Lawrence Seaway. A failing railway system led to consolidation and the establishment of the government-owned Canadian National Railway in 1920, which together with the Canadian Pacific Railway gave Canada two transcontinental systems. The development of air travel produced Trans-Canada Airlines in 1937, a trans-continental monopoly owned and operated as a federal Crown corporation. Today, Canada has approximately 95,000 km. of railway track, over 840,000 km. of roads and highways, 25 large, deep water ports and 475 smaller harbours, and over 1300 licensed airports with 10 of the largest handling 80 percent of all traffic. The airline, rail, trucking and shipping industry earns about $50 billion annually, and provides direct and indirect employment for over one million Canadians. Total private and government investment in transportation exceeds $150 billion.

Canada is a trading nation and transportation is vital in moving products not only within the country, but between Canada and other countries. A significant portion of the country's prosperity stems from the sale of its raw materials and manufactured goods in foreign markets. To maintain its trade position Canadian goods must be competitive in international markets. An efficient, cost-effective transportation system can contribute to making Canadian industry competitive in these markets.

Early recognition by the Canadian government of the vital role of transportation in the future growth and prosperity of the country led to heavy government direct and indirect involvement in the construction of transportation facilities as mentioned earlier, and in the regulation of these facilities. Several objectives of this intervention have been identified. First, the government attempted to ensure that basic transportation services were provided and there was continuity of service. A second objective was to ensure that transportation services were provided to areas that the market, if left alone, might not service. These included remote and sparsely populated areas that depended on basic transportation services for survival but might not generate sufficient traffic to be profitable to private entrepreneurs. Third, transportation services were to be provided at reasonable or fair prices. The various components of the transportation sector lend themselves to monopoly, either on a national or regional basis, with potential for excessive rates and profits. Finally, the government was committed to ensuring a satisfactory level of safety standards in the various modes of transportation.

Regulation of transportation can be traced to the Railway Act of 1851, which provided that all railway rates were subject to the approval of the Governor-in-Council.[1] In 1903, regulatory power was placed in the hands of a Board of Railway Commissioners. The Board was vested with the authority to regulate

---

[1] For an early history of transportation regulation in Canada and the roles of the Board of Railway Commissioners and the Board of Transport Commissioners, see A.W. Currie, *Economics of Canadian Transportation*, 2nd ed. (Toronto: University of Toronto Press, 1959), Ch. XVI.

practically all aspects of rail services including rates and fares, stations, branch lines, and safety. In 1937, when Trans-Canada Airlines was established as a monopoly in air transportation, the Transport Act changed the name of the Board to the Board of Transport Commissioners and gave it added jurisdiction over transportation by air and water. At the provincial level, several provincial governments began to intervene with regulations in the trucking industry just prior to World War II as a means of providing some stability to a highly competitive industry characterized by frequent periods of destructive competition and consequent bankruptcies and disruption of services.

In 1967, the National Transportation Act established the Canadian Transport Commission (CTC). The Act gave the CTC responsibility for regulating all modes of transportation under federal jurisdiction. In addition, the CTC was granted regulatory authority over pipelines, extra-provincial trucking, telegraph service, and telephone service in areas not serviced by provincially-owned telephone companies.[2]

The CTC obtained its powers from the National Transportation Act, which created the commission, as well as from other statutes such as the Aeronautics Act, the Railway Act, and the Transport Act. The CTC was a quasi-judicial body with powers to make decisions in individual cases and broad powers to develop regulations. Its decisions were binding and could be reviewed only by appeal to the Cabinet or by appeal to the Supreme Court of Canada on a question of law or jurisdiction. Therefore, while the CTC enjoyed a considerable degree of autonomy, it was not completely independent. In addition to the restrictions that appeals placed on the functioning of the CTC, it also had to share certain functions with the Department of Transport (Transport Canada). Transport Canada retained responsibility for overall national transportation policy, coordinated transportation activities, controlled navigation and provided navigation aids, and set safety standards. The CTC monitored and assisted in the development of transportation policy, but its main function was to license and regulate commercial transportation carriers.

The CTC exercised its powers through a system of committees, with a committee for each major mode of transportation, such as the Railway Transport Committee, the Air Transport Committee and the Water Transport Committee. The Railway Transport Committee had jurisdiction over construction, maintenance, and operation of railways, including the location of lines, crossings, safety of train operations, investigation of accidents, abandonment of lines, and operating rules. The other committees similarly were responsible for regulating a wide range of transportation activities under their respective jurisdictions.

In 1984, the federal government announced plans for the complete overhaul of its national transportation policy. A primary objective of the new policy was to bring transportation regulations more in line with the demands of industry and

---

[2] The role of the Canadian Transport Commission is discussed in Ivan R. Feltham, "Transport Regulation in Canada," in K.W. Studnicki-Gizbert, ed., *Issues in Canadian Transport Policy* (Toronto: Macmillan Co. of Canada, 1974), pp. 309–343.

consumers. This involved the identification and removal of obsolete regulations which stifled initiative, competition, and growth. In 1984, an agreement with the provinces resulted in the reform and deregulation of the trucking industry and produced the 1987 Motor Vehicle Transport Act. On January 1, 1988, a new National Transportation Act came into effect. The Act contained a declaration of national transportation policy whose general objective was stated to be:

> a safe, economic, efficient and adequate network of viable and effective transportation services making the best use of all available modes of transportation at the lowest total cost ... to serve the transportation needs of shippers and travellers and to maintain the economic well-being and growth of Canada and its regions.[3]

Several more specific principles and objectives were outlined in the Act. First, the highest practicable safety standards were to be given top priority. Some of the initiatives taken to improve transportation safety included: amendments to the Aeronautics Act to improve aviation safety; a National Safety Code for more uniform and rigorous truck and bus safety standards; extensive new regulations and stronger enforcement under the Transportation of Dangerous Goods Act; a new Railway Safety Act to reform and modernize railway safety regulations; and, legislation for a new, independent board to investigate air, rail, and marine accidents.

Second, the new Transportation Act placed emphasis on competition and market forces as the best means of providing users with effective transportation at the lowest possible cost. Third, economic regulation was to be applied only to those services and regions where regulation was determined necessary to serve the transportation needs of users, and the regulations were not to impede or limit a carrier to compete freely with other carriers or other modes of transportation. And, finally, carriers were to apply fares, rates, and conditions that would not result in unfair disadvantages to competitors or create obstacles to access to transportation. A new agency, the National Transportation Agency, was created to replace the CTC and to oversee the new policy.

It was in this new environment of regulation that changes were gradually implemented in the airlines industry, in which rates were deregulated and obstacles to new entry were removed. The process of regulation and deregulation of the airlines industry is analyzed in the following section.

Air Transportation: Historical Development

By the end of World War I Canada was manufacturing aeroplanes, had developed a small air force, and was using air transportation to service primarily areas not accessible by other modes of transportation. By 1922, civil aviation services were being provided by over two dozen companies. These services were first regulated by an Air Board, but regulation was soon transferred to the Department

---

[3] Canada, *Statutes of Canada 1988.*

of National Defence. In 1936, control over civil aviation was transferred to the Civil Aviation Division of the Department of Transport. This Division was authorized to regulate air routes, license commercial pilots and other aviation personnel, and to inspect and register aircraft and airports.

The rapid increase in air passenger service, freight, and mail service prompted the federal government to propose that the two railway companies, Canadian Pacific Railway (CPR) and Canadian National Railway (CNR), form a joint company to provide a transcontinental air transportation system. The proposal was rejected by the Canadian Pacific Railway, which led to the passage of the Trans-Canada Air Lines Act in 1937 and the establishment of Trans-Canada Airlines (TCA).[4] The airline was established as a subsidiary of the CNR Company, with the shares to be held by the CNR. There was a provision, however, that the Department of Transport could, upon government approval, acquire the shares and make the airline a government Crown Corporation divested from the CNR. The Minister of Transport, subject to the approval of the Governor-in-Council, was authorized to enter into a contract with TCA regarding the types of aircraft the corporation would use, the routes, and the schedule of services. Passenger and freight rates were to be on a competitive basis with other carriers in North America. The contract also provided for Parliamentary-appropriated subsidies to cover any deficits incurred by the corporation.

Trans-Canada Airlines was granted a monopoly on trans-continental and mainline routes and was required to operate certain routes on the instruction of the government. Regional and local routes which were considered supplementary to mainline routes, however, were to be left to private enterprise. Smaller airlines that were expected to service supplementary routes included Canadian Pacific Airlines, a subsidiary of the CPR Company. In essence, TCA was established as an instrument of the government to provide cross-Canada air services and this policy was continued into the 1940s.

In 1943–44 the government re-iterated its policy on air transportation. TCA had been established as a non-profit system of air transportation, and would continue to be the sole provider of mainline, trans-continental and international air services. Despite pressure from a rapidly expanding Canadian Pacific Airlines for permission to compete in trans-continental and international air services, the government maintained that the role of private airlines was supplementary, and competition between airlines on the same route continued to be prohibited.[5]

In 1944, responsibility for regulating air transportation was transferred to a newly-established Air Transport Board, which would operate under the provisions of the Transport Act and the Aeronautics Act. The Board's responsibilities

---

[4] A description of the establishment of Trans-Canada Airlines and its early operation is contained in C.A. Ashley and R. Smails, *Canadian Crown Corporations* (Toronto: MacMillan Co, 1965), Ch. 15; in Philip Smith, *It Seems Like Only Yesterday; Air Canada-The First Fifty Years* (Toronto: McClelland and Stewart, 1986); and, in A.W. Currie, *Economics of Canadian Transportation*, 2nd ed. (Toronto: University of Toronto Press, 1959), Ch. XX.

[5] Smith, *op.cit.*, pp. 102–105.

included the power to issue, amend, and revoke licences to carriers, to approve routes and rates, and to advise the government on air transportation matters. The Air Transport Board, however, did not enjoy the same autonomy as the Board of Transport Commissioners. All decisions of the Air Transport Board were subject to the approval of the Minister of Transport, who also heard appeals on such issues as licences. Appeals on legal or jurisdictional matters, however, were heard by the Cabinet or the Supreme Court of Canada. It appears that the reason for granting the Air Transport Board more of an advisory role rather than the semi-judicial status enjoyed by the Board of Transport Commissioners was that air transportation was still in its infancy and government policy on air transportation was still developing. In such an unsettled environment it was believed desirable for the government to maintain its policy-making function rather than to delegate it to regulatory agency.[6]

In certain matters of air transport, such as the relations between the air carriers and the Post Office, the Air Transport Board had no jurisdiction. Indeed, the Post Office played a significant role in the early development of air services in Canada. Airmail formed an important component of the airlines' business. Relations between the Post Office and the air carriers were governed by contract negotiated between the air carriers and the Post Office. Rates were negotiated on the basis of volume and weight and if Trans Canada Airlines suffered a loss on the service it would be compensated by a government subsidy.

In 1967, the National Transportation Act created the Canadian Transport Commission (CTC) as a quasi-judicial agency responsible for regulating all modes of transportation. Air transport regulation was made the responsibility of the Air Transport Committee of the CTC. Under the Aeronautics Act, the Committee was responsible for the economic regulation of commercial air services in Canada and air services between Canada and foreign countries, and also played a role in bilateral negotiations with foreign countries for exchange of traffic rights. The Committee was responsible for the classification of air-carriers, and issued regulations dealing with commercial air services, traffic rates and fares, service schedules, routes and base of operations, records and reports, and various other matters.

The technical side of civil aviation includes such matters as aircraft registration, licensing of personnel, establishment and maintenance of airports, air traffic control, and air safety. These matters were, until 1986, administered by the Canadian Air Transport Administration (CATA) of Transport Canada. In 1986, the CATA was divided into two sections, namely, the aviation group and the airports authority group, and responsibilities were allocated accordingly.

By the early 1970s the airline industry in Canada had evolved into a well-established system. Commercial air-carriers consisted of four main types of carriers; namely, mainline toll per unit carriers, regional toll per unit carriers, local

---

[6] Currie, *op. cit.*, pp. 353–355.

TABLE 8–1: Canada's Air Carrier System 1974

Air Carrier	Operating Revenue (% of total)	Revenue Passengers ('000)	Revenue Passengers Miles ('000,000)
National & International	71		
Air Canada		10,700	10,200
Canadian Pacific Airlines		2,200	3,100
Regional	12		
Pacific Western Airlines		1,900	670
Eastern Provincial Airways		594	239
Nordair		157	--
Quebecair		592	248
Transair		405	225
Other	17		
(Charter, Local and Commuter—approx. 600 airlines) Wardair Great Lakes Airways Time Air Others			

SOURCE: *Canada Year Book 1975* (Ottawa: Statistics Canada, 1975).

and commuter carriers, and charter carriers. Canada's air carrier system as it operated in 1974 is illustrated in Table 8-1.

Specifically the air transportation system was made up of the following:

1. Canada's national and international mainline carriers consisted of Air Canada and Canadian Pacific Airlines. Air Canada, a Crown corporation incorporated in 1937 as Trans-Canada Airlines, provided passenger, commodity, and mail services over a cross-Canada network and to various foreign points. Up until the mid 1970s, Air Canada dominated the nation's air carrier industry with approximately 80 percent of mainline traffic. Canadian Pacific Airlines (CP Air), a private company owned by Canadian Pacific Limited, was only about one-quarter the size of Air Canada measured in terms of passenger revenue. CP Air was restricted by the Canadian Transport Commission to transcontinental services linking Vancouver, Edmonton, Calgary, Winnipeg, Toronto, Ottawa, and Montreal, to some interior services in British Columbia and the Yukon, and some foreign destinations primarily in the Far East. It's share of the

busiest transcontinental traffic route—the Montreal-Toronto-Vancouver route—was restricted to 25 percent of the traffic. In 1974 Air Canada and CP Air together earned 71 percent of the total operating revenues of Canadian commercial air-carriers.

2. Regional carriers operated within the various regions of the country and supplemented the mainline carriers. Each regional airline was restricted to a fairly well-defined area with little or no competition from other regional carriers. In effect, the regional carriers could be classified as regional monopolies. There were five regional carriers in operation in the 1970s prior to deregulation, each of which was a private enterprise. In 1974 these five regional air-carriers earned 12 percent of the total operating revenues of Canadian commercial air-carriers.

The five regional air carriers were Pacific Western Airlines, Eastern Provincial Airways, Nordair, Quebecair, and Transair. Pacific Western Airlines operated in the interior of British Columbia, northern Alberta and the Northwest Territories, and had routes between Vancouver and Calgary, and Calgary and Edmonton. The airline also operated international charter passenger services from Vancouver, Edmonton and Calgary, and operated extensive freight services over the entire scheduled domestic route system.

Eastern Provincial Airways was the regional carrier for the Atlantic provinces. It provided service between various centers in the four provinces and Labrador. Nordair maintained extensive air service between Montreal and points in Northern Quebec and the arctic islands. It also operated scheduled services between Montreal, Ottawa, Hamilton, Windsor, and Pittsburgh, a northern charter service based in Frobisher Bay in the Northwest Territories, and domestic charter flights within Canada and international charters from eastern Canada to the southern United States and the Caribbean.

Quebecair offered scheduled services between a large number of small communities in Quebec and Labrador. Service was also provided between Quebec and Montreal, together with charter flights within Canada and to the United States, the Caribbean, and South America.

Transair Ltd., headquartered in Winnipeg, operated scheduled services in Manitoba, western Ontario, and the Northwest Territories, and charter flights from Canada to the United States, Mexico, and the Caribbean. Transair was purchased by Pacific Western Airlines in 1979.

3. Local and commuter carriers provided residual services within the regions but operated much shorter routes in general than the regional carriers. They provided short-haul service primarily between the large urban centers and small surrounding communities. They included such companies as Great Lake Airways of London, and Time Air of Timmins, Ontario.

4. Charter carriers were licensed to provide air passenger service on only a charter basis. The principal charter carrier during this period was Wardair Canada Ltd., based in Edmonton. It concentrated on international service between the main Canadian cities and foreign destinations, including Europe, the Far East, and the Caribbean. Charter services, both domestic and international, were also provided, as outlined earlier, by the mainline and the regional carriers, although their primary activity consisted of toll per unit service.

Economic Regulation of Air Carriers

The regulatory authority of the Air Transport Committee of the Canadian Transport Commission was established by the Aeronautics Act.[7] Its powers of regulation covered licences, routes, rates and fares, accounting procedures, mergers, aircraft leasing, and various other matters relating to the operations of commercial air services.

Licences

Entry into the air carrier industry was controlled through the licensing system. The CTC was responsible for classifying air services and issuing licences, and establishing conditions and restrictions to the licence. No licence could be issued, however, until an air carrier was certified by Transport Canada that it was adequately equipped and able to conduct a safe operation as an air carrier.

The primary criterion in issuing a licence was public convenience and necessity. The Aeronautics Act stipulated that the Commission "shall not issue any licence … unless it is satisfied that the proposed commercial air service is and will be required by the present and future public convenience and necessity." [8] In issuing the licence the Commission could prescribe the routes to be followed or the areas to be served and could attach any conditions considered necessary or desirable in the public interest. These included conditions respecting schedules, carriage of passengers and freight, and insurance. The Commission also possessed the authority to amend, suspend, or cancel any licence or any part of a licence if such action was deemed in the public interest.

Traffic Routes

The Air Transport Committee had the responsibility of approving air carrier routes and changes in these routes. Routes for a carrier were generally specified in the grant of an operating licence to the carrier. A carrier could, however, file applications to the ATC for additions or deletions to its route system. As part of its function of allocating routes, the ATC was authorized to identify route types

---

[7] Canada, *Revised Statutes of Canada 1970*, Ch. 2, 5.1 Sec. 16(3); and, *Revised Statutes 1985*, C. A–3, 5.1, Sec. 21(6).

[8] *Ibid.*, 1985, Sec. 21(6).

by determining what constituted a regional route compared with a trunk route or a route served by a third level carrier, such as a commuter or local carrier. The ATC did not apply a fixed formula in determining types of routes as it did not believe it desirable or possible to develop a fixed formula that could be applied to every application for a route or route change across the country. Instead, a number of criteria were used, but with considerable flexibility. These criteria included the size of the aircraft that was proposed for the route, the distances of the segments of the route, the number of passengers to be transported, and the size of the population being served at each point.[9]

In its consideration of applications for new routes, the Committee was bound under the provisions of the Aeronautics Act to grant or deny them on the basis of the general criteria that the proposed service was required by the present and future public convenience and necessity. It remained, however, for the applicant to prove that present and future convenience and necessity required the service. This general criteria for the approval of proposed routes continued in effect until the carrier industry was deregulated in 1986.

The following is an example of some of the issues that would be considered by the Air Transport Committee in its examination of an application for new routes. In 1974 Nordair Ltd. applied to the Air Transport Committee to add two points, Sudbury and Thunder Bay, to its licence which authorized services between Montreal, Ottawa, Hamilton and Windsor.[10] Air Canada opposed the application on the grounds that the route in question was a mainline route and that Sudbury and Thunder Bay were already serviced under the licences of Air Canada and had been for over twenty years. A small local air carrier, Voyageurs Airways, also opposed the application on the grounds that Voyageurs provided services between Ottawa, North Bay, and Sudbury and would lose traffic if Nordair entered that market. After considering the evidence of the applicant and the intervenors, the Committee ruled to disallow Nordair's application. Applying the test of public convenience and necessity, the Committee found that it was not readily apparent that the public would receive better and cheaper service from the regional carrier, Nordair, than from Air Canada. Indeed, Air Canada's rates were lower than those proposed by Nordair. There was the added question of the desirability of increasing the degree of competition between regional and trunk line carriers. The Committee expressed the fear that Nordair, in attempting to compete with Air Canada in servicing the two new points, might be forced to charge rates which were insufficient to cover the costs of operating in these routes, and try to recover the losses by increasing rates on its monopoly routes. The situation raised the possibility of a classic case of cross-subsidization, by which losses in a competitive area of operation are covered by profits in monop-

---

[9] Canadian Transport Commission, *Canadian Transport Cases, 1975* (Ottawa: Supply and Services Canada, 1977), p. 684.

[10] Canadian Transport Commission, *Canadian Transport Cases 1974* (Ottawa: Supply and Services Canada, 1976), pp. 674–689.

oly areas. Nordair could not give the Committee an assurance that this would not occur.

Another area of concern to the Committee was the effect on the third-level carrier, Voyageurs Airways. Licensing of Nordair for the Ottawa-Sudbury route would reduce Voyageurs' traffic and the Committee believed that it would be unjust for the Committee to use its licensing function to ruin the third-level carrier's business. On the other hand, the Committee was vested with the responsibility of ensuring that the best possible service was provided to the public at the least possible cost. The Committee determined that Voyageurs Airways in this case was providing satisfactory service.

Mergers

Committee approval was required for any change of control, transfer, consolidation, merger or lease of commercial air services or of any carrier. Applications for any such changes were required to be made to the Committee along with all the necessary information and documentation for the Committee to make a decision. The air regulations required that the Committee's decision be based on whether the transaction would "unduly restrict competition or otherwise be prejudicial to the public interest."[11] If the Committee's findings showed that there was a good possibility that this would occur, the merger would not be approved.

Rates and Fares

The Air Transport Committee was authorized to regulate rates and fares (tariffs) and was empowered to disallow proposes tariffs and to prescribe other tariffs in lieu of the tariffs disallowed. Air carriers operating unit toll and charter services were required to file their tariffs with the committee at least thirty days in advance. These tariff applications had to be very detailed and explicit, listing the names of the points being serviced and the tolls to and from each point. The fares and rates would come into effect as filed unless disallowed or suspended by the Committee. In examining proposed rates, the Committee was empowered to ensure that the rates were just and reasonable and non discriminatory. The Committee had the jurisdiction to suspend or disallow any tariff that in its opinion was contrary to this criteria.

The following is an example of an Air Transport Committee hearing on a requested rate increase, illustrating some of the issues and concerns taken into account in a rate increase review.[12] In late 1978, the two mainline air carriers and the five regionals collectively applied to the ATC for permission to raise their

---

[11] Canada, *Consolidated Regulations of Canada 1978*, Chapter 2, Aeronautics Act, Air Regulations, Part III. Sec. 21, 22.

[12] Canadian Transport Commission, *Canadian Transport Commission Reports, 1979* (Ottawa: Supply and Services Canada, 1987) pp. 44–97.

domestic air fares by an average of 5 percent, effective January, 1979. The ATC suspended the proposed fare schedules pending a public hearing, which was scheduled for March 1979. In the meantime, the air carriers were asked to file additional information with the Committee. The main objector to the rate increase was the Consumers' Association of Canada.

The airlines cited increased operating costs as justification for the rate increase. Air Canada estimated that its average costs would increase due to inflation by 7 percent between 1978 and 1979. Salaries and wages accounted for over 40 percent of total expenditures and were expected to increase by 9 percent. Other cost increases included a 26 percent increase in landing fees, an 11 percent increase in food and bar, and an 8 percent increase in aircraft material. Productivity improvements included a projected 6 percent increase in ton miles flown per employee in 1979 and a higher-density seating program. Air Canada concluded that these productivity improvements would absorb some of the projected 7 percent inflationary cost increase, but the remainder would have to be covered by the proposed 5 percent increase in rates. Air Canada also cited a deteriorating financial position. Even though the proposed fare changes would produce additional domestic revenues, the return on investment for 1979 was projected to be 8.2 percent in comparison to a return of 9.5 percent in 1978.

The rate of return on investment was the measure of profitability in the industry and was calculated by dividing net income and interest expense by total assets. The formula applied by the airline industry used the average long-term debt plus average equity as the value of assets or the rate base. The formula was expressed as follows.[13]

$$ROI = \frac{\text{After Tax Earnings} + \text{Interest}}{\text{Average long-term debt} + \text{average equity}}$$

CP Air also provided evidence in support of the 5 percent requested increase. It estimated an average cost increase for 1979 of 8.3 percent, but did not attempt to obtain full cost recovery with the rate filing because of the fear that rate increases in excess of 5 percent might lessen demand and adversely affect overall revenues. Based on the fare increase, CP Air forecast a domestic rate of return on investment of 11.5 percent. Combined with an anticipated rate of return on international services of 10.5 percent, the overall rate for 1979 was projected at 10.9 percent. CP Air contended that an appropriate rate of return on its operations would be in the range of 13.5 to 14 percent. CP Air presented statistics on its historical performance as follows: [14]

---

[13] *Ibid.*, p. 63.

[14] *Ibid.*, p. 55.

Year Domestic	Rate of Return (percent)
1973	1.8
1974	.7
1975	.8
1976	2.9
1977	10.0
1978	14.5
1979	9.8

Citing evidence on its productivity, CP Air suggested that a good measure of productivity was revenue-ton-miles flown per employee. Applying this measure, CP Air had posted a 10.5 percent increase in 1976, 8.6 percent in 1977, and 9.4 percent in 1978. CP Air produced statistics on the growth of the Consumer Price Index over the previous ten year period and attempted to show that air fares had risen by a smaller amount than the prices of other goods and services and had remained below the increase in the CPI since 1969.

The regional air carriers in turn presented their submissions, also citing increased operating costs as justification for their requested fare increases. Rates of return for the regionals tended to fluctuate similar to the trend shown for CP Air. For example, Nordair presented data showing that its rate of return for 1978 was approximately 15 percent, but the historical average was in the 6–7 percent range. The year 1978 was the most successful in the air carrier's history, enabling Nordair to reduce its long-term debt, which in turn reduced the rate base and caused an increase in the rate of return on investment. However, Nordair planned to purchase new aircraft and finance the purchases by acquiring new debt that would increase the rate base. Nordair argued that the proposed rate increase was necessary to help finance the new debt and maintain an appropriate rate of return on investment.

The objectors raised a number of issues and questions in opposition to the proposed fare increase. The contention was that Air Canada and CP Air were allocating an unreasonable share of their costs to the domestic sector, thereby requiring higher prices and revenues than was justified. It was argued that revenue from domestic trunk service was cross-subsidizing the international service sector of these two airlines.

The Consumers' Association of Canada called on the expertise of witnesses in presenting its case against the proposed fare increase. The witnesses were critical of the cost and revenue allocation procedure. It was argued that the cost formula was arbitrary and did not reflect actual costs of operations in the various sectors. Therefore, fares based on this arbitrary costing formula would tend to be arbitrary and produce discriminatory and unjust pricing. The Committee was urged to reconsider the entire procedure under which rate structures were determined. The Association questioned the manner in which the air carriers constructed their rate bases and questioned whether rate of return should be viewed as returns realized on common equity as opposed to overall invested capital. The air carriers considered returns as returns on overall invested capital, but if rate of return on equity was taken as a measure of profitability, the Consumers' Association contended that Air Canada's rate of return for 1979 after the fare increase would be 18 percent, compared with the 8.2 percent stated by the airline.

Concern was also expressed over the efficiency of Air Canada's operations. The Consumers' Association noted that the airline's load factor declined from 66 percent in 1978 to a forecasted 63 percent in 1979. It was contended that Air Canada was providing excess capacity, flying with 63 percent of its aircraft full, and this tended to cause average costs per passenger to increase.

The Air Transport Committee examined the rate increase request on the basis of the various issues raised. It recognized the problems of cost and revenue allocation but concluded that the air carriers were conforming to established and accepted allocation and accounting practices. The Committee continuously monitored these practices and the data submitted and was satisfied that the allocation methods were reasonable. The Committee had earlier determined that just and reasonable fares should, in principle, be cost related. The cost formulae used by the air carriers included an average terminal cost per passenger plus average distance-related costs. Pacific Western Airlines, for example applied the following formula for fare construction for 1979:

0–100 miles	$28.00
101–200 miles	$28.50 + 15 cents per mile for distance over 100 miles
201–300 miles	$43.50 + 14 cents per mile for distance over 200 miles
301 miles & over	$57.50 + 12.5 cents per mile for distance over 300 miles.[15]

Pacific Western believed that this type of formula gave recognition to the different costs associated with long routes compared with short routes. Other air carriers applied similar formulae.

The Air Transport Committee accepted the general principle that each route should cover its variable costs in the long run and make some contribution to overhead, although it was recognized that in the short run there might exist situations which did not make this possible and where cross-subsidization of routes might be desirable. For instance, in developing a new short-haul route, time may be required before sufficient traffic was generated to cover average operating costs at reasonable rates. The Committee's long-standing position was that it was impractical to structure air fares on the basis of rigid formulae.[16] The Committee accepted discrepancies in rates of return on domestic operations versus international services. In 1978 and 1979, the airline carriers showed higher rates of return on their domestic operations. The Committee, on examination of the evidence, did not believe that this was due to an improper burdening of domestic services in order to cross-subsidize and keep international fares lower.

---

[15] *Ibid.*, p. 58.

[16] Canadian Transport Commission, *Canadian Transport Cases, 1975* (Ottawa: Supply and Services Canada, 1977), pp. 304–309.

Records for the previous eight years showed periods when the opposite was true and international operations produced higher relative yields than domestic operations.

The Committee also accepted the principle of "on-peak" and "off-peak" pricing, with the former designed to reduce congestion on any particular route, and the latter designed to stimulate traffic in slow periods. In a decision in 1975 the Committee acknowledged accepting many such fares. In doing so, the Committee stipulated that such fares were primarily market determined, and that it should be left to the carriers to make judgments on the use of "on-peak" and "off-peak" pricing rather than have such fares imposed on carriers by a regulatory authority.[17]

The Air Transport Committee appeared to have been a relatively passive regulator of air carrier tariffs. It had the power to initiate inquiries into air carrier operations but for the most part did not take the initiative in restructuring air fares. It tended to act on air fares and rates only when approached by the air carriers for changes in these rates. Requests for rate increases were generally made on an annual bases and sometimes more frequently. For example, between September 1976 and September 1979, the Air Transport Committee approved five rate increases requested by the air carriers. The average domestic fare increase approved for Air Canada were: September 1976—4.5 percent; March 1977—6.5 percent; April 1978—5.5 percent; April 1979—5.0 percent; and, September 1979—4.0 percent.[18] The evidence and documentation presented by the carriers in support of requests for rate increases were generally accepted by the Committee and the requests were invariably granted.

In general, regulation in the air carrier industry produced a rigidly structured and stable industry. Competition in air fares was practically non-existent, and competition for passengers on most routes was minimal. The established mainline and regional carriers were not subjected to pressures from new entrants since new licences were not common. Air Canada, the dominant carrier, undoubtedly benefited the most from the government's regulatory policies since it had the lion's share of the market and this share was essentially protected by regulation.

Airline Deregulation

During the 1970s pressure began to build to liberalize the regulatory system and to allow more competition in the air-carrier industry in Canada. These pressures came from the regional airlines, from CP Air and Wardair, and from consumer groups.

CP Air in particular wished to expand its domestic and international operations and to compete openly without restrictions with Air Canada. Up to this time CP Air had been severely restricted in its operations. For example, under the

---

[17] *Ibid.*, p. 306.

[18] *Canadian Transportation Commission Reports 1979, op. cit.*, p. 97.

watchful eye of the Canadian Transport Commission, CP Air had been limited to only a twenty-five percent share of the traffic on its Montreal-Toronto-Vancouver route, which was its primary competitive route. Air Canada enjoyed seventy percent of the domestic mainline traffic and naturally opposed the concepts of deregulation and open competition. In its opposition, Air Canada argued that competition from new entrants into the airlines industry would fragment an already relatively small market. Market fragmentation would lead to excess capacity, a reduced load factor, and lower revenues. This would make it more difficult for Air Canada to maintain a technically modern air fleet and would reduce its ability to compete in the international market. Air Canada was already operating on only a sixty percent load factor. The system then in operation, Air Canada argued, had provided Canadian travellers with the lowest domestic air fares in the world, with more aircraft flying more departures and to more destinations per capita than most countries. Proponents of competition countered that deregulation and competition would force greater efficiency into airline operations, reduce costs, and would provide the public with better service, a wider choice of schedules, and lower air fares.

Cracks began to appear in Air Canada's domestic mainline monopolistic system in 1975 when the government began to permit CP Air increased flexibility in its operations. By 1980, CP Air had been permitted unrestricted competition with Air Canada on the lucrative Montreal-Toronto-Vancouver route. While the CTC continued to maintain regulatory control over air fares, a wider range of discount fares was being allowed, such as those involving advance booking and frequent flier plans. By 1980, approximately thirty percent of domestic passengers were travelling on some form of discount rate.

In early 1984 the government announced plans, to be introduced in two phases, for further deregulation of domestic airlines. In phase one, the Cabinet was to encourage the CTC to allow new carriers to enter the industry, and existing carriers to expand their routes in cases where the CTC judged that benefits to the public would accrue from increased competition. New charter service was also to be encouraged. Price regulation was to be relaxed with fewer restrictions on fare reductions, although fare increases were closely supervised on non-competitive routes. Effective September 1984, airlines were allowed to offer discounts on individual routes ranging up to 30 percent below economy fares without filing advance notice with the CTC. Fare discounts in excess of 30 percent, however, had to be accompanied with certain conditions, such as advance booking and minimum-stay periods by passengers at their points of destination.

In the second phase of deregulation, the government proposed that the CTC examine the question of total deregulation, including possible effects on small communities, and the role of government-owned Air Canada in a totally deregulated environment. CP Air had charged that, in open competition, Air Canada would possess an unfair advantage because it was backed by the government and had access to government financial resources when it encountered financial difficulties. It was suggested that a competitive, deregulated environment would require the conversion of Air Canada to private enterprise.

The government's announced plans for deregulation were interrupted with the defeat of the Liberal government in the Fall of 1984, and it was not until July 1985 that the new Conservative government announced its air transportation policy. The Minister of Transport issued a White Paper calling for practically total removal of federal regulations in the airline industry, and this was to be completed by the end of 1986. The ensuing legislation was finally passed and came into effect January, 1988, as the new National Transportation Act. This Act made deregulation and competition in the airlines industry official, although the industry, in effect, had been operating on the deregulated, competitive basis outlined in the Act since 1986.

The National Transportation Act created a new organization, the National Transport Agency (NTA), to replace the Canadian Transport Commission, but with greatly reduced regulatory powers. The Act made it much easier for new carriers to enter the industry and for existing carriers to expand, change routes, establish rates, etc. New entrants were no longer subjected to the "public convenience and necessity" test. To obtain an operating licence, they were simply required to show that they were "willing and able" to provide transport services and meet safety standards. In addition, air carriers operating in the domestic market had to have 75 percent Canadian ownership. They also had to possess sufficient insurance liability, and were required to meet aircraft maintenance and operation standards established by Transport Canada. Air carriers were required to give a 120 day notice to the NTA if they wished to drop a route or to limit flights on a particular route to fewer than one per week. Air carriers, however, no longer had to file rates with the regulatory agency, but simply had to make their list of fares available to the public. Only in the northern air services sector did more stringent regulations apply. On many of the routes in the sparsely-populated northern regions, traffic was insufficient to sustain more than one carrier. Air carriers servicing the north were, therefore, allowed to question any proposed entry of competitors. The fares of these monopolistic carriers could in turn be questioned before the NTA by passengers and affected parties.

Effects of Deregulation

As outlined in the previous section, deregulation and competition in the Canadian airline industry was introduced gradually over a period of several years, and culminated with the National Transportation Act in January, 1988. Relaxation of regulations on entry, fares, and services was introduced in stages. The effects of deregulation were therefore neither sudden nor dramatic, but could be observed as developing in the form of particular trends in the structure and operations of the air carriers.

TABLE 8–2: Structure of Canada's Air Carrier System 1989

A. MAINLINE CARRIERS AND AFFILIATES

1. Air Canada and Affiliates

Airline	Percentage Owned by Air Canada	Destination
Air Canada		Canada, USA, Caribbean, Europe, Southeast Asia
Air BC	85%	BC, Alberta, Whitehorse, Seattle
NWT	90%	North West Territories, Edmonton, Winnipeg
Air Ontario	75%	Ontario, Winnipeg, Montreal, Northeastern, USA
Air Alliance	75%	Quebec, Ottawa, Boston
Air Nova	49%	Newfoundland., Nova Scotia, PEI, NB, Montreal, Ottawa, Boston
Commuter Express	100%	Toronto, Ottawa

2. Canadian Airlines International and Affiliates

Airline	Percentage Owned by PWA Corp.	Destination
Canadian Airlines (CPA, PWA, Nordair, Quebecair, Eastern Provincial Airways)	100%	Canada, USA, Europe, Central & South America, South Pacific, Asia
Wardair	100%	Montreal, Ottawa, Toronto, Winnipeg, Calgary, Edmonton, Vancouver, Europe, Caribbean
Time Air	46%	BC, Alberta, Saskatchewan, Winnipeg, Minneapolis
Calm Air	45%	Manitoba, North West Territories
Ontario Express (Canadian Partner)	49%	Ontario, Winnipeg, Pittsburg
Air Atlantic	45%	Newfoundland, Nova Scotia, NB, PEI, Montreal, Ottawa, Boston

B. INDEPENDENT REGIONAL AND COMMUTER CARRIERS

Airline	Destination
Air Toronto (linked with Air Canada)	Toronto, Northeastern USA cities
First Air	Canadian North
City Express	Toronto, Ottawa, Montreal
Frontier Air	Northern Ontario
Air Quebec	Northern Ontario
Intair	Quebec, PEI, NB, Ottawa, Toronto
Others	

C. NATIONAL AND INTERNATIONAL CHARTER AIR CARRIERS

Worldways Canada / Nationair Canada / Canada 3000 Airlines / Vacationair Inc. / Odyssey International / Points of Call / Minerve Canada / Others

SOURCE: Canadian National Transportation Agency, Ottawa, 1989.

Industry Restructure

One of the major developments in the industry following deregulation was the creation and entry of new air carriers, the expansion of some of the existing carriers and the restructuring of the industry. Early in the deregulation process the two mainline air carriers, Air Canada and CP Air, began to manoeuvre to try to improve their competitive positions and strength in anticipation of increased competition. Desiring to expand its domestic network, CP Air purchased two regional air lines, namely Nordair in 1985 and Eastern Provincial Airways in 1986. In 1986, however, CP Air was itself purchased by Pacific Western Airlines Corporation, which owned Pacific Western Airlines. This new amalgamated air carrier was renamed Canadian Airlines International. Canadian Airlines embarked on a program of expansion with the creation of new regional and commuter carriers and the total or partial purchase of a number of smaller air carriers[19]. Purchases included Quebecair, Time Air, Norcanair, and Air Atlantic. Some of these airlines continued to operate under their original names while others were merged and renamed. For example, Quebecair was merged with Nordair Metro and Quebec Aviation to become Inter-Canadian. By January 1988 it was estimated that Canadian Airlines controlled 44 percent of the domestic air traffic market. In January 1989, Canadian Airlines purchased the financially-troubled Wardair, which had posted a financial loss in 1988 of $110 million. Canadian Airlines announced plans to scale down and rationalize Wardair's operations, but initially to continue to operate Wardair as an independent, scheduled airline. These plans were changed in late 1989 when, in an effort to control costs, the management of the two airlines was merged, along with reservations staff and ground crews. At the same time, Canadian Airlines announced that it would sell Wardair's entire fleet of jet aircraft for a reported $760 million.

Air Canada responded to the challenge from Canadian Airlines with an expansion of its own to develop a connector airline network. It purchased either totally or in part such regional and local air carriers as Air Ontario, Air Alliance, Commuter Express and Air BC. Air BC, 85 percent owned by Air Canada, had been established in 1980 as a small commuter airline in southern British Columbia, but by 1988 it has become Canada's fourth largest scheduled carrier, operating a fleet of small, short-distance air craft and servicing British Columbia and parts of Alberta, including the lucrative Edmonton-Calgary route. The alignment of the various carriers wholly or partly owned by the two mainline carriers is illustrated in Table 8–2. In the partly-owned carriers, the shares not held by the two major airlines are in private hands and are traded on the major Canadian stock exchanges.

In addition to the total purchase of smaller air carriers, the major airlines formed alliances and affiliations with many of the smaller carriers by purchasing a partial interest in the carriers or through special arrangements with independent

---

[19] An outline of Canadian air carrier mergers and acquisitions is contained in Statistics Canada, *Air Charter Statistics, 1987*, Ottawa, pp. 8–9.

carriers. In these alliances and affiliations, the small carriers became feeder or connector airlines to the mainline carriers. The small airline would book connections for its passengers with the mainline, thereby providing travellers from small communities with assured connections and service to their destinations. Similarly, passengers originating their travel on a mainline carrier would be assured of connections to the smaller air carrier if their destinations were not serviced by the mainline carrier.

While few independent carriers remain, some have found it economical to participate in the connector system. An example is Air Toronto, an independent carrier which has formed an alliance with Air Canada. Air Toronto operates small aircraft from Toronto to mid-sized U.S. cities such as Columbus, Ohio and Louisville, Kentucky. It's clientele consists mostly of business travellers who desire a direct flight rather than being forced to change planes in Detroit or Chicago. Air Toronto is affiliated with Air Canada and feeds passengers to the trunk routes, but Air Canada has no equity in the airline.

Some of the smaller carriers on the other hand, have not been completely satisfied with their affiliations. For example, Inter-Canadian Airlines announced in late 1989 that it wished to sever its ties with Canadian International Airlines and operate as a completely independent carrier. Inter-Canadian was 31 percent owned by PWA Corp. and operated as a feeder service for Canadian International and Wardair in Ontario and Quebec. Inter-Canadian claimed that it cancelled its agreement with Canadian Airlines because it desired to expand its operations beyond those of a purely regional and feeder airline. Inter-Canadian executives offered to purchase the 31 percent interest held by PWA Corp. and to change the name of the airline to Intair Inc. As an independent carrier, Intair would compete on many short routes in these two provinces with Air Alliance, which was affiliated to Air Canada, and expand to compete directly with the two mainline carriers. There was speculation that Intair planned to provide feeder services for some U.S. airlines that desired to increase their presence in Canada and compete with the Air Canada and Canadian International. The mainline air carriers, in their attempts to rationalize air service and reduce costs, have transferred some of their shorter routes to their affiliates. Some of these routes were serviced by jet aircraft such as the DC–9, which had a capacity of about 100 passengers, but they are now being serviced by smaller, fuel-efficient propeller-driven aircraft such as the Dash–8. In 1989, Air Canada removed its large jet aircraft from several routes in the Maritimes, Quebec, and Ontario and turned the service in these areas over to its affiliates Air Ontario, Air Alliance, and Air Nova. In Ontario, for example, Air Canada stopped flying its DC–9 jet aircraft to Windsor, Timmins, Sudbury, and North Bay. Despite opposition to this move by these communities, Air Canada maintained that service would improve in terms of a larger number of flights between the larger cities and these smaller cities. For example, whereas there had only been three Air Canada jet flights between Toronto and Windsor a few years ago, by 1989 Air Ontario and its Canadian Airlines' rival Canadian Partner (Ontario Express) together offered as many as

25 flights a day between the two cities. Similarly, Canadian Airlines withdrew its jet service from some small communities in British Columbia in favour of service by its affiliate Time Air, which operates a fleet of new 52-seat, Dash 8 aircraft out of Lethbridge. Despite the increase in the frequency of flights to these communities, however, many passengers have expressed some discontent, arguing that the switch from the larger jet aircraft to the smaller turbo-propeller driven planes made flying less comfortable and offered inferior services.

The development of the system of alliances, or what is known as the connection system, by the mainline carriers serves a purpose similar to the development of the "hub and spoke" system in the U.S. following deregulation of the airlines in that country. Each mainline U.S. carrier concentrated on a major city as its airport hub and developed feeder services into the hub from outlying centres. These centres would feed traffic into the hub where passengers would make connections to their destinations. In this way, an airline would increase the number of potential destinations for a passenger, although it meant fewer non-stop flights for the passenger. The primary benefits to the airline accrued from the use of smaller, more fuel-efficient aircraft in providing service from the outlying areas into the hub, and an increased load factor on flights from the hub to long-distance destinations. This system also tended to make it more difficult for a competing airline to establish service in the area and resulted in a system of regional monopolies.

Because Canada's air carriers operate in primarily a linear east-west market, it is less feasible to develop a hub-and-spoke system. The system of alliances serves a similar purpose, however, with the smaller regional and commuter air carriers providing feeder services into the major centres serviced by a mainline carrier. While the aircraft of these affiliated, feeder air carriers are primarily smaller and slower turbo-props, they are much less expensive to operate and can offer a greater number of flights between cities and towns than the larger jet airliners.

Competition not only exists between the two mainline air carriers, but extends to competition between the affiliates of the two and between an affiliate of one trunk and the other trunk itself. In Ontario, Canadian Airlines established Ontario Express to compete against Air Canada's Air Ontario, and the two have been strongly competitive. In other areas, Air BC, an Air Canada affiliate, offers intense competition to Canadian Airlines on some west coast routes and the Edmonton-Calgary run.

When Wardair decided to switch from completely chartered services to full-scheduled domestic services on mainline routes in competition with Air Canada and Canadian Airlines, a gap was created in charter services. New charter air carriers were quick to become established to fill this gap. Several small two-three plane charter airlines sprang up in the latter part of the 1980s with leased or purchased aircraft. These included air charter companies such as Odyssey Airlines, Canada 3000, Vacationair, Nationair Canada, and Worldways. Canada 3000 Airlines began flying to destinations in Florida, Mexico, and the Caribbean, and by early 1989 was leasing two modern 757 aircraft with a capacity of 250 passengers each and making 26 flights per week. Other charter air carriers such as Worldways and Nationair Canada decided to purchase older aircraft instead of leasing in the belief that it was more economical to establish a fleet through purchasing than leasing.

A major development during this period of deregulation and industry restructuring was the privatization of Air Canada. While Air Canada had opposed deregulation, the company used deregulation to support its drive to become a private enterprise. Air Canada officials argued that privatization was required to give the company the flexibility to compete in a deregulated market. The Canadian government at first opposed privatization. During the mid–1980s, however, faced with large budgetary deficits, the federal government sought ways to cut federal expenditures. Air Canada, at the same time, was pressuring the government for increased funds to finance proposed capital expenditures, primarily to modernize its air fleet. Agreement was finally reached in the fall of 1988 to privatize the airline. Shares in the company were sold to the public in two stages. In October, 1988, approximately 32 million shares representing 45 percent of the airline's equity were sold. The privatization process was completed in July 1989, when the remaining 41 million shares were sold, and the former Crown corporation become a widely-held company in the private sector. Proceeds of the sale of Air Canada totalled over $700 million.

Industry Performance[20]

Tables 8–3 to 8–7 illustrate trends in some economic indicators of the airline industry prior to and following deregulation. The poor performance of the industry, in terms of operating revenue and passenger kilometres flown, during the period 1981–83 is partly a reflection of the world-wide energy crisis and the high costs of aviation fuel. Operating revenue remained constant during 1981, 1982 and 1983, while passenger kilometres flown declined from 34,525 million kilometres in 1982 to 31,131 million kilometres in 1983 and did not recover until 1985. The rate of return on investment also plunged for most airlines during 1982 and 1983. The economic indicators show an upward trend since 1983. Operating revenue for Air Canada increased from $2145 million in 1983 to $2,684 million in 1987. For the same period, operating revenues for the airlines constituting Canadian Airlines increased from $1400 million to $1843 million. Deregulation and the consequent increase in competition reduced Air Canada's share of the market over this period. From 1981 to 1987, Air Canada's share of total scheduled passenger kilometres fell from 65 percent to 52 percent, while total operating revenues were reduced from 56 percent of the total for the industry to 53 percent.

---

[20] A historical account of the performance of the air carrier industry in Canada is presented in Statistics Canada, *Aviation In Canada* (Ottawa: Supply and Services, 1986).

TABLE 8–3: Air Carrier Operations—Passenger Load Factor 1981–1987

Air Carrier	1981	1982	1983	1984	1985	1986	1987
Air Canada	65.5	62.7	64.9	67.5	65.3	67.4	69.8
CP Air	68.7	65.5	69.9	70.0	69.8	69.0	a
Eastern Provincial	56.3	47.8	50.1	55.9	58.0	57.6	a
Nordair	50.3	-	-	-	51.6	52.4	a
PWA	54.3	52.3	53.7	50.4	51.4	53.0	69.1[a]
Quebecair	52.9	59.8	52.7	58.2	50.1	58.7	62.2
Wardair[b]	-	-	-	-	78.7	71.6	67.7
Air BC	-	-	-	-	-	-	46.9

[a] Operating as Canadian International Airlines
[b] Operating regular scheduled service beginning in 1985.

SOURCE: Statistics Canada, *Air Carrier Operations in Canada,* 1981–1987, Ottawa.

Deregulation and competition appear to have brought increased efficiency to air carrier operations in terms of capacity utilization. As shown in Table 8–3, the passenger load factor for Air Canada increased over the period 1981–1987 from 65.5 to 69.8. CP Air maintained a relatively high passenger load factor, with an average of close to 70. Other airlines experienced an increase in passenger load factors following the energy-crisis period.

In terms of its rate of return on investment, the industry as a whole does not appear to have suffered. Table 8–6 illustrates the rate of return for the industry and each major airline on an annual basis from 1978 to 1987. The rate of return for the industry shows a declining trend from 1978 to the early 1980s, reflecting the large increase in fuel costs during this period. Since 1982, the rate of return has been following an increasing trend. A similar trend is shown for most of the individual carriers, except for Eastern Provincial and Nordair.

Table 8–7 shows a major change in price trends of air passengers service following full-scale deregulation in 1986. While the increase in the consumer price index (CPI) and the price index of the transportation sector remained relatively constant around the 4 percent mark over the period 1984 to 1988, the air transportation component of the CPI increased by 12.1 percent between 1984 and 1985 and by 17.0 percent between 1985 and 1986. This trend was broken in 1987 when the air transportation price index increased by only 3.2 percent between 1986 and 1987, and dramatically declined by 16.1 percent between 1987

TABLE 8–4: Air Carrier Operations—Scheduled Passenger Kilometres,[1] 1981–1987

Air Carrier	1981	1982	1983	1984	1985	1986	1987
				(millions of kilometres)			
Air Canada	22,489	20,540	19,554	20,996	21,842	21,765	20,794
CP Air	9,644	8,902	9,159	10,233	10,511	11,158	[a]
Eastern Provincial	-	563	439	632	774	921	[a]
Nordair	487	233	337	399	542	577	[a]
PWA	1,661	1,494	1,438	1,419	1,625	1,748	15,476[a]
Quebecair	244	212	204	232	255	299	172
Wardair[b]	-	-	-	-	69	2,400	3,407
Air BC	-	-	-	-	-	-	174
Total	34,525	31,944	31,131	33,911	35,618	38,868	40,203

[1] A passenger-kilometre represents the carriage of one passenger for one kilometre. The figures are obtained by totalling the number of kilometres flown by each passenger.
[a] Operating as Canadian International Airlines.
[b] Operating regular scheduled service beginning in 1985.
SOURCE: Statistics Canada, *Air Carrier Operations in Canada*, 1981–1987, Ottawa.

TABLE 8–5: Air Carrier Operations—Operating Revenue, 1981–1987

Air Carrier	1981	1982	1983	1984	1985	1986	1987
			($ million)				
Air Canada	2,161	2,171	2,145	2,335	2,520	2,636	2,684
CP Air	819	849	864	933	1007	1100	a
Eastern Provincial	87	93	75	94	115	122	a
Nordair	134	113	140	158	183	188	a
PWA	310	315	321	323	342	348	1,843[a]
Quebecair	81	70	71	91	127	115	59
Wardair[b]	244	271	254	283	329	360	392
Air BC	-	-	-	-	-	-	50
Total	3836	3882	3870	4217	4623	4869	5028

[a] Operating as Canadian International Airlines.
[b] Operating regular scheduled services beginning in 1985.
SOURCE: Statistics Canada, *Air Carrier Operations in Canada*, 1981–1987, Ottawa.

TABLE 8-6: Air Carrier Operations—Rate of Return on Investment[1]

Air Carrier	1978	1979	1980	1981	1982	1983	1984	1985	1986	1987
Air Canada	7.2	6.6	5.9	5.1	1.6	3.8	5.2	3.9	5.7	5.8
CP Air	9.6	5.8	4.6	2.7	2.6	2.6	4.5	3.0	5.2	a
Eastern Provincial	14.9	8.1	6.9	12.1	7.7	.3	(4.1)	(4.1)	(4.3)	a
Nordair	10.0	3.6	6.4	6.1	1.2	7.5	4.7	3.7	2.1	a
PWA	4.7	8.4	8.3	10.3	6.6	5.9	8.5	4.7	5.2	4.0[a]
Quebecair	5.8	3.9	2.5	.4	(7.7)	(15.6)	(2.7)	.3	12.4	15.1
Wardair	5.6	(8.0)	16.0	2.5	(1.1)	(2.7)	5.6	7.5	3.7	5.8
All Carriers	7.3	6.1	6.3	5.1	2.2	3.2	5.0	3.6	5.4	5.4

[1] Calculated as the ratio of net income plus interest expense to total assets.
[a] Operating as Canadian International Airlines.
SOURCE: Statistics Canada, *Canadian Civil Aviation*, 1982, 1987, Ottawa.

TABLE 8–7: Transportation Price Index 1984–88
(1981=100) Annual Average

Price Index Component	1984		1985		1986		1987		1988	
	Index	% Change	Index	% Change	Index	% Change	Index	% Change	Index	% Change
Consumer Price Index	122.3	4.3	137.1	4.0	132.4	4.2	138.2	4.4	143.8	4.1
Transportation Sector	124.8	4.2	130.8	4.8	134.9	3.2	139.9	3.6	142.6	1.9
Inter-City Air Transportation[a]	142.7		159.9	12.1	187.1	17.0	193.0	3.2	162.0	-16.1

[a] The inter-city air transportation component of the transportation sector price index is not shown separately in Statistics Canada data prior to 1984.
SOURCE: Statistics Canada, *The Consumer Price Index*, 1984–1989, Ottawa.

and 1988. The major reduction in the air transportation price index in 1988 was the result of an extensive "seat sale" in January, 1988 following formal deregulation of the industry on January 1, 1988. The index fell from 195.4 in December, 1987 to 142.0 in January 1988. By April of that year it had increased to 193.2, and peak season rates during July and August kept the index at 177.4 and 179.5 respectively. But, by December, 1988, the index had once again dropped to 146.8.[21]

An examination of the monthly air transportation price index shows much more significant fluctuations in passenger fares after deregulation took effect in 1986. In 1984, the index fluctuated from a monthly low of 133.0 to a high of 158.9, a 19 percent movement, while in 1985 there was a 27 percent movement from the monthly low to the high. In 1986, the monthly index fluctuated from a low of 162.1 to a high of 224.4, or a movement of 38 percent.[22] In 1987 and 1988, fluctuations of 35 percent and 36 percent respectively were recorded. The increased magnitude of the fluctuations, beginning in 1986, reflect the greater freedom the airlines were permitted in setting peak-season rates and excursion discount rates, along with introducing various lower-rate schemes, such as frequent flier plans.

In summary, the gradual liberalization of regulations in the air carrier industry in Canada ushered in some major changes, the most significant of which was the restructuring of the industry. Once dominated by Air Canada, the industry is now comprised of the two major air carriers—namely, Air Canada and Canadian International Airlines, and their affiliates. Basically, the industry has been transformed into a duopoly. On domestic trunk routes Air Canada and Canadian Airline, compete head-to-head, while on regional routes the competition is either between the two trunk airlines, between one of the two trunk airlines and an affiliate of the other trunk, or between the affiliates of the two trunks. With the absorption of Wardair by Canadian International, and the existence of few truly independent carriers that are relatively small, the duopoly has become more or less complete on practically all domestic scheduled passenger routes. It remains to be seen whether this duopoly structure will provide Canadian passengers with adequate services and competitively low rates or administratively structured rates through potential tacit collusion or other duopoly practices.

---

[21] Statistics Canada, *The Consumer Price Index*, 1984–89, Ottawa.

[22] *Ibid.*

9

TELECOMMUNICATIONS: THE TELEPHONE INDUSTRY

Historical Development [1]

In 1876, Alexander Graham Bell pioneered the world's first long-distance telephone transmission, a 16 km., one-way transmission between Brantford and Paris, Ontario. In 1880 the Bell Telephone Company of Canada (Bell Canada) was incorporated through an act of Parliament and chartered to provide telephone service to all of Canada. In effect, the charter provided the Bell Co. with a virtual monopoly which lasted for five years. In 1885, the government revoked Bell Canada's patents, an action which opened the market to numerous small companies offering telephone services in competition with Bell. In 1885, the Telephone Co. of Prince Edward Island was formed, followed by the formation in 1988 of the New Brunswick Telephone Co. and the Nova Scotia Telephone Co. In 1911, the PEI Telephone Co. and the Nova Scotia Telephone Co. were absorbed by the newly incorporated Maritime Telegraph and Telephone Co. As these companies developed, Bell Canada sold its facilities in these provinces and withdrew its services, deciding to concentrate its services in Ontario and Quebec. It wasn't until the 1960s that Bell Canada acquired majority interest in the Maritime Telegraph and Telephone Co. and the New Brunswick Telephone Co. In Newfoundland, the Avalon Telephone Co. was formed in 1919 by private interests. In 1976, the company was changed to the Newfoundland Telephone Co. with Bell Canada acquiring a majority of its publicly-traded shares.

The settlement and development of western Canada caused Bell Canada, along with some competitors, to expand to provide telephone service in the west. In 1908 and 1909, however, the telephone operations in Alberta, Saskatchewan and Manitoba were acquired by the provincial governments to be operated as provincially-owned public utilities. In British Columbia, telephone service was provided by the British Columbia Telephone Co. (BC Tel), a subsidiary of General Telephone and Electronics Corp. of the United States. To provide services in Canada's north, the federal government created Northwestel.

---

[1] Information on the early development of the telephone industry in Canada can be found in Canada, Dept. of Communications, *Canadian Telecommunications: An Overview of the Canadian Telecommunications Carriage Industry* (Ottawa, 1987), and English, H.E. (Ed) *Telecommunications for Canada* (Toronto: Metheun Publications, 1973).

In addition to the telephone companies listed above, which account for most of the telephone service in Canada, there are some 150 small systems operating in various parts of the country. In Ontario, approximately 30 small systems exist, accounting for 5 percent of the telephones in the province. In total, Bell Canada interconnects with 42 independent telephone companies in Ontario and Quebec. Examples of some of the smaller systems are: Edmonton Telephones, a municipally-owned and operated company providing service in the City of Edmonton; the Thunder Bay Telephone System, another municipal operation; Terra Nova Communications, owned by the Canadian National Railway and operating in Newfoundland; Quebec Telephone and Telebec in the province of Quebec, and the Island Telephone Co. in PEI. In total, in 1985, Canada's telephone system had a 98.2 percent household penetration rate, one of the highest in the world.

In essence, Bell Canada, BC Tel, and the provincial telephone companies operate as regional monopolies in the provision of telephone services in Canada. There is no competition in local telephone service in these regions, nor in long-distance service within the region. Long-distance telephone service between the regions and across Canada is provided through the interconnection of these regional companies.

The interconnection of the various independent telephone systems to provide a cross-Canada network began in 1921 when the telephone companies entered into a loose consortium, called the Telephone Association of Canada, to explore the development of a national telephone system. Up to that time, many long-distance calls between Canadian cities were routed through the American telephone system because of lack of trans-Canadian telephone circuits. By 1928, the Telephone Association of Canada had completed an all-Canadian line, linking Montreal and Winnipeg. The Association was replaced by the Trans-Canada Telephone System (TCTS) whose objective was to construct and maintain an all-Canadian network from coast to coast. This trans-continental, long-distance telephone network was completed in 1931.

In 1969, Telecast Canada was created to administer satellite communications, and in 1977 it became a member of TCTS. In 1983, TCTS was renamed Telecom Canada, consisting of the nine major telephone companies plus Telesat Canada.

Telecom Canada is neither a company nor a corporate entity and owns no property. Its facilities are owned and operated by its member companies who, by means of a master agreement, have interconnected their facilities to provide a nationwide telephone network. Telecom Canada is managed by a board of directors comprised of one representative from each of the member companies. These directors appoint a full-time president to oversee the operations of Telecom Canada. Decisions require the board's unanimous consent. The member companies are obligated to observe the agreed terms so long as they remain members. There also exists a system of committees involving representatives from all member companies, assisted by a supporting staff made up of employees on loan from the member companies and located in Ottawa. Telecom Canada itself is not regulated by any government. Each member company files the Telecom Canada rate schedule with its respective regulatory agency, which may examine and review the schedule. One of the main functions of Telecom Canada is the division of revenues generated by long-distance, inter-provincial telephone calls. In addition to the Telecom master agreement, members may enter into other arrangements for the interchange of telecommunications traffic between them or enter agreements with the independent telephone companies.

Terrestrial and space systems were integrated in the country in 1977 when Telesat Canada became a member of Telecom Canada. The development and launching of satellites, which had begun in the late 1960s, ushered in a new era in telecommunications. Canada was the first country to use satellites for domestic communications and launched the Anik series of satellites, beginning with Anik A-l in 1972. Telesat was created by the federal government in 1969 to operate and oversee Canada's satellite program and to establish a domestic commercial satellite system. Established as a joint public-private venture, 50 percent owned by the federal government and 50 percent owned by the major Canadian telecommunications carriers, Telesat was given a monopoly over domestic communications satellites and operates as a carriers' carrier. It owns the satellites and leases satellite channels to the telecommunications carriers, and to television and cable companies. The creation of Telesat, therefore, added satellite transmission facilities to Telecom's existing coaxial cable, fibre-optic cable, and microwave facilities.

CNCP Telecommunications was established as a consortium of the telecommunications branches of the Canadian National and the Canadian Pacific railway companies. These two companies served as the main providers of telegraph service in Canada and operated competitively until 1967, when they formed a partnership to provide telegraph services, as well as to operate a nationwide microwave system offering private-line and data communication services for the business community. CNCP operates its own microwave relay system and switching centres but leases local loops from local telephone companies. In 1979, CNCP Telecommunications was authorized by the CRTC to interconnect with the local exchange facilities of Bell Canada and BC Tel telephone networks. The interconnection permitted CNCP customers dial access through the public telephone network for private-line voice and for data transmission services.

Completing the Canadian telecommunications structure is Teleglobe Canada, originally established as a federal crown corporation to provide Canada with satellite and cable telecommunications connections overseas. Teleglobe was privatized in 1987, when it was sold to Momotec Data Incorporated.

An outline of the structure of Canada's telephone and telecommunications carrier system is contained in Table 9–1, along with an identification of the regulation jurisdiction in each case. Table 9–2 shows the various telecommunications services offered and identifies the carriers involved in these services.

TABLE 9–1: Major Telephone Companies and Telecommunications Carriers

Company	Ownership	Territory	Regulator[1]
Bell Canada*	Bell Canada Enterprises (Investor)	Ontario, Quebec, Eastern NWT	Federal
BC Tel*	General Telephone & Electronics (Investor)	British Columbia	Federal
Alberta Gov't. Telephones*	Alberta Crown Corp.	Alberta	Province
Saskatchewan Telecomm.*	Saskatchewan Crown Corp.	Saskatchewan	Province
Manitoba Telephone System*	Manitoba Crown Corp.	Manitoba	Province
Maritime Telegraph & Telephone*	Bell Canada & Investor	Nova Scotia	Province
New Brunswick Telephone*	Bell Canada & Investor	New Brunswick	Province
Newfoundland Telephone*	Bell Canada & Investor	Newfoundland	Province
Island Telephone Co.*	Investor	Prince Edward Island	Province
NorthwesTel	CNR	Yukon, NWT, Northern BC	Federal
Quebec-Telephone	General Telephone & Electronics (Investor)	Quebec	Province
Telebec Ltee	Bell Canada Enterprises (Investor)	Quebec	Province
Edmonton Telephones	Municipal	Edmonton	Municipal
Northern Telephone	Investor	Ontario	Province
Thunder Bay Telephone	Municipal	Thunder Bay	Province
CNCP Telecommunications	CNR (Crown Corp.) & CPR (Investor)	Canada	Federal
Telesat*	Federal Gov't & Major Telephone Cos.	Canada	Federeal
Teleglobe	Investor (Memotec Data Inc.)	International	Federal

* Member of Telecom Canada.

[1] In terms of total revenues of the telephone companies and the carriers, the federal government regulates almost 75 percent of the telephone and telecommunications carrier service. SOURCE: CRTC, *Annual Report* 1987–88, Ottawa: Supply and Services Canada, and Canada, Department of Communications, *Canadian Telecommunications: An Overview of the Canadian Telecommunications Carriage Industry*, Ottawa, 1987.

TABLE 9–2: Telecommunications Services and Carriers—Overview

Services	*Carriers*
Voice Telephony Public switched	Telecom Canada & other telephone companies
Leased circuits (private lines)	Telecom Canada, other telephone companies & CNCP
Telegraph	CNCP
Switched Teleprinter and other text	CNCP (Telex) & Telecom Canada (TWX)
Data	
Public switched	Telecom Canada & CNCP
Leased circuits	Telecom Canada & CNCP
Program Transmission	
Audio and Video	Telecom Canada & CNCP

SOURCE: Canada, Department of Communications, *Canadian Telecommunications: An Overview of the Canadian Telecommunications Carriage Industry*, Ottawa 1987.

Objectives In Telephone Service Regulation

In its early years the telephone industry was non-regulated. The withdrawal by government of Bell Canada's patents in 1885 was intended to produce a competitive industry and competition was viewed as the vehicle to ensure reasonable rates and adequate services. By the turn of the century, however, there was considerable dissatisfaction with the operation of the industry. Consumers complained of excessive rates and of poor services. The telephone companies tended to concentrate their services on the more populated areas of the country and were hesitant to extend services to the low-populated rural areas. Small, independent operators in competition with Bell Canada complained of anti-competitive practices by Bell, including predatory pricing and the refusal of Bell to permit the independents to interconnect with Bell's local and long-distance lines.

In 1906, following an investigation of the telephone industry by a special committee of Parliament, the federal government introduced regulation into the industry. Revisions to the Railway Act brought Bell Canada under the authority of the Board of Railway Commissioners, which also had jurisdiction over transportation in Canada. The Board was authorized to approve all telephone rates of Bell Canada and was empowered to permit the interconnection of other telephone companies to the Bell network. In 1967, the responsibility of regulating the portion of the telephone industry under federal jurisdiction was transferred to the Canadian Transport Commission, and in 1976 to the Canadian Radio-Television and Telecommunications Commission (CRTC). The CRTC continues to regulate to ensure that telephone rates are reasonable and just, and that services are provided, including interconnection, under terms and conditions which are viewed as fair and equitable.

Telephone companies not under the jurisdiction of the federal government came to be regulated by provincial and municipal governments as illustrated in Table 9–1. The government-owned telephone systems in Alberta, Saskatchewan, and Manitoba are regulated by public utility boards in those provinces. Edmonton Telephones is regulated by the Edmonton City Council. Some municipally-owned systems, such as the system in Thunder Bay, Ontario, are regulated by the provincial government.

Bell Canada and BC Tel are the two largest telephone companies in Canada. Given the number of telephone and telecommunications carriers in the country, the companies regulated by the CRTC account for almost 75 percent of the total operating revenues and for 70 percent of the total number of employees in the industry.

Inter-provincial long-distance rates and other aspects of services provided by Telecom Canada are regulated jointly by the CRTC and its provincial regulatory counterparts. When the Telecom Canada members agree on uniform rates and practices offered collectively or on a cross-Canada basis, these rates and conditions become effective by being approved as part of each member's tariff.

CRTC regulatory powers over telephone and telecommunications carrier services derive primarily from the Railway Act. The Act stipulates that all tolls must be "just and reasonable," and that tolls for all traffic of the same description over the same route "be charged equally to all persons at the same rate."[2] Furthermore, it is stipulated that with respect to tolls, services and facilities a telephone company will not discriminate against any person or company or give any unreasonable preference to anyone.

As the federal communications regulator, the CRTC has established the following commitment:

> ... to preserve and enhance communications systems in Canada in the interests of the Canadian public ... the CRTC will foster an environment characterized by a wide diversity and availability of Canadian services and facilities offered by adequately resourced entities.[3]

Within the context of the general objectives established by legislation, the CRTC has enunciated five specific goals in telecommunications. These are: (1) to ensure the provision of efficient, just, and reasonably priced telecommunications services; (2) to ensure universal accessibility of basic telephone service; (3) to prevent telecommunications carriers from taking advantage of any monopoly position in their dealings with the public and competing carriers; (4) to ensure

---

[2] Canadian Radio-television and Telecommunication Commission, *Annual Report, 1987–88* (Canada: Minister of Supply and Services, 1988) p. 3.

[3] *Ibid.*, p. 4

that telecommunications operators are financially fit to provide quality services; and, (5) to determine where regulation can be reduced or made more flexible and where regulation can be complemented by reliance on market forces.[4]

As of 1989, the CRTC was composed of five directorates—namely, telecommunications, broadcasting, strategic planning, the general counsel, and the secretariat—and consisted of over 400 personnel. The staff members of the telecommunications directorate are charged with the responsibilities to: analyze tariffs and agreements filed by carriers; prepare recommendations on major revenue requirements and rates; respond to complaints and enquiries from the carriers and their customers; and, develop new regulatory procedures to ensure that rates are fair and regulation is in the public interest.[5]

The focus of regulation by the CRTC is on rates, the extent and quality of services, and the carriers' construction programs, including issues of depreciation and renewal and amortization of their equipment. In the regulation process, the Commission has committed itself to the "fullest possible public participation." [6] Public hearings are scheduled on major issues, and when a public hearing is planned or an application is received, public comment is solicited by the Commission. The views of the public are considered an integral part of the decision-making process through which policies are established and amended, licences issued or revoked, and other matters are settled. During 1987–88, for example, the CRTC held 28 public hearings in centres across the country on matters under its jurisdiction. In the same period, the Commission replied to over 2,500 verbal and approximately 1,500 written inquiries and complaints involving telecommunications.

All telephone and telecommunications carriers under federal jurisdiction must apply to the CRTC for approval to change their rates or change the conditions of services. Commission approval is also required by the carriers to issue shares, to conclude connecting agreements with other telecommunications companies, and a variety of other issues.

Once the regulated companies receive CRTC approval to change rates or services, they are required according to the CRTC rules of procedure to notify customers and other interested parties before they can proceed with the changes. For example, telephone subscribers are informed in advance of an increase in telephone rates by a notification included in their monthly billing statements.

---

[4] *Ibid.*, p. 5

[5] *Ibid.*, p. 17.

[6] *Ibid.*, p. 4

Telephone Rate Regulation

The obligation of the Canadian government to ensure that telephone rates are just, reasonable, and non-discriminatory date to the early period of telecommunications regulation. In the early days of telephone services, local rates covered the costs of the local network, while long-distance rates were set to cover the costs of interconnection, that is, joining local networks together. Over time, however, the costs of interconnection have greatly fallen, but the relationship between long-distance and local rates remained unaltered, so that the relationship between these rates and corresponding costs was lost.[7]

The CRTC, like its predecessors, has relied on the rate of return on invested capital as the yardstick determining telephone rates. The rate base used was average invested capital or the equity of the company. A fair or adequate rate of return was viewed in terms of whether it was sufficient to permit the company to raise required capital in the financial markets. The prime concern of the regulatory agency was, therefore, the total revenue need of the various carriers and how this revenue was distributed among the two major services—namely, long-distance voice (message toll service) and local telephone service.

The determination of the capital structure and the capital base was traditionally left to the carrier management, and the CRTC and the earlier regulator, the Board of Transport Commissioners, were unwilling to substitute their judgment on capital base for that of the management. This raised the potential for needless or excessive capital assets to be acquired and incorporated in the rate base and result in the need for increased prices to customers to yield sufficient revenues to maintain an established rate of return. This potential for over-capitalization is, of course, well recognized in the theory and practice of rate of return regulation.

In 1978, as part of an inquiry into telecommunications carriers' costing and accounting procedures, the CRTC reviewed rate base requirements and the methods carriers were to apply in calculating their revenue needs.[8] The Commission decided to continue to apply the average invested capital rate base for calculating telephone carriers' revenue requirements. The CRTC reiterated that all carriers calculate their revenue requirement on a net asset rate base consisting of: the sum total of the book cost of telecommunication property (including capitalized leases), plus materials and supplies, plus working capital (and that portion of the assets of affiliated companies considered to be integral by the Commission), minus accumulated depreciation and deferred taxes. The rate base would be a monthly average of the amounts involved.[9]

---

[7] *Federal-Provincial Examination of Telecommunication Pricing and the Universal Availability of Affordable Telephone Service*, Working Papers (Ottawa; Supply and Service, 1986), p. 474.

[8] CRTC, *Telecom Decision CRTC 78–1*. Inquiry Into Telecommunications Carriers' Costing and Accounting Procedures. Phase I: Accounting and Financial Matters (Ottawa: 1978).

[9] *Ibid.*

The pricing system applied in the industry requires that a telephone company's total costs of services are covered in the aggregate. Rates for individual services are not necessarily set to cover the costs of each service, however, but are generally averaged over all of the services.

All of the telephone companies follow similar pricing principles and practices and have developed similar rate structures. The two basic principles adopted in rate-making are company-wide averaging and value-of-service pricing. Company-wide rate averaging means that rates for services with the same features are the same throughout. Within an exchange, all customers pay the same basic local service rate for a given class of service, regardless of their usage or distance from the central exchange. In the case of long-distance, company-wide averaging results in the same rates for equal-distance routes, independent of cost. Therefore, while costs may vary, a 200-mile call from one location is the same as a 200-mile from another location. This is sometimes call "route-averaging" and is practiced by all telephone companies.[10]

The value-of-service principle recognizes that telephone services are more valuable to some classes of customers than to others. This principle is applied to local service and is responsible, for example, for the differences in rates between residential and business subscribers.

Local service is generally provided on a flat-rate basis, although in some areas, local measured service (LMS) has been available to private-line business customers. Extended area service (EAS) is also available, allowing customers in neighbouring exchanges to call one another on a flat-rate basis without incurring long-distance charges.

Long-distance or message toll service (MTS) is priced on a distance and usage-sensitive basis. Discounts may be provided for customers, generally during off-peak periods. Customers, such as businesses, which have large long-distance requirements may enjoy considerable savings by leasing private-line voice services or leasing Wide-Area Telephone Service (WATS), a form of bulk long-distance service where a subscriber leases a channel for service to specific zones. Three long-distance services are therefore offered by the telephone companies, namely, MTS, WATS, and private-line. Long-distance rates are based on distance and call-duration. A single per-minute charge is applied to all classes of calls over the same distance, and increases as distance increases but not proportionately. The per-minute rate for a 200 mile call is about one-half the rate for a 2000 mile call.[11]

Developing technology in telecommunications over the last two decades ushered in a host of new and varied equipment, facilities, and services and has made regulation much more complex. The period since 1968 has witnessed the introduction of satellite communications, the use of fibre optics for telecommunica-

---

[10] *Federal-Provincial Examination of Telecommunications Pricing and the Universal Availability of Affordable Telephone Service* (Ottawa: Supply and Service, 1986), p. 7.

[11] *Ibid.*, p. 12.

tions transmission, digital technology, and widespread use of computers. New and varied services have been introduced including data transmission, teleconferencing and video-conferencing, widespread use of private lines, and various computer-enhanced telecommunications services. These developments have forced the CRTC to be concerned with rates for the varied services and to analyze how revenue requirements are distributed among different types of services and different types of users. In addition, the entrance of new companies offering many of these services, and the extension of existing carriers into these new areas raised a concern for the CRTC to ensure that monopoly services were not used to cross-subsidize competitive services.

In 1972, the Canadian Transport Commission initiated an inquiry into telecommunications carriers' costing and accounting procedures, which was transferred to the CRTC in 1976 when the latter was given jurisdiction over federally-regulated telecommunications carriers. This inquiry was a planned, six-phase program of public hearings and decisions on costing and accounting procedures. Phase I dealt with depreciation and accounting charges and procedures, and rate-base calculations for regulatory purposes. Phase II considered the type of information the Commission would require from carriers filing tariffs for new services. Phase III was designed to identify costing approaches and related information requirements needed by the Commission to determine the costs and revenues associated with certain competitive and monopoly services. The Commission attempted to ensure that carriers who operated in both monopoly and competitive markets did not price their competitive services below cost in an attempt to gain an advantage over competitors while subsidizing such services from excessive rates on monopoly services. In 1985, the CRTC ordered the telecommunications carriers under its jurisdiction to prepare costing manuals (following methods set down by the CRTC to establish the costs of several categories of services) and to file, by 1987, their first set of separated revenue and cost figures. This would enable the Commission to identify the costs and revenues associated with these services and to identify the nature and extent of any cross-subsidies among categories. Phase IV would establish the information requirements to be filed in support of a carrier's general rate increases and for rate structure charges. Phase V was to clear up miscellaneous issues such as rate of return and capital structure. Phase VI would establish reporting systems for the information to be filed with the Commission by the carriers on an ongoing basis. These would include information relating to such areas as quality of service and construction programs as well as issues arising from the various earlier phases of the Inquiry.

CRTC Inquiries: Case Studies

To demonstrate the types of issues and considerations in rate increase applications submitted by telephone companies and in CRTC hearings on these applications, consider two cases representing typical applications for rate increases. The first case to be described is an application submitted to the CRTC by BC Tel in

1982 for a general increase in telephone rates. The second is an application for increased rates by Bell Canada in 1988.

Case I: BC Tel Application, 1982[12]

In June 1981, BC Tel announced that it intended to file an application on November 2, 1981, requesting a general increase in rates to come into effect on May 1, 1982. The application filed in November proposed to increase monthly rates for residence primary service by 28 percent and for business primary services by percentages ranging from 37 to 48 percent. For the connection of primary services, BC Tel proposed to increase service charges by approximately 37 percent. An increase from 10 cents to 25 cents was proposed for local coin telephone service, along with an increase in the rate for directory assistance calls from 25 cents to 50 cents. Several increases in rates for long-distance services were also proposed including an increase in the per-minute rate on station-to-station calls from 70 cents to $1.00, and an increase in operator service charges on person-to-person calls from $1.70 to $2.00. BC Tel estimated that these increases would add $106 million to its revenues in 1982. The reasons cited for the proposed increases included the impact of inflation, the need to improve the company's rate of return, and the need to finance its construction program. BC Tel requested an increase in its allowed rate of return on common equity from 14 percent to a range of 17.5 to 19 percent to compete, it argued, with other alternatives available to investors.

Following a pre-hearing in early February to deal with matters of confidentiality and to make arrangements for the conduct of the hearing, the central hearing was held from February 16 to March 12, 1982. The CRTC received a total of 278 interventions in the proceeding, including several petitions containing numerous signatures. The main hearing was held in Ottawa, with four days of regional hearings in four different cities in British Columbia. The central issues considered and reviewed at the hearings were: the quality of service; the company's construction program; operating revenues and expenses; and, the rate of return.

With regard to the quality of service, the CRTC continued to be of the view, as in previous cases, that a proper determination of just and reasonable telephone rates involved an assessment of the quality of service provided by the company to its subscribers. In judging the quality of service, the Commission relied on quarterly data provided by BC Tel for 1981 governing 23 indicators. These indicators covered such aspects of operations as repairs, network performance, operator services, directory and billing accuracy, and complaints. The CRTC concluded that, although there had been some improvement in overall quality of service by BC Tel, the quality remained unsatisfactory in a number of respects. The company failed to meet standards for installation orders, repeat repair ser-

---

[12] CRTC, *Telecom Decision CRTC 82–5*, British Columbia Telephone Company, General Increase in Rates (Ottawa: 1982).

vices were unacceptably high, and the percentage of direct-distance dialled calls not completed due to equipment failures was below standard in a number of geographical areas.

BC Tel submitted a five-year capital plan for the period 1982–86. Estimated expenditures totalled $2.7 billion for the following purposes: 74 percent on primary telephone service; 12 percent on modernization; 5 percent on service improvement; 4 percent on operations improvements; and 5 percent on administrative support. The expenditures were related, claimed BC Tel, to growth in subscriber requirements for existing telecommunications services and were needed to replace obsolete plant and equipment. After reviewing the evidence, the CRTC found the proposed expenditures to be reasonable.

In its application, BC Tel estimated that its operating revenues for 1982 would be $1.14 billion, of which $106 million would be revenues from the proposed rate increases. The estimate of revenues was based on forecast demand for services. Several intervenors questioned BC Tel's forecasting methodology, but the CRTC considered it to be reasonable. The Commission did, however, question BC Tel's estimates of expenses, which determined its revenue requirements, and reduced the company's 1982 expense estimate and consequently its revenue requirement by $10 million.

BC Tel submitted a request for a rate of return on average common equity of 17.5 percent with a permissible range of 17.5 to 19.0 percent. The company argued that interest rates were high and that this level of return was necessary for the company to gain access to the financial markets to finance its construction program. BC Tel relied on outside experts to provide evidence that a fair and reasonable rate of return on equity for BC Tel, given the rates of interest the company was paying on its long-term debt, was between 18.0 to 18.5 percent. Intervenors, on the other hand, countered that a rate of about 15.5 percent would be adequate. The CRTC concluded that an appropriate permissable range for the rate of return on average common equity for BC Tel was between 16.5 and 17.5 percent, but, as the company had not attained the level of service quality deemed satisfactory by the Commission, the Commission decided to approve the lower limited of 16.5 percent as the rate of return for BC Tel for 1982.

To attain its proposed revenues requirements and rate of return, BC Tel had proposed rate increases of 28 percent for residential local services and 37 percent for basic business service. The CRTC was not persuaded that these rate increases were necessary to attain the approved rate of return and accordingly approved rate increases of 18 percent for residential services and 23 percent for business services. The resulting change in the residence-to-business rate ratio was justified on the basis of value-of-service. The CRTC accepted BC Tel's arguments that the earlier liberalization of rules concerning the attachment of terminals to the network had increased the value of business services generally through the widening of service options available to business subscribers.

With regard to intra-BC Message Toll service, BC Tel proposed per-minute rate increases based on a demand model using elasticity estimates derived from monthly calling data assembled in the period 1973–78. The CRTC requested more recent data, but BC Tel claimed that such information was not available. The Consumers Association of Canada questioned the elasticity estimates and argued that rate increases should be kept in line with the rate of inflation. The CRTC finally decided to accept BC Tel's data and approved the intra-BC MTS rates requested. Of the proposed rate increases for the other services, the CRTC for the most part approved smaller increases than those proposed by the company.

Case II: Bell Canada Application, 1988[13]

In February, 1987, Bell Canada filed an application and tariff notice with the CRTC outlining a proposal for telephone rate revisions and rebalancing. Specifically, Bell proposed to reduce long-distance rates and to increase local rates so that the two rates more adequately reflected the costs of the two services. In July, 1987, the CRTC approved interim rate reductions for intra-Bell MTS services by 2.8 percent, but refused to consider local-rate increases, or a rebalancing of local and long-distance rates, to reflect costs, without a full public hearing. Such a hearing was scheduled for late 1987 to establish Bell's 1988 revenue requirement, rate of return on average common equity, and telephone rates and rate structures. An unexpected surge in Bell's finances during early 1987 furthermore raised the issue that Bell's rate of return for 1987 might exceed the range that had earlier been established for 1987. In the hearing held from October 27 to December 11, 1987, the CRTC received a total of 36 interventions and 381 comments, with representations from such organizations and entities as the Old Age Pensioner's Organization, the Senior Citizens Organization, BC Tel, Canadian Manufacturers' Association, Canadian Bankers' Association, Consumers' Association of Canada, CNCP Telecommunications, Department of Consumer and Corporate Affairs, Ontario Telephone Association, and the Telecommunications Workers Union.

As in previous hearings on rate increases, the CRTC examined Bell Canada's application from a number of perspectives, including quality of service, expenses and revenue requirements, and rate of return.

In 1985 the CRTC had approved a set of quality of service indicators in Bell Canada's territory[14] and applied them in the 1987 hearing. Assessing the company's performance for 1986 and early 1987 with respect to 41 indicators pertaining to provision of service, repair service, local service, long-distance service, operator services, and directory assistance and billing service, the CRTC found Bell's service performance to be above standard with the exception of two service-quality indicators in the areas of provision of service and repair service.

---

[13] CRTC, *Telecom Decision CRTC 88–4*, Bell Canada—1988 Revenue Requirement, Rate Rebalancing, and Revenue Settlement Issues (Ottawa: 1988).

[14] CRTC, *Telecom Decision CRTC 85–20* Bell Canada—Standards for Quality of Service Indicators (Ottawa: 1985).

The commission directed the company to pursue corrective action in the two areas where indicators were below standard.

In estimating demand and revenues for 1988, Bell Canada relied on estimates of the price elasticity of demand for intra-Bell MTS that were based on econometric models. Employing these models and using data for 1984–85, Bell estimated the price elasticity of demand for customer-dialled services to be .44 and .49 for the peak and off-peak periods respectively. A number of intervenors conducted extensive cross-examinations of Bell's witnesses on price elasticity, raising questions on the design of the models used, and expressing doubts about the accuracy of the company's elasticity estimates. Concern was expressed over the aggregation of residence and business services in the computations, and it was submitted that disaggregated models would provide higher elasticity coefficients, and therefore higher projected revenues accompanying rate reductions. The Canadian Business Telecommunications Alliance submitted that the CRTC should use an elasticity figure for Bell that is not less than .6. Bell, however, argued that disaggregation was precluded because of lack of adequate data, but that such models could be developed as the quality of data improved. The CRTC believed that it would be valuable to develop disaggregated models, but given the information available at the time, the level of disaggregation used in Bell's models was considered appropriate. Taking the evidence into consideration, the Commission decided that a price elasticity of demand of .5 would be applied to intra-Bell customer-dialled MTS in the peak period, with an elasticity coefficient of .53 for the off-peak period.

Bell Canada's econometric elasticity models played an important role in determining its revenue forecasts for 1987 and 1988 by simulating the effect on revenues of rate reductions and the proposed 10 percent sales tax on telecommunications services, which took effect January, 1988. Given the proposed rate reductions, the Commission estimated, however, that the higher elasticity coefficients applied by the Commission served to increase Bell's forecast revenue for 1988 by $18 million, yielding total estimated revenues of approximately $6.5 billion for 1988.

The CRTC next examined Bell Canada's forecast of expenditures for 1987 and 1988. Bell submitted that these expenditures were expected to rise by 6.8 percent and 8.2 percent respectively. The company provided details of its forecasts by categories of expenses and identified the reasons for the increases, which included inflation and growth in demand for services. The company also provided various measures of its performance to attempt to show that cost increases were not caused by inefficiency. These measures included an index of factor productivity and such specific indicators as operator services expense per operator-handled call. The indicators all pointed to continuing performance gains for 1987 and 1988. Some intervenors challenged the costs as being inflated, arguing that Bell intentionally and regularly inflated its forecasts in the expectation that they would be reduced. They took the position that any cost increases in excess of a one-half percentage point above the Consumer Price Index should be viewed with suspicion. Intervenors zeroed in on some specific expenditures as being excessive. These included vehicle maintenance expenses and marketing expenses. The Commission concluded that it was satisfied that Bell's estimates of its operating expenses for 1987 and 1988 were reasonable. It noted, however, that performance gains were lower than in earlier years and cautioned Bell that it expected the company to continue its efforts toward additional operational improvements. The CRTC maintained that by approving rates designed to achieve a rate of return in excess of the lower range established for 1988, the commission provided Bell "with the means to enhance its return to shareholders through additional efficiency improvements."[15]

In this hearing, the CRTC also examined Bell Canada's procedures for purchases of equipment from its affiliates. The Commission was concerned that inappropriate pricing could occur between Bell and an affiliated company in the absence of any controls. If the company did not secure the best terms possible from its affiliates, an additional burden would be placed on Bell's subscribers. The CRTC announced its intention of initiating a hearing to examine various purchase procedures, including a competitive tender process where an affiliate is a potential supplier.

Bell Canada forecast its rate of return for 1988 to be 13.0 percent, which it claimed was a reasonable reflection of its demand and revenue forecasts for 1988. The company employed outside expert witnesses to prepare evidence as to what would be a "fair and reasonable" rate of return. The witnesses emphasized the importance to Bell of maintaining a high credit rating to ensure access to international financial markets at reasonable rates to finance its construction program. It was submitted that a reduction in Bell's rate of return would result in a downgrading of Bell's credit rating by Moody's Investor Service and Standard and Poor's Corporation, and that these ratings were crucial in the money markets. An increase in the cost of capital, it was argued, would have to be passed on to Bell's subscribers. Despite counter-arguments by intervenors, the CRTC accepted Bell's position on the need to maintain and support its credit rating. Taking into account Bell's large external financing requirements, and the conditions existing in the capital markets, the Commission approved an allowed rate of return on common equity of between 12.25 percent and 13.25 percent for 1988. The Commission applied the middle point of this range, that is, 12.75 percent for the purpose of determining Bell Canada's 1988 revenue requirements. But the established rate of return range, the Commission held, would provide Bell with an opportunity to increase profits above 12.5 percent and up to the 13.25 percent maximum level through additional gains in efficiency.

The approved interim rate reductions in July, 1987, had given Bell Canada a rate of return of 13.2 percent for the entire year, which fell within the prescribed range of 12.25 percent and 13.25 percent for 1987. Given the forecasts of operating expenses and revenues for 1988, however, the CRTC calculated that a reve-

---

[15] *Ibid.*, p. 52.

nue reduction of some $90 million was required for 1988 to achieve the 12.75 percent prescribed rate of return for that year. The CRTC decided that this excess revenue would be applied to secure a reduction in toll rates, giving Bell subscribers a reduction in MTS and WATS rates without the necessity of any rate increase on subscribers to local services. The Commission accordingly authorized reductions in MTS/WATS rates. In recognition of costs, it was determined that the intra-Bell MTS rate reductions would be greater for long-haul services than for short-haul services.

As these case studies show, the revenue requirements for the telephone companies are determined in relation to costs and a rate of return as set by the CRTC. Realized revenue, however, may sometimes exceed forecast revenues, raising the possibility that the rate of return earned for the year may be in excess of the range established by the CRTC. This occurred in 1985 and 1986. The CRTC had established Bell's maximum permissible rate of return on common equity to be 13.75 percent for 1985 and 13.25 percent for 1986. Bell Canada exceeded these rates and had earned excess revenues of $63 million and $143 million in each of the respective years, for a total of $206 million. The Commission, therefore, ordered Bell to provide subscribers with a one-time credit on its billings for basic local services. The amount of credit each subscriber would receive was to be determined by pro-rating the $206 million of excess revenues in relation to each subscriber's billing for the specific basic monthly local service. The Commission estimated that the amount of credit received by each customer would be approximately equal to two months' regular billing charges for basic local service.

Bell Canada appealed the CRTC's order to give this one-time credit to its subscribers before the Federal Court of Appeals on the grounds that the CRTC did not have the jurisdiction for such an order. In July, 1987, the Federal Court agreed with Bell's position and ruled that the Commission exceeded its jurisdiction in issuing the order. The CRTC appealed the Federal Court's decision to the Supreme Court of Canada. In June, 1989, the Supreme Court overturned the Federal Court decision and ruled that the CRTC did indeed have the authority to order a rebate, and also ruled that Bell Canada return to its subscribers, in the form of a credit, the excess amount of revenues for 1985 and 1986 as determined by the CRTC.

Deregulation and Competition

Within the last two decades there has been a trend toward deregulation and increased competition in telecommunications services in both Canada and the United States. Telecommunications in the U.S. had for years been the monopoly of the American Telephone and Telegraph Co. (AT&T) or the Bell System. The challenge to this monopoly began in the 1960s when the Federal Communications Commission (FCC) removed restrictions on the attachment of non-Bell terminal equipment to the Bell system's telephone lines. This opened up the telecommunications equipment market for new entrants in competition with

Western Electric company, AT&T's equipment manufacturing subsidiary. Competition in the equipment industry accelerated the development and marketing of new and innovative telecommunications equipment and provided increased choices for telecommunications users. Competition in telecommunications transmission services was also promoted with a number of FCC decisions that liberalized regulation of telecommunications carrier services. In 1971, the FCC Specialized Common Carrier Decision authorized the entry of specialized service carriers in the interstate business and data transmission market. Basic telephone service, however, continued to be supplied on a regulated, monopoly basis by AT&T. In 1978 the FCC launched a far-reaching market structure proceeding to determine whether the public interest was best served by a continuation of this regulated, monopoly structure. In its historic MTS/WATS decision in 1980, the FCC determined that the public interest would be best served by allowing all interstate telecommunications services, including message-toll service and wide-area telephone service, to be provided competitively. Other FCC decisions during this period deregulated all services except basic telephone services supplied by AT&T. The FCC continued to regulate AT&T because of its dominant position in the industry and consequent potential for preventing new entrants from becoming established in the industry through predatory pricing and other anti-competitive practices.

The federal and provincial regulatory agencies in Canada followed the path of the FCC in liberalizing regulations dealing with terminal attachments and, to a degree, in transmission services. Liberalization in the latter, however, was restricted to private-line and data transmission. Traditional long-distance voice and local telephone services remain a monopoly of Bell Canada and the provincial telephone companies.

Terminal Attachments

In Canada, the statutory provisions regarding terminal equipment attachments to telephone lines have traditionally differed at the federal and provincial levels. Legislation enacted by those provinces with jurisdiction over telephone rates and services within the respective province expressly stated that connection of privately-owned terminal equipment could be prohibited. The reason most commonly given was that connection of allegedly inferior equipment could result in the impairment of the telephone service. Federal statutes declared that Bell Canada was required to show that a policy of restrictive tariffs prohibiting privately-owned terminal attachments was reasonable. For years the CRTC upheld Bell's restrictions in barring the connection of any equipment to Bell's lines that was not approved and supplied by Bell. Bell's equipment manufacturing subsidiary, Northern Electric Company (more recently changed to Northern Telecommunications Inc.) was, therefore, provided with a monopoly on the manufacture and sale of equipment for the Bell telephone system.

Two cases arose during the 1970s to challenge Bell's monopoly in terminal attachments. Challenge Communications Inc., a small company in Ontario, desired to offer a mobile telephone service and applied to the CRTC to allow the connection of its equipment with Bell facilities. Bell Canada sought to prohibit interconnection through the establishment of discriminatory tariffs. In 1977, the CRTC ruled the tariffs unlawful and gave Challenge the right to install automobile phones with access to the Bell network. The Federal Court of Appeal dismissed a Bell appeal and the Supreme Court of Canada denied Bell leave to appeal further.

The second case arose when a small firm in Quebec, Harding Communications, proposed to offer a service to the Bank of Montreal called divert-a-call. After Harding had persuaded the Bank to purchase its equipment, Bell Canada refused to permit the connection of the equipment to its system. Harding sued Bell before the Quebec Superior Court, which issued an injunction preventing Bell Canada from interfering with Harding's business. Bell Canada viewed these decisions as a direct threat to its ability to control attachments to its facilities. Bell's general regulations had provided that no equipment, apparatus, or circuit which was not provided by Bell could be attached to or used in conjunction with the company's equipment or wiring in any way, except where specified in the tariffs of the company or by special agreement. In the event of a breach of this rule, the company could suspend or terminate its services to the party or parties involved.

Concerned that the Challenge and Harding cases would establish the precedent that customer-owned, non-Bell equipment could be connected with the Bell system without any controls by the company, Bell Canada asked the CRTC in 1979 to convene a hearing to determine if the connection of such equipment was in the public interest, and proposed certain conditions under which interconnection would be permitted. Bell opposed the liberalization of policy governing terminal attachments on a number of grounds. First, Bell argued that it would lead to large increases in imports of telecommunications equipment resulting in unemployment and reduced research and development in Canada's high technology electronics and telecommunications industry. Bell estimated that in 1978 the company had purchased $160 million of Canadian-manufactured terminal equipment. Second, Bell argued that interconnection of non-Bell equipment would result in a loss to Bell of up to $110 million annually in revenue from the lease and sale of equipment, and this loss would have to be made up by increasing rates in basic telephone service. In effect, Bell argued that its revenues in the equipment area were cross-subsidizing other areas such as local telephone service. And, finally, Bell argued that the attachment of alleged, cheaper, inferior equipment would harm the integrity of the telephone system, reducing the quality of service.

Intervenors argued extensively that interconnection of subscriber-owned equipment was in the public interest. It was contended that interconnection would lead to the establishment of new producers and importers of telephone equipment in competition with Northern Electric. Competition would stimulate technological development and provide telecommunications customers with equipment possessing a greater and improved range of features and capabilities. They argued that equipment provided by Bell was frequently outdated with limited capacity for up-grading to meet future needs.

In 1980, the CRTC brought down an interim decision on Bell's proposed requirements for interconnection. The Commission disallowed the requirements as unreasonable. The interim decision permitted interconnection with certain conditions until a final decision could be reached. The CRTC agreed that subscriber-provided terminal equipment attached to Bell's network should not cause harm to the network, and accordingly specified technical standards to afford adequate protection to Bell's network. One of the requirements for terminal equipment specified by the CRTC was that the equipment be of the same quality as that provided by Bell Canada to its subscribers. In addition, the interim decision limited telephone subscribers to the ownership of extension telephone sets. The primary set was to be leased from Bell.

In November, 1982, the CRTC issued Telecom Decision 82–14, its final decision regarding the terms and conditions under which subscriber ownership and attachment of telephones and other terminal equipment would be permitted. The decision applied to all federally-regulated telecommunications carriers. The CRTC concluded that since its 1980 interim decision, no convincing evidence had been provided to show that the attachment of privately-owned equipment to Bell facilities and competition in the terminal equipment market had been harmful, and that subscribers should continue to enjoy the potential benefits of this competition. The interim policy was varied to permit residential subscribers to own all their telephone sets, not just extension sets. Subscribers would now have the choice of owning or leasing all of their telephone sets, although the associated inside wiring for residential subscribers would remain the property of the telephone companies. Customers purchasing their own telephones from either Bell or other sources would pay a basic monthly charge for access to the network. They would also be responsible for the repair and maintenance of their own sets upon expiry of any seller's warranty. Under the rate unbundling arrangements, customers continuing to rent their equipment from Bell Canada would pay separate rates, one rate for lines and another for the rental of telephone sets and other equipment, with the monthly rental rate continuing to include full repair service.

The 1980 decision legalizing interconnection of non-Bell equipment led to a rapid proliferation of new telecommunications equipment manufacturers and sellers. By the end of 1982 there were approximately 120 terminal attachments vendors in Ontario, Quebec, and British Columbia. Bell Canada aggressively responded to the growing competition in telecommunications equipment by establishing a subsidiary, Bell Communications Systems, to market business telecommunications equipment manufactured by Northern Telecom Ltd. and actively engaging in price competition (with reductions, for example, of the prices of the more expensive, fancy telephones by 25 percent).

At the provincial level, the provincial regulatory agencies were slow to follow the CRTC example in liberalizing their terminal attachments policies. The provincial telephone companies argued, as had Bell Canada before the CRTC, that interconnection of subscriber-owned equipment would result in the deterioration of the quality of service of the network. Interconnection would also produce a loss of revenues to the telephone companies from the consequent reduction in lease and sales of their telephone equipment. In response, in 1980 the Saskatchewan government passed an amendment to the Saskatchewan Telecommunications Act strengthening the monopoly position of the Saskatchewan Telecommunications Corporation (Sask Tel.). Under the amendment, no person could attach or connect to any part of a telecommunication line of Sask Tel. any equipment, and no one was permitted to advertise or offer for sale any such attachments unless specifically permitted by the regulators. In Manitoba, the Manitoba Telephone Act prohibited the connection to the system of terminal attachments not authorized by the Public Utilities Board. The provincially-regulated telephone companies, however, had in general more open buying policies than Bell Canada, primarily because they were not vertically integrated. This gave independent sellers an opportunity to sell their products through telephone company channels, if not directly to the public.

The first step in the liberalization of provincial interconnect and other regulatory policies came in 1981 in Alberta. After an extensive inquiry, the Alberta Public Utilities Board divided telecommunications into two categories; basic telecommunications services, and non-basic services. The former were those with monopolistic attributes and which were generally considered essential public services. These services would continue to be regulated. Non-basic services were those for which there was more than one provider and which were not considered essential. These services would be open to competition, and they included the manufacture and sale of terminal equipment. Subscribers would no longer rent equipment from Alberta Government Telephones but were given the choice of purchasing the equipment from the telephone company or from an independent supplier.

Other provinces gradually followed the CRTC and the Alberta examples of liberalizing their terminal attachments policies.

Telecommunications Services

In June 1976, CNCP Telecommunications filed an application with the CRTC for an order that would require Bell Canada to allow the interconnection, at a fair price, of certain CNCP facilities to Bell's local switched public telephone networks.[16] The services CNCP proposed to supply through this interconnection included communication between computers and between terminals and computers, teleprint message, and private-line voice services. CNCP was already providing these data and voice services to users through its own network but desired to extend the services to cover a larger number of users. CNCP claimed that its application was directed to the competitive segment of the Canadian telecommunications market, which represented about 13 percent of total revenues of the industry. The interconnection CNCP sought involved "dial access," which would connect CNCP telecommunications facilities to Bell's central telephone switching equipment in a given community.

CNCP argued that increased competition in the areas of service listed above was in the public interest and would result in greater consumer choice of services and improved services at reasonable prices, more innovative facilities and systems, increased efficiency, and quicker response to changing consumer demands.

The CNCP application was vigorously opposed by Bell Canada. The arguments put forward by Bell Canada were very similar to those used earlier by AT&T in the U.S. in its fight against transmission interconnection and competition. First, Bell Canada argued that the telephone industry was a natural monopoly, with large economies of scale producing efficient, low-cost services. To introduce competition would destroy all the advantages and benefits accruing from the natural monopoly. Second, Bell contended that revenues from interprovincial tolls and other long-distance transmission facilities subsidized basic telephone service (local calls) and service in rural, low-populated areas. Bell argued that CNCP would engage in "cream-skimming," that is, it would enter and compete in the most lucrative areas of telecommunications, and reduce the volume of business of Bell and other Telecom Canada members, who would also have to continue to provide the less lucrative services and service the high-cost, rural areas. Cream-skimming by CNCP would reduce revenues of the established carriers, shrink the revenue pool for subsidizing local telephone service, and force the telephone companies to increase local rates.

The question of whether the telephone industry was a natural monopoly was widely debated, with both the pro-monopoly and anti-monopoly sides presenting studies and evidence before the CRTC to substantiate their claims. The general conclusions reached in various independent studies during these hearings, and in the subsequent period, was that there was little evidence to suggest that Bell Canada was a natural monopoly with respect to all of its main services. The debate focused on the issue of economies of scale which characterize natural monopoly. The econometric models that were developed failed to produce reasonable and statistically significant estimates of economies of scale with any

---

[16] CNCP Telecommunications, *Application for Interconnection to Bell System: An Overview* (Montreal, 1976).

degree of consistency for the industry as a whole. Similarly unconvincing, was the evidence produced by the models on economies of scale in selective services such as private-line service. The tests failed to reject the hypothesis that private-line services could be provided on a competitive basis without efficiency loss. In one particular study, a multi-output econometric cost function was employed to develop a procedure to determine changes in production costs attributed to factor price changes, scale economies, and technological change.[17] This approach, however, was unable to distinguish between the cost-reducing effects of technical change with those of economies of scale. An alternative approach involving attempts to model economies of scope in telecommunications services also produced unsatisfactory results. A general finding of these studies, and one which corresponded to findings in studies for the FCC in the U.S., was the inability of existing analytical techniques to separate efficiency gains into those accruing from economies of scale and those due to technological change.

In reply to Bell Canada's contention that local telephone rates would rise, CNCP argued that interconnection would not result in any loss of revenue to Bell and, therefore, there would be no need for local rates to be increased. Indeed, CNCP's position was that the competitive services for which CNCP sought interconnection were being operated at a loss by Bell Canada and were being subsidized by revenues from Bell's monopoly services, particularly long-distance message toll service.

In 1979, the CRTC finally handed down its decision in favour of the CNCP application and permitted interconnection of CNCP facilities with the Bell system for data transmission and private-line voice transmission.

Having put its foot in the door, CNCP's next step was to attempt to expand its range of telecommunications services in competition with Bell Canada and Telecom Canada. In 1982, CNCP petitioned the CRTC to permit it to provide business customers with packages of long-distance telephone services, called bulk intercity voice facilities, at rates below those of Bell Canada for similar services. Bell Canada objected on the grounds of unfair competition, and the CRTC denied the CNCP proposed tariffs unless it could be shown that the lower tariffs reflected a material difference in the value of CNCP services as perceived by users.

In 1985, CNCP applied to the CRTC for permission to provide long-distance telephone voice services in the areas under CRTC jurisdiction. Competition, CNCP argued, would reduce long-distance rates by an amount ranging from

---

[17] See, for example, Denny, M. *et al*, "Estimating the Effects of Diffusion of Technological Innovations in Telecommunications: The Production Structure of Bell Canada," The *Canadian Journal of Economics*, Feb. 1981, pp. 24–93; Fuss, M. and Waverman, L. *The Regulation of Telecommunications in Canada*, Economic Council of Canada, Technical Report #7, March, 1981; CNCP Telecommunications, "Here is What University of Toronto Professors Wilson, Waverman and Fuss Say About Interconnection," Presentation to the CRTC on CNCP Application for Interconnection, 1977; Kiss, F, *et al*, "Economies of Scale and Scope in Bell Canada: Some Econometric Evidence," Paper presented to Conference on Telecommunications in Canada, Montreal, March 4–6, 1981.

10–20 percent for about 10 million telephone users. Bell Canada and BC Tel vigorously opposed this application, arguing that competition in long-distance voice services would reduce their revenues and therefore the amount available for subsidization of local services. Without the subsidy, Bell argued, there would be no alternative but to increase local rates to cover the full cost of local services. In a major decision in 1985, the CRTC denied the CNCP application to complete with Bell Canada and BC Tel in the provision of traditional long-distance telephone service. The CRTC was careful to point out, however, that its decision was based on the merits of this particular application, and that the decision did not reflect a Commission position with respect to increased competition generally in the long-distance telephone market. The Commission stated that it recognized potential benefits from increased competition, including lower long-distance rates, increased customer choice, and more rapid introduction of new technology. In 1986, CNCP Telecommunications requested the CRTC to review its decision but the request was denied. The issue, however, would not die and CNCP announced plans to continue to press for a second long-distance voice network in competition with Telecom Canada. CNCP's position was strengthened in 1989 when Rogers Cable systems, the largest cable company in Canada, purchased a 40 percent interest in CNCP Telecommunications and announced that it would combine its resources and influences with CNCP to obtain authorization for a second national telecommunications network.

In addition to CNCP Telecommunications, other telecommunications companies also continue to chip away at Bell Canada's monopoly position in message toll and local telephone services. Call-Net Communications, a small Toronto-based operation, began providing private-line, long-distance services to several hundred small businesses in the Toronto and Montreal areas. Call-Net leased private lines from Bell Canada, then resold the services to companies at a discount. Bell charged that through these discounted services, Call-Net was attempting to compete with Bell's long-distance monopoly service. In 1988, the CRTC agreed with Bell Canada's position and gave Bell authority to disconnect Call-Net's lines. Call-Net appealed to the federal Cabinet arguing that its services were enhanced services rather than traditional long-distance voice. The Cabinet ordered the CRTC to re-examine the issue and the CRTC continued to study the matter into 1989.

In other provinces, CNCP Telecommunications sought interconnection arrangements for data and private lines with the provincial telephone companies similar to the interconnections the CRTC had authorized with Bell Canada and BC Tel. In a charge before the Federal Court of Canada, directed at Alberta Government Telephones (AGT), CNCP contended that AGT was subject to the Railway Act and to federal regulations because it offered interprovincial services. The Federal Court in 1984 found that AGT was a non-local undertaking and as such was subject to federal jurisdiction, but since AGT was also a provincial crown corporation it was not subject to federal legislation or statutes. AGT appealed the decision that it was subject to federal jurisdiction. In 1985, the

Court of Appeal confirmed the earlier decision that AGT was a non-local under-taking subject to federal jurisdiction, but disagreed that AGT, as a provincial crown agent, was not subject to federal legislation. The Court ruled that the interprovincial activities of AGT were indivisible from the rest of its activities and therefore all of its activities were subject to federal regulation. AGT appealed the decision to the Supreme Court of Canada, which rendered its judgment in August 1989, in essence upholding all of the major points of the ruling of the Federal Court in 1984. The Supreme Court was unanimous in its finding that AGT, and by implication every other telephone company, was an inter-provincial, as opposed to a local undertaking, and therefore subject to the exclusive authority of the federal government. The Court stated that AGT's involvement in the transmission and reception of electronic signals at the borders of Alberta were sufficient to mark AGT as an inter-provincial operation. The Supreme Court also found, however, that the existing wording of federal law prevented Ottawa from exercising this new-found jurisdiction because AGT was a provincial Crown corporation and the Railway Act gave such entities immunity from federal laws. A parliamentary amendment to the Railway Act, nevertheless, could remove this impasse and make provincial telephone utilities subject to regulation by the CRTC.

In effect, until such time as the legislation was amended, the provincial telephone companies were in a regulatory vacuum in which no authority regulated them. It was not until October, 1989, however, that the federal government tabled a bill in Parliament proposing to strip the provincially-owned telephone companies of their Crown immunity, making them subject to regulation by the CRTC. The federal government interpreted the Supreme Court decision to apply only to members of Telecom Canada, and therefore was acting to take jurisdictional control over seven provincially-regulated telephone companies, namely; Saskatchewan Telecommunications, Alberta Government Telephone, Manitoba Telephone System, New Brunswick Telephone Co., Maritime Telegraph and Telephone Co., Newfoundland Telephone, and Island Telephone Co. The federal government exempted smaller telephone companies that were provincially or municipally regulated and providing service to about 3 percent of telephone subscribers.

Pending the enactment of the legislation, the Maritime Telegraph and Telephone Co. serving Nova Scotia, announced its submission to CRTC jurisdiction when its provincial regulator refused to hear applications from the utility because of the Supreme Court decision. Non-federally-regulated telephone companies in other provinces were not so quick to submit to the CRTC. The governments of Alberta, Saskatchewan, and Manitoba were very critical of the federal government's proposal, and contended that regulatory jurisdiction should be legislated back to the provinces. The New Brunswick Telephone Co., owned by private investors, also criticized Ottawa's move. The federal government defended its action, arguing that jurisdiction over all telephone service under one regulatory agency, the CRTC, would enable the federal government to establish a national telecommunications policy and permit all telephone subscribers to be treated equally, with the same degree of competition and choice that the CRTC had allowed in federally-regulated regions. The provincial telephone companies countered that provincial regulatory agencies were more responsive to regional and local interests than would be the case with one central agency such as the CRTC.

Bell Canada Reorganization

In 1982, Bell Canada proposed a major corporate reorganization. It proposed to establish Bell Canada Enterprise Inc. (BCE) as the new company of the Bell group of companies, including Bell Canada. Bell Canada's holdings in other companies and affiliates, including its 55 percent interest in Northern Telecom, would be transferred from Bell Canada to BCE. Both Bell Canada and Northern Telecom would be subsidiaries of BCE. The primary objective of the reorganization was to separate Bell's regulated activities from its non-regulated activities. The federal Cabinet, acting under the authority of the National Transportation Act, directed the CRTC to hold a public hearing on the proposal to inquire into potential effects on Bell Canada services and its subscribers. The CRTC was directed to examine the potential effects on subscriber rates and on the CRTC's ability to carry out its mandate, and the limitations, if any, that should be placed on the scope of potential activities that may be conducted by the Bell group of companies. Such activities included the holding of broadcast licences by Bell. Up to that time, Bell Canada had been prohibited from such activities. The CRTC reported to Cabinet in 1983, recommending that the reorganization be allowed to proceed, subject to the enactment of certain legislative safeguards. These safeguards related to the regulatory access to information about Bell companies' activities, the scope of the operations of the regulated versus unregulated companies in the Bell group, and certain statutory duties and limitations. Bell's reorganization plan was subsequently implemented.

BCE controls some 80 companies of the Bell group, and in addition to telecommunications is involved in real estate, financial services, pipelines, printing and publishing, and consulting services. The bulk of the revenue of BCE, however, accrues from telecommunications operations and telecommunications equipment manufacturing. For example, in the first half of 1989, telecommunications operations generated $3.9 billion of revenue; telecommunications equipment produced $3.4 billion; financial services yielded $ .2 billion; and, $ .4 billion of revenue came from other operations.[18]

---

[18] BCE Inc., Letter to Shareholders, Second Quarter, 1989.

TELEVISION: BROADCAST, CABLE, PAY

Nature of the Television Market

The television market is composed of three components—namely, broadcast, cable, and pay television. The objective of the operators in all three components is to attain mass audiences through the provision of entertainment and information. Some basic differences exist between broadcast television and cable and pay television, however, including the way in which the entertainment and information services are financed. The nature and characteristics of the various components of television and their operation in the North American market have implications for government regulation in Canada.

Broadcast Television

In broadcast television, the production and presentation of television programs is but the means of attaining the primary objective—to provide audiences for advertisers. The consumer product is the television program. It is an intermediate good which is provided free of direct change to consumers or viewers. The end product is the access to audiences that the programs produce, and it is this access to audiences which is bought and sold in the market. Advertisers seek audiences who are potential consumers of the advertised product, and it is advertising that finances television programs and services and enables them to be brought to the household via the airwaves, and to be brought free of direct charges to the household. In the final analysis, the markets that provide broadcast television services are the consumer markets of the goods and services advertised on television. The consumers of these goods and services ultimately pay for television services since advertising is but one of the costs of production of goods and services and is reflected in the market prices of these goods and services.

In general, the larger the audience produced by a television program, the more the advertisers are prepared to pay for the advertising time allotted to the program. The size of the audiences produced by programs is monitored very closely by television operators and advertisers. The success of a program is gauged by the Nielsen rating system, which measures the proportion of television households tuned into the program. The Nielsen ratings of audience size is, therefore, crucial to the profitability of a television station operator.

The structure of the television broadcasting industry is organized along the lines of networks, plus a number of independent television stations. A network is a group of interconnected stations simultaneously broadcasting the same programs, as well as the same commercial advertisements. It may be nationwide or regional. Television stations organize into networks for the simple reason that networking is economical. Networks can supply a national audience for advertisers and serve to economize on the costs of arranging for nationwide advertising. They employ a single agent to deal with national advertisers. Each affiliated station, therefore, is saved the expense of soliciting advertisers, and the advertisers are saved the expense of dealing with individual stations. Similarly, networks provide economies through centralized program purchase and distribution. The program producer or distributor has only to negotiate with the network rather than the many television stations. The network affiliated stations, on the other hand, provide air time for network programming and are assured of a secure source of programs, as well as access to costly programs which an individual station might not otherwise be able to afford.

Basically, the economies of networking stem from the nature of television programs. A television program broadcast over the airwaves is a public good. Characteristics of a public good include non-rivalry in consumption and non-excludability. Non-rivalry means that one person's consumption of the good or service does not affect or interfere with another person's consumption. Furthermore, unless the signals are scrambled, consumers cannot be excluded from receiving the signals. In essence, the marginal cost to the distributor of additional users of a public good is zero. The basic cost in broadcast television is the cost of the program, which represents a fixed cost. As more viewers tune into the program, this fixed cost is spread over a larger and larger number of viewers, so that the average cost of the program per viewer declines. Given that the program is financed by advertising, the average cost of advertising per viewer declines as the number of viewers increases. Networks can provide large audiences and spread the costs of programming and advertising over a large number of viewers. They can, therefore, more readily afford expensive, quality programs than can individual stations which are restricted to small local audiences.

Cable Television

Cable television, otherwise known as community antenna television (CATV), is a system by which television signals are brought into households on a subscription basis by co-axial cable or optical fibre. A CATV system makes it possible for a household to receive broadcast signals it could otherwise not obtain, either because of the distance from the broadcasting station or because of interference from geographical barriers.

Unlike a broadcast television station, which provides only one channel, CATV has multi-channel capacity. Some systems in the U.S. are capable of providing as many as 200 channels. This difference in capacity produces differences in the economies of broadcast television compared with CATV. As outlined earlier, a broadcast television station possesses a single channel and its objective is to maximize audiences, subject to cost constraints, at all times on its one channel. Programming is geared to this maximization goal. Various types of programs, such as situation-comedy, action-adventure, police-detective, talk shows, etc., can be shown, but variety in programming is restricted in particular viewing periods to those programs that are most popular in a particular period. In a period such as prime time, for example, there tends to be a lack of diversity of programs on network television. CATV, on the other hand, uses its multi-channel capacity to provide diverse programming in any viewing period. The objective of CATV is to maximize the combined audiences for all the channels, and this is best achieved by programming for specific audiences in addition to general audiences. In any one particular viewing period, there will be some viewers who wish to see a situation-comedy, others may wish to see an action-adventure program, still others may prefer a musical variety program. By appealing to these specific tastes on its many channels, cable television attempts to attract as many subscribers as possible.

Another distinctive economic feature of CATV is that cable stations tend to operate as regional monopolies. A cable operator obtains a licence for a specific region or area. In Canada, these are for the most part exclusive licences so that the cable operator does not face competition from other cable operators. The exclusive licensing system stems primarily from the economies of scale inherent in CATV and its tendency toward natural monopoly. It is more economical and efficient for one cable company to wire a community for cable signal distribution than for several cable operators to duplicate facilities and compete for subscribers. Once a system is in place the costs of delivering programs is relatively low and tend to decrease as the number of subscribers increases. The cost of a program to the operator is a fixed cost, and therefore the larger the number of subscribers, the lower is the average cost of a program per subscriber.

Pay Television

Pay television is a system by which television signals are brought into subscribers homes for a fee for each individual channel. The signals may be carried over the air in scrambled form, for which a descrambler or decoder must be used by the subscriber, or through coaxial cable or optical fibre. The major difference between cable and pay television is that the former carries primarily broadcast television programming not available due to distance or interference and is multi-channel, whereas pay television consists of specialty channels carrying programs such as movies, sports, music, etc. not shown on regular broadcast television. Furthermore, pay television is usually limited to one channel.

Pay television is closely associated with cable television in that cable operations usually act as the distributors of the pay television programs. A pay channel will distribute its programs to cable operators via microwave or satellite transmission facilities and the cable operators use their cable facilities to feed the signals to pay television subscribers. Indeed, the two systems have become so closely linked that they are viewed in combination as paycable services, and most cable subscribers also subscribe to one or more pay specialty channels. It has been argued that it was only with the introduction of pay television that the cable television market in the United States began to expand. Most television viewers in the U.S. had access to the commercial and public networks and saw little need for cable television. But, when the specialty movie, sports, music and other pay channels came into existence, they combined with basic cable to expand very rapidly. In Canada, the situation was somewhat different. Unless a household was located near enough to the U.S. to pick up American signals, those signals were unavailable via the airwaves. But they could be made available via cable. In addition, given the vast spaces in Canada, even Canadian broadcast signals could be better received through cable than through the airwaves. Cable television consequently become popular and widespread in Canada several years before its expansion in the U.S. Pay television, on the other hand, developed more slowly in Canada as the CRTC, the federal regulatory agency of communications, was slow to permit or legalize pay signals in this country. This was part of a deliberate policy of communications regulation which had a direct effect on broadcast, cable and pay television in Canada.

In the following sections an attempt will be made to explain why and how television communications have been regulated in Canada, the objectives of regulation, and the extent the government achieved these objectives through its communications regulation policies.

Operation and Regulation of Broadcast Television

In the Canadian broadcast television market not only do Canadian television networks compete with each other, they face competition from American networks both via the airwaves and through cable. In essence, Canada and the U.S. form a common market, particularly for American broadcast signals, and this has had a significant impact on Canadian television programming and government regulatory policy.

Broadcast television in the U.S. consists of two components: commercial television, supported by advertising; and, public television, supported by contributions from government, institutions, and individuals. The three major commercial networks are the Columbia Broadcasting System (CBS), the National Broadcasting Corporation (NBC), and the American Broadcasting Corporation (ABC). Together, these three networks accounted for over 90 percent of the American viewing audience in the early 1970s. Competition from public television, pay-cable television, and from Fox Broadcasting (a newly-established fourth network) reduced the audience share of the three networks to approximately 70 percent by the late 1980s. Public television was introduced in 1967 when Congress passed the Public Broadcasting Act and created the Public Broadcasting Service. This service links some 300 public television stations in a loose network which focuses on educational-type programming and competes with the commercial networks.

The Canadian broadcast television industry features two major networks. The Canadian Broadcasting Corporation (CBC) consists of over 30 federal government-owned television stations, with an additional 30 affiliates and several hundred rebroadcasting stations. The second major network is the privately-owned CTV, a consortium of 16 affiliated television stations, each an equal partner in the network. In addition, the CTV network includes several supplementary affiliates and rebroadcasting stations. Global Television is a third but much smaller network, consisting of one program originating station and several rebroadcasting stations. In addition to these three networks, there exist several independent stations located primarily in large urban areas, plus Province-owned and operated television stations, such as TV Ontario.

The two private networks, CTV and Global, are commercial networks and are financed through advertising. The publicly-owned CBC is financed through a combination of advertising and public funds appropriated by Parliament. The purpose and functions of the CBC are governed by the Broadcasting Act. Its mandate is to provide a Canadian broadcasting system that is Canadian in content and character which would enrich and strengthen the cultural, social, political and economic fabric of Canada. This objective, as outlined in the Broadcasting Act, was to apply to all broadcasting in Canada and the CBC was one vehicle by which this was to be achieved. The other vehicle was the regulation of private broadcasting.

The broadcast television industry is regulated by the Canadian Radio-Television and Telecommunications Commission (CRTC), which obtains its television regulatory authority from the Broadcasting Act. Among its functions, the CRTC is responsible for issuing licences to television stations. All licences must be periodically reviewed for renewal, and the CRTC has the power to cancel licences of stations not meeting established conditions. Licences are only issued to Canadian-owned and Canadian-controlled stations. Advertising on Canadian television is governed by CRTC regulations. The CBC is allotted ten minutes of advertising per hour, while private television stations are permitted up to twelve minutes per hour.

A primary function of the CRTC, in keeping with the objective of promoting and strengthening Canadian culture, is the regulation of television programming content. Current programming content regulations require that Canadian programs account for sixty percent of programming between the hours of 6:00 am and midnight, averaged over one year. Between the hours 6:00 pm and midnight, fifty percent of air time must be devoted to Canadian programming. The remaining time can be used to show Canadian or foreign programs.

The justification for Canadian-content regulations stems from the proximity of the U.S. market and the costs of programs. Canadian viewers have ready access to U.S. television signals, either directly via the airwaves, if they reside in border areas, or through cable television. Canadian cable operators and rebroadcasters can readily pick up U.S. television signals, and broadcast television stations and networks can purchase U.S.-made programs at a fraction of the cost of Canadian-produced programs. In addition to their lower cost, U.S.-made programs usually generate a larger viewing audience and consequently larger advertising revenues and profits. The general rule of thumb is that it costs a Canadian network ten times as much to produce a program as to purchase an equivalent American program. It is claimed that without Canadian-content regulations, the private Canadian television stations and networks would show very few Canadian-made programs other than the news. If left alone, the Canadian television operators would follow profit-maximizing behaviour of minimizing costs while attempting to maximize advertising revenue. If American programs cost less, but produce larger viewing audiences and therefore advertising revenues, it is rational for Canadian television operators to show American programs and ignore producing their own programs or purchasing programs produced by Canadian independent producers.

Content regulations are costly to Canadian television. In 1985, it was estimated that in meeting Canadian-content requirements, television networks and stations spent 70 percent of their program budgets on Canadian programs and 30 percent on foreign programs. But Canadian programs accounted for only 30 percent of their total revenue, whereas foreign programming brought in 70 percent of total revenues.

The estimated average costs of producing various types of programs in the U.S. in 1988 were as follows:

One week of afternoon soap operas *(5-one hour episodes)*	$300,000
One week of daytime game shows *(5-one-half hour episodes)*	$250,000
A one-half hour situation-comedy for prime time	$350,000–$600,000
A one-hour prime time drama	$.5–$1.5 million

The last category would include such programs as Miami Vice ($1.3 million per episode); Dallas ($1 million per episode); Dynasty ($1.6 million per episode); and, LA Law ($1.1 million per episode). The cost of producing a quality one-hour drama in Canada, such as Danger Bay, was approximately $500,000, although a fairly popular drama, Degrassi Junior High, was produced for only $250,000 per episode. A one-half hour comedy series cost approximately $35,000–$100,000 to produce in Canada. These are extremely high costs, however, in comparison to the price that Canadian television stations paid for acquiring American programs. In 1987–88 it was estimated that, on the average, the cost to Canadian stations and networks for American programs was $15–$20,000 for a one-half hour program, and from $35–$50,000 for a one hour drama.[1]

In addition to the general content regulations, special regulations have been applied to the two Canadian private networks, CTV and Global. In renewing Global's licence in 1986 for a five-year period, the CRTC ordered Global to

---

[1] *Variety*, Nov. 25, 1987, p. 72.

double its spending on Canadian programs, including dramas, documentaries, and children's programs. This condition required Global to spend $5 million per year to broadcast 200 hours of original Canadian programs.

In 1987, when the licence of CTV was renewed for a five-year period, the CRTC set out several conditions governing the network's programming. First, CTV was required to increase its expenditures on Canadian programs from the $230 million it spent in the previous five years to $400 million over the 1987–92 period. Second, the network was required to increase its weekly number of hours of Canadian drama from 2.5 hours to 4.5 hours by the end of the five-year period, and only one of these hours could be broadcast before 8: 00 pm. Third, CTV was required to broadcast 24 hours of Canadian series per year in prime time. Fourth, a minimum of 6 hours per year was to be devoted to programs featuring new Canadian musical talent. And, finally, the network was ordered to establish self-regulatory guidelines to reduce violence in its programming.

An objective of the Canadian-content regulations was to promote the production and exhibition of Canadian television programs and assist in the development of an independent television program production industry in Canada. While Canadian-content regulations have been in existence from the early days of television, however, they tended to have a negligible impact on developing an independent television program production industry in Canada. Independent producers faced a number of difficulties in their struggle to develop and survive. One of these difficulties was the lack of demand for their products. In the past, there was a tendency for the networks, the CBC and CTV, to produce their own programs ("in-house" production) rather than to rely on independent producers. The networks appeared to show little interest in Canadian independent producers' ideas or products. Furthermore, these producers found it extremely difficult to penetrate the foreign market, and were generally restricted to programs such as wildlife documentaries and educational-type programs which enjoyed a small penetration in external markets. It was estimated that in the 1970s, Canadian independent television program producers rarely covered more than 30 percent of their production costs with revenue from Canadian markets. When independent programs were purchased by CTC or the CBC, these networks were generally not prepared to pay amounts sufficient to cover the costs of the programs because, it was contended, these programs did not generate a sufficient amount of advertising revenues. American producers, on the other hand, could afford to sell their programs to Canadian television at a fraction of program production cost since the cost would have been recovered or amortized in the U.S. television market. Consequently, Canadian producers were restricted by market conditions to the production of low-budget programs and this precluded production of programs with mass audience appeal, such as dramas, comedies, and action-adventure programs.

These market and cost factors influenced network productions as well as the productions of independent program producers. Without specific regulations governing types of programs required to be shown, the general content quotas were filled by CTV with relatively inexpensive musical and variety programs, talk shows, game shows, documentaries and re-runs rather than dramas. Over 90 percent of the drama programs shown on Canadian television was foreign-made. Consequently, no pool of talent was developed in the Canadian television program production industry to produce dramas, comedies, and action-adventure programs that could compete with the programs available from the U.S.

In 1984, the Canadian government established the Canadian Broadcast Program Development Fund to be administered by Telefilm Canada (formerly the Canadian Film Development Corporation, an agency whose function had been to administer financial assistance to Canadian feature film producers).[2] The Fund provided financial assistance to Canadian independent television program producers under certain conditions. To qualify for financial assistance a private Canadian production company had to raise two-thirds of the budget for a program from private sources and have a guarantee from a Canadian broadcaster for prime-time exposure for the program. The funds could be made available by Telefilm Canada as a loan, a loan guarantee, an equity investment, or some combination of these financing methods. In addition, under a new marketing assistance scheme, Telefilm Canada would pay a Canadian exporter of Canadian-made programs up to 50 percent of the cost of advertising in international media with the objective of penetrating international markets.

This policy was welcomed by the Canadian independent producers since it concentrated on both the supply and demand components of the market. The policy provided funding to help finance the supply of programs, and through the guarantee provision from a Canadian broadcaster, ensured that no program would be funded unless it had prime-time exposure.

The Broadcast Program Development Fund was allocated $35 million of federal government funds in 1984, to be increased to $60 million by 1989. By 1987 over one-half of the fund was invested in mini-series drama and was credited with such reasonably successful programs as Degrassi Junior High, Danger Bay, Mont Royal, and Diamonds. These programs were produced by independent Canadians production companies working closely with either CBC, CTV, or the Global network. They were relatively high-budget productions with an average cost per one-hour episode of approximately $500,000. The improved quality of these Canadian productions was reflected in their relative success in foreign markets, including Europe, Hong Kong, and some African countries. It was reported that the series Danger Bay reaped approximately $2 million in revenues in these external markets. Another example of a highly successful Canadian television program was the mini-series "Anne of Green Gables," which was distributed to over 60 countries. It was expected that, as Canadian-produced drama began to be marketed profitability, more small private investors would be attracted to invest in Canadian productions with the expectation of earning a

---

[2] A description and evaluation of the Canadian Program Development Fund is found in C. Hoskins and S. McFadyen, "The Canadian Broadcast Program Development Fund: An Evaluation and Some Recommendations," *Canadian Public Policy*, Vol. XII, No. 1, March, 1986.

return on their investments, and contribute to the development of a financially viable and independent Canadian television program production industry. The policy combination of funding the supply and assuring the programs of a market appears to have considerable potential in helping to develop a program production industry, whereas the policy of simply regulating the use of air time through content quotas failed to achieve this goal.

Paycable Television Services

Cable Television

As mentioned earlier, cable television (CATV) developed in Canada much more rapidly than in the U.S. owing to the geographical difficulties of transmitting broadcast signals in this country. Both Canadian and U.S. broadcast signals could be better received through cable in many parts of Canada than over the air. In 1988, there were 812 cable systems in operation in Canada, with approximately 5.5 million subscribers and a penetration rate of over 60 percent of Canadian households. Canada is one of the most cabled countries in the world relative to population. In contrast, paycable penetration in the U.S. is less than 30 percent. Five large cable companies in Canada accounted for over 50 percent of the national share of the market. These companies were: Rogers Cablesystems (22 percent of the national share); Videotron (14 percent); Maclean-Hunter (6 percent); Shaw Cablesystems (5 percent); and, CUC (4 percent).[3]

Canadian cable operators primarily import U.S. border stations' signals via microwave and re-transmit these signals to subscribers via cable. Cabled Canadian households are thereby given access to U.S. network programming. This access to American network programs has been primarily responsible for cable's popularity in Canada and for the high household penetration rates. Cable has also been responsible for further fragmenting the Canadian television market and eroding network power as the stations they offer compete with the CBC and CTV for viewers.

Prior to January 1990, Canadian cable operators did not pay for the signals that they retransmitted. Under the terms of the Canada-U.S. free trade agreement, however, Canada had to amend federal copyright legislation requiring cable companies to pay royalties for retransmission of signals, starting January 1990. American groups who will receive royalties include the commercial television networks, the Public Broadcasting System, and major sports leagues including football, baseball and basketball. Canadian beneficiaries will include the television networks and other television broadcasters. The amount of the royalties will be determined by a copyright board and the cost of royalties are expected to be passed on to cable subscribers in the form of higher subscription rates.

CATV is regulated by the CRTC. All cable operators must be licensed by the CRTC, but cable is not subject to the same Canadian-content regulations as

---

[3] CRTC, *Annual Report, 1987–1988* (Ottawa: 1988).

broadcast television. The main requirement for a licence is the inclusion of a local community channel to broadcast local and Canadian affairs. The remaining channels in basic cable carry programs of a variety of network, public broadcasting, and independent stations. The CRTC, however, requires Canadian cable operators to substitute the Canadian television station's or network's program if the Canadian and U.S. stations are broadcasting the same program simultaneously. From the beginning, the CRTC regulated subscription rates charged by cable companies but in 1985 relaxed its regulations to permit cable operators to increase rates, subject to a 40 day notice to subscribers, to reflect increases in their capital spending and in the consumer price index. The result has been virtually automatic annual rate increases, although the CRTC has the authority to suspend rate increases. For example, in September, 1989, the CRTC decided to block cable television rate increases sought by Rogers Cable TV Ltd. pending a public hearing into capital spending plans on which the rate increases were partly based. The CRTC was concerned that some of the capital spending might be related to other telecommunications services in which Rogers was involved and was not solely for providing basic cable television service.

The CRTC continues as a form of watchdog over CATV rates and operations and can subject the various aspects of cable to intense scrutiny. In 1988 the CRTC revised its regulations governing the installation of basic cable services. Previously cable companies charged a single flat fee for installation, but following complaints from cable customers the CRTC decided to issue new rules by which cable operators would have to design rates that more closely reflected the costs of installation. The CRTC reviews the appropriateness of cable rates in terms of the rate of return on net fixed assets as well as quality of service, and claims that it has the authority to order a roll-back of rates of any cable company where the service is deemed unsatisfactory even if its rate of return is low.[4]

In late 1989 the CRTC announced plans to call for a hearing to examine various aspects of cable operations, including how cable companies determine installation fees and the manner in which they calculate annual rate increases. The Commission proposed to consider the elimination of the provision in the regulations entitling cable companies to an annual rate increase. In addition, the Commission announced plans to examine the feasibility of applying rate of return regulation to cable operators similar to that applied to telephone companies. Underlying these proposals was the CRTC's desire to ensure that cable services remained available to households at affordable prices, while at the same time fostering the development of Canadian programming services.

CRTC Policy for Pay Television

While cable television was quite readily accepted by policy-makers in Canada, and rapidly expanded and flourished once permitted, the same was not true of pay television. Indeed, pay television has had a rather controversial and tenu-

---

[4] CRTC statement as reported in the *Globe and Mail*, February 9, 1989, p. B7.

ous history. The era of pay television began in the U.S. in 1972 when Home Box Office began to offer a movie channel to subscribers for a specific fee. By the 1980s specialty-program channels ranging from sports to country music to all-news were available on the pay format in the U.S. The American experience started a prolonged debate in Canada over pay television. The primary issues were whether it should be permitted in this country and, if so, what form should it take.

Canadian television networks opposed pay television on the grounds that it would further fragment the already fragmented, small Canadian market and cause the loss of viewers and advertising revenues for the networks. Cultural groups feared that pay television would carry primarily U.S. programs and would increase American dominance over Canadian culture. Canadian television program producers and feature film producers argued that if the pay structure was permitted it should be regulated and that its programming be required to carry a high degree of Canadian content. Pay television with a high Canadian content would, it was contended, create an additional outlet for Canadian productions and serve to stimulate the television program and film industry in Canada.

There was also considerable doubt expressed whether the size of the Canadian market was sufficiently large to sustain profitable pay services. It was argued that Home Box Office, the largest pay television operator in the U.S., only became profitable after it had attracted some four million subscribers. It was noted that this number almost equalled the total number of cable subscribers in Canada, and that pay television was not likely to appeal to all cable subscribers. Others countered that pay, when merged with cable as the carrying vehicle, would make an attractive combination and would lure additional subscribers to cable and pay services. As pay television expanded in the U.S. many Canadians began to purchase and install satellite receiving antennas to pirate the signals of American pay stations as they were beamed from telecommunications satellites. While the installation of such antennas was not legal without a licence, the government neglected to press charges against their owners. As these antennas proliferated and public pressure began to build for pay systems, the CRTC finally decided to permit pay television in Canada.

In its March, 1982, decision on pay television the CRTC outlined certain objectives that the pay system was to achieve, along with conditions governing the structure and operations of the system.[5] Among the stated objectives was an increase in the diversity of television programming available to Canadians. Another objective was development of high quality Canadian programming from new programming sources. Pay television was viewed as providing new opportunities for exhibiting Canadian productions and a new source of revenue for these productions. And, finally, pay television was to become an integral part of the

---

[5] Canadian Radio-Television and Telecommunications Commission, *Decision CRTC 82–240, Pay Television*, March 18, 1982 (Ottawa: 1982).

Canadian broadcasting system, helping to promote and foster Canadian culture and the objectives of the Broadcasting Act.

The pay television system initially licensed by the CRTC took the following form:

(a) One national, general interest service which was required to provide both an English language and a French language channel. The licence for this service was granted to a company appropriately calling itself First Choice Canadian Communications Corp.;

(b) Three regional, general interest services. The successful applicants in this category were Star Channel, serving the Atlantic region; Superchannel, serving central Canada; and, Allarco, serving the western region. Programming on these channels was to appeal to a wide audience, but it was anticipated that programming would consist mostly of movies, variety, drama, and sports.

(c) One national, specialty-cultural channel featuring the performing arts. A licence was granted to C-channel for this service; and

(d) One regional, multi-lingual service in British Columbia, primarily Vancouver with its diverse mix of cultures. This channel was required to present 60 percent of its programming in languages other than English and French.

These were the initial licences granted, but the CRTC did not rule out the licensing of additional channels in the future, particularly regional and specialty channels.

The intention of the CRTC in 1982 was to create a competitive pay television structure. The coexistence of a national service along with regional services was expected to produce an element of competition in pay services. In the opinion of the CRTC, a competitive structure was more likely to enhance program diversity for viewers and provide greater opportunities for Canadian producers than would a monopoly structure. Indeed, various submissions to the CRTC had pressed for a monopoly structure, contending that monopoly would provide more revenues for program production because it would benefit from economies of scale and consequently operate with greater efficiency than a competitive system. The counter-argument, which was accepted by the CRTC, was that competing channels would provide program producers with more opportunities to sell their programs, compared with a monopoly which would in effect act as a monopsony (one-buyer) for programs. In addition, competition between the pay channels would serve to regulate subscriber rates and preclude the need for CRTC rate regulation. Rate regulation was thought to be unnecessary not only because of competition between the pay channels but also because of the competition the pay channels presumably would face from cable television, conventional broadcast television, and video-cassette recorders.

Various other conditions and restrictions were imposed by the CRTC in its grant of licences. No existing television stations, broadcasters or consortium of cable companies were granted licences for pay television services. The CRTC wished to avoid vertical integration in pay operations, whereby a licensee would be a program producer, a distributor of the program, and an exhibitor. Under the approved system, the licensees would only put together packages of programs. Programs to meet Canadian-content requirements were expected to be produced by independent Canadian producers.

Stringent regulations were established governing Canadian content in pay television programming. The national and regional general interest licensees were required to devote a minimum of 30 percent of their programming time to Canadian-produced programs. This content was gradually to be increased to 50 percent by the end of the five-year licence period. Furthermore, 30 percent of programming in the evening hours 6:00 pm to 10:00 pm was to be devoted to Canadian content. The decision to require only 30 percent of total programming to be Canadian in the initial years was in recognition that the operators would incur high start-up costs and would likely have difficulty acquiring a sufficient number of quality Canadian programs to meet higher content quotas and the need to attract enough subscribers to cover the high start-up costs.

The CRTC also specified for each licensee the proportions of gross revenue and total programming budget that had to be allocated to the acquisition of Canadian programs. For example, First Choice, the national-general interest channel, was required to spend annually on the investment in, and acquisition of, Canadian programs a minimum of 45 percent of its total operating revenues. Furthermore, a minimum of 50 percent of the funds spent on Canadian programs had to be devoted to television dramas, including dramatic feature films (as opposed to talk and game shows which, it was deemed, did little to develop Canadian artistic talent and Canadian scriptwriters). The CRTC undertook to monitor programming to ensure that these regulations were followed, and that the pay channels were providing new programming services which complemented rather than duplicated those available on conventional, broadcast television.

No advertising was to be permitted on the pay channels. This medium was to provide a new source of funds for Canadian television program producers and not divert funds that were already committed to the broadcasting system.

All of the licensees proposed to make use of existing cable television facilities for their signal delivery systems. For example, First Choice proposed to originate its programs from its studio in Toronto and use existing communications satellite facilities to distribute its signals to local cable operators, who in turn would deliver the signals via their cable systems to subscribers. Cable operators, however, would be free to choose whether they wished to participate in these services. For those who participated, First Choice proposed a monthly rate of $7.50 per subscriber charged to the cable operator, and it was expected that the cable operator's fee would also be approximately $7.50 for a total monthly charge of $15.00 to the subscriber. First Choice also envisaged a form of direct broadcast service to subscribers in areas not serviced by cable. Signals would be beamed in scrambled form to a communications satellite and subscribers would set up receiving antennas and rent decoders to receive and unscramble the signals.

Pay Television Performance Under Regulation

The early progress of pay television in Canada was much slower than expected. Start-up expenses were greater than anticipated and the number of subscribers did not materialize as projected. In the first year of operations, instead of the millions of subscribers predicted, the pay channels had succeeded in attracting only about 500,000 customers or a meager ten percent of the potential market. First Choice had estimated that it would attract forty percent of the cable subscribers, but by 1987 its penetration rate was only sixteen percent. All pay services experienced operating losses in their early years of operation. The C-channel, offering arts and cultural programs, went bankrupt in its first year of operation. Star Channel in the Atlantic region and the multi-lingual channel in British Columbia folded early. Allarco, the western regional network, and Super-channel, the central regional service, merged to become a second national general interest service in competition with First Choice. The viewer market, however, proved too small to accommodate two competing national channels, so in 1984 the CRTC permitted the two channels to divide the country into two non-competitive markets. First Choice would operate east of the Manitoba-Ontario border, and Allarcom Pay TV Ltd. (the combination of Allarco and Super-channel) would operate west of this border as Superchannel. The result of these early failings and restructuring was no longer a competitive system, but a system consisting of two regional monopolies.

High subscription rates and disappointment by subscribers with the service combined to contribute to this very shaky start for pay television. The higher-than-expected subscription rates of approximately $16.00 per month discouraged potential subscribers. Many early subscribers began to cancel their subscriptions, producing a very high turnover rate. By the end of the first year, the industry was losing as many customers as it was gaining. The dissatisfaction stemmed from the fact that pay television had promised more than it could deliver. First Choice devoted its programming to movies, and the shortage of quality movies available to the channel meant seemingly endless repetition, with a movie being shown three to four times a day and continuing in the schedule for weeks. Subscribers complained about the low quality of Canadian content. Canadian-made movies being shown included many that had been box-office and critical disasters when exhibited in movies theatres, and some which were so poor that they were never exhibited in theatres.

The pay operators complained that a contributing factor to the low number of subscribers was the proliferation of illegal decoders and theft of the signals. The illegal decoders enabled households to pirate pay channel signals without subscribing to the channel. The pay operators in Quebec estimated that in 1983 there were approximately 50,000 legal decoders in use and about 20,000 unauthorized decoders. In 1987, Videotron, the largest CATV operator in Quebec, filed suit against a Quebec-based company for allegedly manufacturing and selling unauthorized decoders that descrambled pay television signals. The Quebec Superior Court ordered an injunction preventing that particular company from making or selling any device capable of descrambling pay-television signals. At the time, Videotron estimated that there were 30,000 unauthorized decoders in the market, which caused potential revenue losses of $7 million for Videotron.[6]

Another contributing factor to the low number of subscribers to pay services was competition from the video-cassette recorder and home movie rentals. The movie pay channels contended that in order to meet this competition they had to show quality movies but were hampered in this respect by the high Canadian-content requirement. There were very few Canadian movies that had been box-office successes, and the majority of the remaining Canadian movies could not compete with those available in video-cassette.

In addition to the restructuring of the pay television industry, the licensed operators began to introduce various other measures in their efforts to survive. In a bid to attract subscribers, both First Choice and Allarcom began to offer more "adult-programming," or what some in the industry labelled as "soft pornographic" programs. Some industry analysts claimed that the introduction of this type of programming could conceivable alienate as many subscribers as it attracted. The CRTC, concerned with the survival of pay services, did not interfere.

Cultural groups began to claim that pay television operators were not abiding by the Canadian-content regulations, and that they were classifying as Canadian content many programs which were not distinctively Canadian. In addition, it was charged that pay companies were not spending the amount of funds on Canadian productions as was specified by their licences. By 1986, the pay channels were required to air 50 percent Canadian material but, it was alleged, were only airing about 30 percent.

The pay television companies defended their actions as a matter of survival and pressured the CRTC for a relaxation of their licence requirements. First Choice argued that it spent more money filling its 30 percent Canadian-content quota than it did on the remaining 70 percent of the programming. By 1984, the pay operators were contending that unless the CRTC reduced Canadian-content requirements, pay services were likely to completely fold. At the end of 1984, First Choice reported a cumulative deficit of $56 million; Allarcom a deficit of $10 million; and, Premier Choix, the French channel of First Choice, a deficit of $14 million. The number of subscribers reported by these companies was 318,000, 78,000, and 78,000 respectively. Without some changes in content requirements, First Choice projected total cumulative losses of $100 million by 1988.[7] It argued that there were just not enough Canadian-made movies to meet the content quota. Those available were shown an average of 22 times, while U.S. movies were played an average of 11 times. First Choice claimed that the

---

[6] *Globe and Mail*, December 10, 1987.

[7] *Globe and Mail*, June 18, 1986.

high repeat factor for the Canadian movies, many of which were of dubious quality and attraction, was a major contributor to the low number of subscribers. In effect, the viewing menu offered simply did not appeal to subscribers. First Choice requested the CRTC to reduce the Canadian-content requirement from 50 percent in 1986 to 15 percent, and to reduce the spending requirements specified in its licence. The pay operators argued that they could not make a profit as long as they had to spend 45 percent of their operating revenues on Canadian programming.

A sympathetic CRTC introduced new regulations in late 1986. The requirements for Canadian content were reduced from 50 percent of viewing time to 30 percent during prime-time hours and 20 percent for the rest of the day. Furthermore, new Canadian productions shown in prime time were to be counted as if they were 1.5 times their actual length. In addition, the spending requirement was reduced from 45 percent of operating revenue to be spent on Canadian programming to only 20 percent. These changes, along with other initiatives approved by the CRTC, such as the introduction of specialty channels, breathed renewed life into the industry. By the end of 1987, the pay television operators were able to report an increase in the number of subscribers and marginal profitability.

In late 1989, Allarcom Ltd. submitted a proposal to the CRTC for permission to operate, on an experimental basis to determine viability, a pay-per-view service for Superchannel subscribers. The proposed test service was to be called Superchannel Main Event. A subscriber to this service would be offered a choice of up to five channels, each offering a movie, in prime time. The subscriber would either punch into a keypad or call a local telephone number to choose one of the channels. It was proposed that the cost of a movie would range from approximately $3.00 to $6.00 depending on how current the movie was. Pay-per-view has operated in the U.S. for about five years and a similar service has been offered in many Canadian hotels.

Specialty Channels

In 1984, in an attempt to inject some economic and financial vitality into the floundering pay television industry, the CRTC, in a major decision, agreed to license specialty channels in pay television. The initial approval was for six specialty channels offering a variety of forms of entertainment. These six channels were: (1) Action Canada Sports Network (TSN), providing 24 hours of sporting events, including hockey, baseball, tennis, U.S. basketball, and international soccer, with 18 percent of viewing time devoted to Canadian events in its first year of operation, increasing to 35 percent by the end of five years; (2) Muchmusic, a 24 hour music-video channel with 10 percent Canadian content in the first year and 30 percent by the fifth year; (3) Arts and Entertainment Network, offering a mix of music, dance, theatrical productions, and classic movies; (4) Nashville Network and (5) Country Music TV, both offering primarily country music along with some quiz shows and sporting events; and, (6) Financial

News Network, providing business news and information. The first two channels were Canadian and were assigned Canadian-content requirements, while the last four were American channels with no Canadian quotas. The only condition established by the CRTC regarding these channels was that in order to subscribe to an American specialty channel, a customer also had to subscribe to at least one Canadian channel. Each of the channels was offered through cable facilities on a pay-per-channel basis.

All of the above specialty channels were permitted to carry advertising but they were restricted to national commercials so as not to compete with local advertising. The commercials were limited to eight minutes per hour on a national level.

Following the initial licensing of these six specialty services, the CRTC began to grant licences to additional specialty channels. The Life Channel, offering medical and childrens' programs, was approved in 1984, followed by 12 more channels in 1987 and several more in 1988. These included channels covering weather, news, public affairs, the stock market, religion, business, performing arts, and childrens' programs. Most of these additional channels were licensed to form part of basic cable services, with only a few offered on a pay-per-channel basis. Included in the latter was the Family Channel, which had been established by Allarcom and First Choice as its major shareholders and obtained 60 percent of its programming from the Disney Channel in the U.S.

Canadian-content requirements were negotiated separately for each of the additional specialty channels and varied considerably. The Family Channel, for example, was required to carry 25 percent Canadian content in its program schedule. The All News channel introduced by the CBC was required to have 90 percent Canadian content. A children/youth service, the YTV Canada channel, was required to carry 60 percent Canadian content, with a minimum of 40 hours a year of original first-run Canadian shows, increasing to 55 hours by the end of its three-year licence term. The license of a French language music channel, Musique Plus, called for 60 percent Canadian content, with 30 percent of overall time devoted to music videos.

The specialty channels were to be financed by a combination of subscriber fees and advertising, or by subscriber fees only. The license of the Family Channel restricted financing to subscriber fees. Other channels were financed by subscriber fees ranging from ten cents per subscriber to seventy five cents, and up to twelve minutes of national advertising per hour.

The licensing of additional channels by the CRTC was not without its critics. It was argued that the Canadian market was too small to support so many channels and that few would survive financially. Evidence was cited from U.S. cable-pay television operators who claimed that it was difficult to sell more than three or four specialty channels to a single customer. A 1984 U.S. survey revealed that, on the average, cable subscribers only watched two more channels than broadcast-only viewers, and that the most popular programs with these viewers were old network series, movies, and sports.

The fragmentation of the Canadian market was underscored when a number of the specialty channels applied to the CRTC to be permitted to be carried as part of the basic cable package offered to subscribers. TSN and Muchmusic, seeing little potential for further growth as separate pay channels, believed that they could increase their market penetration as part of basic cable. TSN, one of the more successful specialty channels, reached a saturation point in 1988 with approximately one million subscribers, whereas the subscription base of cable exceeded five million customers. While TSN would receive considerable less revenue per viewer as part of basic cable, it was believed that the larger number of potential subscribers would more than compensate for the reduced rate and produce increased profits. The applications of both TSN and Muchmusic to be included in basic cable were approved by the CRTC in 1988. Indeed, by the end of 1988 all of the original specialty channels except First Choice, Allarcom, and the Family Channel were part of either the basic cable or a basic cable extended package in which a group of specialty channels would be added to basic cable for an additional monthly rate, but subscribers could not choose which channels they wished from the group. Only First Choice, Allarcom and the Family Channel remained truly individual, discretionary pay television channels which could be added or deleted separately rather than in combination with other channels.

Paycable television operators package programs in a variety of ways. In central Canada, a typical basic cable package consists of 30–35 channels including Canadian and U.S. networks, U.S. public television, and a number of specialty channels. In 1989, a typical basic package would cost subscribers about $18.00 per month. A variety package may include basic plus several specialty channels, such as Muchmusic, TSN, Arts & Entertainment, Nashville Network, news services, and others for approximately $20.00 per month. The most comprehensive package would include basic and the specialty channels plus First Choice and the Family Channel at a monthly rate of $33.00.[8] The CRTC, however, restricted the packaging of the Family Channel. It could not be packaged with more than five channels containing exclusive U.S. satellite service. All cable companies must also ensure that the total number of Canadian channels offered is always greater than the number of foreign channels and that priority is given to programming over non-programming services.

In summary, the final structure of the pay television industry was considerably different than that envisaged when pay television were first launched in 1982. Most pay channels have become part of basic cable services and are indistinguishable from basic cable. Only three separate pay per channel services remain in Canada: Allarcom in the west, First Choice (and its French counterpart Premier Choix) in central Canada, and the Family Channel. The marriage of traditional cable television with pay services has become so complete that the service is generally known as paycable service or simply cable television.

---

[8] Trillium Cable Communications Ltd., Windsor, Ontario.

The CRTC continues to regulate many aspects of cable and pay television services. The operations of each company are subject to review during applications for licence renewal, including the review of Canadian content in the case of specialty pay channels. The CRTC continues its long-standing concern to provide broadcasting service to remote and underserviced parts of Canada and continues to issue licences to new cable companies proposing cable service to these areas. The CRTC also continues to examine developing technologies, such as Direct-To-Home service, which have potential for more economical and feasible means of distributing and extending television signals.

11

FINANCIAL INSTITUTIONS

Features of the Canadian Finance Industry

The finance industry in Canada consists of a variety of financial institutions.[1] It includes the Bank of Canada, domestic chartered banks, foreign chartered banks, credit unions, trust companies, mortgage companies, investment and securities dealers, the securities exchanges, small loans companies, insurance companies, and provincial treasury and savings offices. The largest companies in the major groups are listed in Table 11–1. This financial system performs a host of indispensable functions in the economy. It controls the money supply and manages the monetary system. It provides the facilities for the safekeeping of funds. It acts as the intermediary between borrowers and savers. It influences interest rates. It provides the links to foreign currencies and the international financial market. It provides essential payment services and acts as a clearing house for numerous types of financial transactions. Without such a financial structure it would practically be impossible for modern economies to function.

The Bank of Canada plays a key role in the Canadian financial system. It is Canada's central bank, established by the Bank of Canada Act, 1934, and is owned by the federal government. The Act and its subsequent revisions govern the authority and functions of the Bank. The Bank of Canada possesses broad powers to influence and control the money supply, interest rates, and monetary policy. It issues paper currency, acts as the banker for the federal government, buys and sells securities in the securities markets, acts as the selling agent for federal securities, and influences general interest rates. It operates in the foreign exchange markets to stabilize the value of the Canadian currency in relation to foreign currencies. The Bank, however, does not engage in commercial and public banking activities.

Although the Bank of Canada operates with a considerable amount of independence it is ultimately responsible to the federal government. Monetary policy is designed to assist the economy to achieve price and employment stability and to provide the conditions for economic growth. In designing and implementing

---

[1] A description of the various financial institutions and their functions in Canada can be found in: R.A. Shearer, J.F. Chant and D.E. Bond, *The Economics of the Canadian Financial System*, 2nd ed. (Scarborough: Prentice Hall Canada Inc. 1984): E.H. Neave and J. Prefontaine, *Canada's Financial System* (Toronto: Methuen Publications, 1987); and, Economic Council of Canada, *A Framework for Financial Regulation* (Ottawa: Supply and Services Canada, 1987).

TABLE 11–1: Largest Financial Institutions in Canada, by Major Category, 1988

Institution	Assets ($ million)
Chartered Banks	
Royal Bank of Canada	110,054
Canadian Imperial Bank of Commerce	94,687
Bank of Montreal	78,908
Bank of Nova Scotia	74,674
Toronto Dominion Bank	59,285
Trust Companies	
Royal Trustco	28,500
National Trustco	12,191
Central Guarantee Trust	11,600
Montreal Trustco	10,202
General Trustco	4,900
(Canada Trustco would be near the top but data was not available	
Credit Unions	
Confederation Caisses Populaires Desjardins	34,246
Vancouver City Savings	1,735
Credit Union Central of Saskatchewan	1,441
British Columbia Central	1,347
Canadian Co-operative Credit Society	932
Life Insurance Companies	
Manufacturers Life Insurance Co.	23,888
Sun Life Assurance Co.	23,188
Great-West Life Assurance Co.	17,257
Confederation Life Assurance Co.	13,599
Canada Life Assurance Co.	11,365

Property and Casualty Insurances	Revenue ($ million)
Co-operators General Insurance Co.	836
Royal Insurance-Canada	791
Zurich Canada Group	789
Economical Group	541
Lloyd's of London	526

Investment Dealers	Total Capital ($ million)	Major Shareholder
Burns Fry Holdings Corp.	285	Security Pacific 30%
RBC Dominion Securities Inc.	270	Royal Bank of Canada 67%
Gordon Capital Corp.	234	Employees
Wood Grundy Inc.	221	C.I.B.C. 62%
Scotia McLeod Inc.	183	Bank of N.S. 100%

SOURCE: *The Financial Post 500*, Summer 1989.

monetary policy, the Bank works in close consultation with the federal Department of Finance.

Chartered banks operate under the charter of the federal government and are subject to the provisions of the Bank Act. A fairly large number of banks were chartered in the early period of banking in Canada. Amalgamations, however, gradually reduced this number, so that for most of the first half of the 1900s the country was served by ten chartered banks with nationwide branch networks. After further amalgamations, five banks came to dominate the system. These were the Bank of Montreal, Bank of Nova Scotia, Imperial Bank of Commerce, Toronto-Dominion Bank, and the Royal Bank of Canada. No new banks were chartered between 1931 and 1953. Beginning in the 1950s, however, several new banks were incorporated including such banks as the Mercantile Bank of Canada (1953), Bank of British Columbia (1966), Northland Bank (1975), Canadian Commercial Bank (1975), Western and Pacific Bank (1982), and the Bank of Alberta (1984). Since 1985, the number of Canadian chartered banks has again declined, this time through bankruptcies and mergers, including mergers with foreign banks.

The chartered banks are publicly owned and their shares trade on the Canadian stock exchanges. Besides providing the public with banking services, these banks have an obligation to earn an adequate return for their shareholders. The banking system consists of both domestic and foreign banks. The Canadian-owned chartered banks are classified as Schedule I banks. Foreign-owned banks are classified as Schedule II banks, and currently there are about sixty of these banks.

Other banking institutions consist of: the Province of Alberta Treasury Branches, which are established by provincial legislation and operate in Alberta; the Province of Ontario Savings Office, which borrows funds for the province by means of deposits; and, various credit unions and caisses populaires, which are consumer-owned financial institutions providing savings, chequing, and loan services. There are over 3000 of these facilities throughout the country.

Trust companies are incorporated either under federal or provincial statutes. They provide executor and trustee services, manage property and investments, and provide banking services including savings deposits and various savings vehicles, such as investment certificates. Other services include loans and mortgages, transfer and registration of securities, disbursement of dividends, registered retirement and pension trusteeship, and financial counselling. There are over a hundred of these institutions, many with full-service branches across Canada. They provide the consumer with the closest alternative to the chartered banks for basic financial services.

Mortgage companies are also registered either by the federal or provincial governments. They may accept deposits and issue debentures, and under the provisions of the legislation most of the funds secured in this way are to be invested in mortgages, with the real estate as security.

Insurance companies are licensed or registered by the provincial governments. Services include life and health insurance, property insurance, and causality insurance. In addition to private insurance companies, there are government-operated agencies which provide insurance services. The private companies are profit oriented and the funds generated from premiums are invested in a variety of loan and investment instruments.

Finally, there are the investment dealers and the securities and commodities exchanges. They provide channels for savings and investments through the purchase and sale of bonds, shares, and future commodity contracts, and are licensed under provincial legislative authority. The five stock exchanges in Canada are found in Toronto, Montreal, Winnipeg, Alberta and Vancouver, with the Toronto Stock Market accounting for approximately three-quarters of the total value of securities traded.

The Financial Regulatory Environment

The regulation of banking and other financial institutions stems from their crucial role in economic affairs, including their influence on the supply of money in the economy. A stable, viable financial system in which consumers and business have confidence provides the backbone for the economy, channelling financial resources to the various sectors and components of the economy. Financial institutions are charged with the trust of peoples' funds and there is natural concern by depositors for the safety of their deposits. Failure and bankruptcy by one institution could lead to a loss of confidence by depositors. A consequent run on the banks or rush to withdraw funds from remaining institutions would jeopardize their survival and the very survival of the financial system. Consumer protectionism and financial stability, therefore, remain prime justifications for government regulatory involvement in the financial system. In addition, there can be a tendency towards concentration and monopoly in the financial industry, and a primary objective of regulation is to promote efficiency through an adequate degree of competitiveness. But active competition can lead to the failures of some financial companies just as in any other industry. Ideally a system should provide competition to achieve efficiency, but at the same time be sufficiency stable to retain the confidence of the public and avoid major disruptions in the economy.

Other goals of regulation that have been cited in the past included the desirability of fostering Canadian ownership of financial institutions, and of preserving the separation of financial and non-financial activities. Canadian ownership was considered desirable for the implementation of Canadian monetary policy objectives. Separation of financial and non-financial activities was considered necessary to prevent possible conflicts of interest which might increase the risk factor in portfolio holdings. A bank with equity holdings in a business enterprise might be more inclined to provide it with loans at favourable terms despite possible high risks of failure of the corporation.

Government regulation of financial institutions in Canada has focused on entry into the financial industry, ownership and transfers, restraints and limitations in the operations of specified categories of institutions, and supervision of operations to ensure financial soundness and consumer protection.

Regulatory jurisdiction is shared by the federal and provincial governments. The constitution gives the federal government exclusive jurisdiction over chartered banks. Near-banks, which includes trusts, insurance companies and mortgage companies, are regulated by both the federal and provincial governments. Those chartered by the federal government are regulated by the federal government. Provincially-chartered trusts, insurance companies, credit unions, caisses populaires, and securities firms come under the authority of provincial governments.[2]

Traditionally, the "four pillars" of the financial system were chartered banks, trust companies, insurance companies, and investment dealers. These four categories of financial institutions were viewed as the backbone of the financial structure, supplemented by credit unions and other savings and loan institutions. The functions of each group were established by legislation and were kept separate. Chartered banks performed the traditional banking function of holding deposits, clearing cheques, and making loans. Trust companies performed a trustee function; insurance companies provided life, property and causality insurance; and, mortgage companies provided loans secured by real estate.

Competition in banking was restricted by both regulatory and economic barriers to entry into the banking industry. As part of the set of regulatory barriers, entrants required a licence or charter. In order to obtain a charter, certain conditions had to be met. The group applying for a charter had to consist of at least 10 individuals who were required to provide a specified amount of capital, but the equity holdings of any one individual investor was limited to 10 percent. Foreign ownership was limited to no more than 25 percent in total. Restrictions were placed on interlocking directorates between banks and other financial institutions, such as trust and mortgage companies, and on the ownership of non-bank institutions by banks. These restrictions made it difficult for other financial firms or new banks to obtain banking charters. The near-banks (trust and mortgage companies) operated under various constraints with more limited powers than the chartered banks and these restrictions reduced their ability to compete with the banks. Even competition between banks themselves was restricted by various statutory provisions, such as interest-rate ceilings and the practice of collective rate setting by banks.

Potential new entrants into the banking industry have faced rather formidable barriers to entry. Depositors tend to be conservative and are reluctant to place their savings in a new institution which would not possess an established track

---

[2] An outline of regulation of Canadian financial institutions is contained in Economic Council of Canada, *Efficiency and Regulation* (Ottawa: Supply and Services Canada, 1976); and, Economic Council of Canada, *A Framework for Financial Regulation* (Ottawa: Supply and Services Canada, 1987).

record of trust or substantial assets as security, although the introduction of deposit insurance has tended to reduce this risk barrier. New entrants, furthermore, have to compete with large established branch networks, with conveniently-established and highly-visible outlets for customers. A potential new entrant is faced with problems of obtaining appropriate branch sites, of establishing a sufficient number of branches in various geographical locations to appeal to customers who travel or move, and would likely be faced with high costs in promotion and advertising to attract customers away from the old, well-entrenched banks which may have earned a reputation for good service, reliability, and trust. Prior to 1967, there was also little incentive to enter the banking industry because of the high opportunity cost. The statutory-imposed interest rate ceiling tended to keep profits and rates of return lower than in most other industries and tended to discourage new capital from entering the industry.

Government regulatory involvement in the financial system ranged from the general control of the money supply and monetary policy through the Bank of Canada to specifications and restraints governing the behaviour of the smallest of the financial institutions. The Bank of Canada was and remains the monetary manager for the federal government. Through its role as a lender of last resort to the banks, its purchase and sale of government securities on the open market, and through moral persuasion, the Bank of Canada influences the supply of money and consequently the level of interest rates and the supply of credit in the economy.

Prior to 1987, in addition to the jurisdiction over banks exercised by the Bank of Canada, chartered banks were regulated by the Office of the Inspector General of Banks. This Office was established in the 1920s within the Department of Finance, and was charged with the function of ensuring that the provisions of the Bank Act were observed and that banks remained in a sound financial condition. The discharge of this function involved annual inspections and reports of irregularities to the Minister of Finance.

The financial areas administered by the provinces came under the authority of a provincial regulatory agency, and in the areas administered jointly by the provinces and the federal government, each level of government established or designated an agency to oversee operations. Insurance and trust companies were subject to regulation by the Department of Insurance at the federal level, and by provincial counterparts. The main regulator of financial firms in Ontario is the Superintendent of Financial Institutions. In some other provinces, this responsibility rests with government departments or agencies exercising authority over consumer and corporate affairs. The securities markets are the responsibility of provincial Security Exchange Commissions, which regulate the markets in accordance with provincial securities legislation. To coordinate the activities of the various provincial securities commissions, the federal government incorporated the Investment Dealers Association of Canada (IDA). The IDA collects financial information from member firms, performs audits, and reports its findings to the stock exchanges and the provincial securities commissions.

In 1987, a new federal agency called the Office of the Superintendent of Financial Institutions was created as an amalgamation of the Office of the Inspector General of Banks and the Superintendent of Insurance. The latter had been responsible for supervising federally-registered financial institutions other than central banks. These included insurance companies, investment, trust and loan companies, credit unions and employer-sponsored pension plans under federal jurisdiction. The new Superintendent of Financial Institutions is responsible to the Minister of Finance for the administration of the Bank Act. The functions of this office continue to include: the examination of the affairs of chartered banks and savings banks to ensure that the provisions of the Bank Act are observed; to examine the financial viability of the banks and ensure the financial security of depositors and creditors; to certify to the Minister and the Bank of Canada whether the returns submitted by the banks on their cash reserves are correct; to inspect banks on behalf of the Canada Deposit Insurance Corporation; and, to serve as an advisor to the Minister of Finance on banking matters.

The Canada Deposit Insurance Corporation (CDIC) was established by statute in 1967 to ensure Canadian currency deposits up to a specified amount. Currently the maximum amount insured is $60,000 for deposits by a customer in any federally incorporated bank, trust, or loan company, and any corresponding provincial deposit-accepting institution which is authorized by the province to apply for deposit insurance. The insurance protects depositors in the event of bankruptcy of the bank or trust holding their deposits and greatly reduces the possibility of a customer run on banks in the event of a bank failure or rumours of its financial difficulties. In 1988, there were 162 financial institutions protected by the CDIC consisting of 67 chartered banks, 58 federal and 37 provincial trust and loan companies. The CDIC finances its operations by levying an insurance premium on its members. In 1986, the premiums were increased from one-thirtieth of 1 percent of their insured deposits, or about 3 cents for every $100 deposit, to one-tenth of 1 percent or 10 cents for every $100.

In an attempt to ensure that rules and regulations were followed by financial institutions, the government had at its disposal a broad range of enforcement powers and sanctions. These included: the authority in certain cases to seize assets; authority to place limits on interest rates, investments, branching, and on borrowings; public disclosure of irregularities; authority to apply for a liquidation order; monetary penalties; civil and criminal charges through the judicial system; and, in the case of banks, the power to appoint a curator to take immediate control of a troubled bank.

A More Competitive System

In 1964, the Royal Commission on Banking and Finance (Porter Commission) recommended major changes in the financial system to create a more open and competitive system. The objectives of its recommendations were to increase efficiency, flexibility, and innovation in the industry. Many of the recommendations were incorporated in revisions to the Bank Act in 1967. Subsequent changes in the rules and regulations governing banks, trust and mortgage companies, credit unions and caisses populaires began to open the Canadian financial system to competition. Competition for deposits and in consumer loans was fostered by eliminating interest rate ceilings, by giving banks increased authority to extend mortgage loans, and by requiring banks to provide customers with better information on the cost of loans. The 1967 revisions to the Act also provided federal deposit insurance for each $20,000 account in banks or near-banks. The revisions enabled banks to compete more aggressively with each other and with near-banks in attracting deposits and in consumer and business loans and mortgages. New financial services were offered, including various types of accounts carrying varying interest rates. The increased competition resulted in lower costs and greater choices for customers.

Additional revisions to the Bank Act in 1980 further loosened the reins of regulation and prompted the acceleration of competition in the financial system. Banks were granted extended powers in factoring and leasing. The former involves financing buyers' purchases of goods and services, while the latter consists of banks purchasing capital equipment to be used by a firm and leasing the equipment to the firm. Leasing was beneficial to small businesses which were short of capital as it avoided the necessity of financing capital purchases. The new Bank Act increased the available assets of banks by reducing cash reserve requirements. The Canadian Payments Association was established as the agency responsible for the cheque clearing system, and the system was opened to near-banks. This placed near-banks on the same level as the chartered banks in cheque clearing and payment services and permitted them to compete more closely with the banks. Entry into banking was facilitated by enabling a new entrant to obtain a charter at the discretion of the Minister of Finance through a letter of patent rather than by an act of Parliament. In addition, the 10 percent ownership rule was relaxed. Banks were divided into two categories or schedules, A and B. Schedule A banks were required to adhere to the ownership rule, while Schedule B banks were not. The latter, however, were subjected to greater limitations, in terms of the total assets and number of branches they were permitted, and they had to meet higher minimum capital requirements in order to obtain a charter. A near bank was permitted to create a Schedule B banks as a subsidiary, and also to combine with a banking subsidiary to become a Schedule A bank if it met the ownership requirements. Restrictions on the entry of foreign banks were relaxed enabling a subsidiary of a foreign bank to be incorporated as a Schedule B bank. In 1988, the two bank categories were changed from designations A and B banks to Schedule I and Schedule II banks respectively, but the criteria for each category remained the same.

In June, 1987, the federal government gave federally-regulated domestic banks, trusts, and insurance companies the green light to enter the securities market. They could do so on their own or through association with an existing securities firm. Rules restricting foreign firms from entering the Canadian securities industry were also relaxed. Beginning in June, 1987, foreign firms could acquire up to 50 percent of an existing, domestic securities firm and, as of June 1988 could acquire 100 percent of such firms. According to the agreement, in-house securities functions of federally-regulated financial institutions would be supervised by the federal office of the Superintendent of Financial Institutions. In an agreement with the Ontario and Quebec Securities Commission, the security subsidiary firm of a federally-regulated financial institution would be regulated by the provincial Securities Commission, but the federal Superintendent would be allowed to receive information on the security firm necessary to insure that the federally-regulated institution retain its solvency. The goal of allowing financial institutions into the securities market was to provide a wider range of services for securities issuers and investors. It was expected that more competition in the investment industry would produce better service at lower costs.

The developments over the past several years have produced an increasingly complex financial system in Canada and a nightmare for federal and provincial regulators. Differences between the functions and operations of the various groups of financial institutions has become more and more blurred as banks, trusts, insurance companies and other financial institutions moved into each other's territory. Stocks can be purchased from banks, demand deposit accounts can be established with investment dealers, mutual funds can be purchased from banks, trusts, credit unions, and investment dealers. Competition has increased, along with a trend towards greater concentration of ownership. There has been a greater mixing of financial and non-financial activities. Banks, trust companies and other financial institutions have diversified by acquiring interest in other institutions. Financial holding companies have been established bringing together a large mix of financial institutions, while some of these holding groups may themselves be part of large non-financial corporations.

Problems and the Need for Regulatory Reform

The relaxation of restraints and the promotion of competition in the financial system since 1967 brought numerous benefits to customers in terms of services, rates, and innovative financial instruments. But this period also witnessed some disturbing and serious problems in the financial system. Prior to 1967, the financial system enjoyed public trust and confidence in its soundness and stability. There had been no bank failures since the failure of the Home Bank in 1923. But the late 1970s and the 1980s witnessed the failure of a number of financial institutions, and solvency problems caused many other financial institutions to seek mergers to strengthen their positions.

Between 1980 and 1985, 22 financial institutions failed in Canada.[3] The failures included two relatively new chartered banks, ten federally-chartered trust and loan companies, four provincially-chartered trust and loan companies, and

---

[3] For a list of the financial institutions which failed, see Economic Council of Canada, *A Framework for Financial Regulation* (Ottawa: Supply and Services Canada, 1987), p. 47.

five general insurance companies. The two chartered banks which failed were
the Canadian Commercial Bank, established in 1975 as Canada's tenth chartered
bank, and the Northland Bank, both based in Alberta with combined assets of
over $2.5 billion. In 1986, the Bank of British Columbia, Canada's ninth largest
chartered bank with 39 branches and assets of $2.8 billion, was purchased by the
Canadian subsidiary of the Hong Kong and Shanghai Banking Corporation. The
Bank of British Columbia was on the merge of bankruptcy, weighed down by
millions of dollars of non-performing loans. In 1987, the Principal Group Ltd., a
holding company with various trust, mortgage, and investment house subsidiaries and $1.2 billion in assets, declared bankruptcy leaving 67,000 depositors
fearful and angry.

Mergers involved banks, trusts, mortgage companies, and even security dealers. In 1986, the Mercantile Bank merged with the National Bank, the Morguard
Bank was taken over by the Security Pacific Bank, and the Continental Bank
merged with the Canadian subsidiary of Lloyds Bank of London. The securities
industry witnessed some 20 mergers between 1981 and 1985, including the
merger of such large firms as Richardson Securities and Greenshields Ltd.

The Canadian Deposit Insurance Corporation (CDIC) paid $276 million to the
Canadian Commercial Bank customers for insured deposits and $332 million to
the Northland Bank's insured depositors. By 1986, the rash of failures of financial institutions had caused a cumulative CDIC deficit of about $1.25 billion. In
1987, the CDIC paid out another $116 million to insured depositors of Principal
Savings and Trust Co., the only Principal Group subsidiary that was CDIC
insured.

Factors contributing to difficulties and failures of financial institutions may be
external, internal, or a combination of both. External conditions can severely
impact on financial business. Recessions and declining economic activities reduce business borrowing requirements for expansion, and may cause business to
close and default on loans. As the economy slows and unemployment increases,
the consequent decline in income reduces customer deposits. Inflation may also
produce difficulties. As interest rates rise, financial institutions have to pay increased rates to retain deposits which counteract the higher rates charged on
loans. High rates furthermore may cause more businesses to default because of
the heavy debt burdens. Institutions with a high proportion of loans in real estate
may suffer considerable losses if the real estate market should collapse. The
exposure to these risks requires astute internal management if financial institutions are to remain solid and viable. The quality of loans, degree of diversification, size of capital base, and the balance between assets and liabilities will be
determining factors in the success of an institution.

The Economic Council of Canada, in an examination of the financial institution failures in the early 1980s, found that while external factors did contribute to
the failures, the dominant factors were internal.[4] The most significant of these

---

[4] *Ibid.*, pp. 46–51.

were inadequate management of assets and liabilities, erosion of the capital base, and questionable loan practices. Aggressive competition caused many institutions to take on a high proportion of low-quality, risky loans. Some institutions, such as the Northland Bank, had 60 percent of its loans in Alberta, with a high proportion of real estate and petroleum-associated investments. When oil prices dropped and the oil industry became depressed, many loans were defaulted. A number of questionable practices were also discovered in which managers attempted to secure gains for themselves at the expense of depositors and investors. Conflicts of interest and fraud were discovered in some of the cases where institutions became insolvent.

The failures of financial institutions occurred despite the mechanisms in place that are designed to reduce or prevent such failures. These include the conditions and restraints attached to an institution's licence or charter, the requirements concerning the capital base and borrowing multiples in relation to that base, disclosure requirements, and the inspection and monitoring of operations by the Office of Inspector General of Banks (OIGB).

While restrictions specified in charters and licences on the activities of financial institutions have the effect of portfolio regulation, the primary mechanism for attempting to ensure solvency and stability was the inspection system. The inspection system consisted of self-inspection by the banks and inspection by the OIGB. The Bank Act requires each bank to have an audit committee consisting of three directors of the bank who are not employees of the bank. The audit conducted for shareholders by outside auditors also plays an important role in this system. In its examination of a bank's activities, the OIGB did not conduct on-site inspections of banks by inspectors but instead depended heavily on the internal and external auditors' reports. Through these reports, information returns, and management interviews, it was expected that the OIGB would be able to detect early signs of any trouble in a bank, such as management weakness, falling earnings, irregularities, lack of diversification, etc., which could potentially lead to insolvency. The monitoring of these variables created a form of early warning system for detecting problems in the banks and the banking system. With respect to trust and loan companies and insurance companies, the agencies at both the federal and provincial levels performed a similar monitoring function as part of an early warning system designed to identify problems in those institutions that could potentially lead to insolvency.

The increasing number of failures of financial institutions during the 1980s, and the difficulties incurred by others, brought the effectiveness of these early warning systems and the regulation of financial institutions into question.[5] Mismatched assets and liabilities, the questionable quality of loans, and lack of diversification were among the causes of the failure of trust companies and the failure of the Northland Bank and the Canadian Commercial Bank. There were

---

[5] A critical examination of the federal government's supervisory methods is contained in Canada, House of Commons, *Canadian Financial Institutions*, Report of the Standing Committee on Finance, Trade and Economic Affairs, November, 1985 (Ottawa: 1985).

also questionable accounting practices in attempts to disguise the true financial status of these institutions. These practices were apparently undetected by the OIGB. In other cases, there was evidence that the early warning systems did indeed detect potentially dangerous situations, but no action was taken by the authorities. This was apparently the situation in the failure of the Principal Group Ltd. in 1987. The Principal Group, based in Alberta, was a financial conglomerate of more than 100 companies, including two major investment companies, First Investors Corporation and Associated Investors Corporation. These latter two companies operated near the borderline of solvency for a number of years. In 1984, the assistant deputy minister of the Alberta Department of Consumer and Corporate Affairs recommended that the two companies be shut down, but the government failed to act. Subsequent audit statements showed continuing and growing losses. In late 1986, the Alberta government appointed an outside auditing firm to examine the operations of First Investors and Associated Investors. The firm recommended that the two companies be closed, but the government instead began negotiating with the Principal Group to establish a rescue and reorganization plan. In June, 1987, negotiations failed and the government finally cancelled the licences of First Investors and Associated Investors and launched an investigation into the matter. But, in August, 1987, the parent company, the Principal Group, itself filed for bankruptcy. The Alberta premier announced that if the investigation, headed by court-appointed inspector Mr. W. Code, found the government to be negligent in the Principal collapse, it would compensate investors. In his report in July, 1989, Mr. Code identified the primary cause of the failure of the Principal Group as the collapse of the real estate market in Western Canada, which comprised a large proportion of Principal's assets. The report also provided evidence of dishonest and fraudulent practices by the Principal Group executives. The report pointed to a failure of the Alberta Minister of Consumer and Corporate Affairs to act on early reports of difficulty and questionable practices within the Principal Group and charged the Minister with a breach in public duty. A few days later, the federal government filed charges against the president and several executives of the Principal Group for misleading advertising and information contained in the annual reviews issued by Principal Group Ltd. Liquidation of Principal's assets returned investors approximately fifty cents on each dollar invested, while the Alberta government announced that it would compensate investors in First Investors Corp. and Associated Investors Corp. for up to 75 percent of their losses. Depositors with funds in Principal's Savings and Trust subsidiary were insured by the Canada Deposit Insurance Corp. and were able to recover losses up to the maximum insurable amount of $60,000.

Regulatory Reform

Numerous studies have been conducted on the structure and operation of the Canadian financial system, with accompanying proposals for changes and reform. As outlined earlier, the Royal Commission on Banking and Finance (Porter

Commission) recommended a comprehensive program for increasing efficiency, flexibility, and innovation in the system through competition and diversification of operations. Many of the Commissions proposals were subsequently incorporated in the changes in the Bank of Act in 1967. In 1976, the Economic Council of Canada produced a study on the regulation and efficiency of deposit institutions. The Council recommended a functional approach to regulation rather than regulation by institution. In 1985, the federal government released a Green Paper setting out details for financial reform, followed by a task force study known as the Wyman Report. These two studies were in turn examined by the House of Commons Standing Committee on Finance, Trade and Economic Affairs, whose findings were released in late 1985 in the Blenkarn Report, and by a Senate Committee on Banking, Trade and Commerce in 1986. In addition, the failure of the Canadian Commercial Bank and the Northland Bank prompted the federal government to establish the Commission of Enquiry on Certain Banking Operations (Estey Commission).

The Green Paper[6] proposed that the federal government strengthen its supervisory structure by creating a centralized federal supervisory agency with extended regulatory powers. The increased blurring of differences between financial industries raised questions about the suitability of having an Inspector General of Banks responsible for regulating banks and a Department of Insurance responsible for supervising the insurance industry. It was proposed that the two separate bodies be amalgamated, and this was done in 1987 with the creation of the Office of the Superintendent of Financial Institutions. The Green Paper also recommended that the federal government modernize its supervisory methods, including stricter standards for granting and renewing licences, and the requirement of ministerial approval for mergers. Other proposals favoured the reduction of barriers among different financial sectors to permit federally-regulated financial holding companies to own diversified financial interests. A new class of Schedule C banks was proposed which consisted of banks that could be owned by domestic financial companies seeking to enter banking.

New sanction and enforcement powers applying to all financial institutions were recommended in the Green Paper. These included: increased grounds for a curator to take control of a troubled financial institution; powers to issue cease and desist orders against an institution or its officials; power to remove management officials and directors; authority to prohibit changes in the control of institutions; power to force divesture of prohibited loans and investments; and, increased civil and criminal penalties for infractions. No legislative action was taken on the Green Paper, and in 1986 the federal government introduced a Blue Paper, a revised policy statement called "New Directions for the Financial Sector," which covered chartered banks, and federally-regulated trust, loan, and insurance companies. The thrust of the proposals contained in the Blue Paper

---

[6] Canada, Department of Finance, *The Regulation of Canadian Financial Institutions: Proposals for Discussion* (Ottawa: 1985).

was to give Canadian financial institutions broader powers by enabling them to diversify into other financial market segments which traditionally were kept separate. All federally-regulated financial institutions would be permitted to operate subsidiaries or, through holding companies, control other regulated financial institutions. Also the non-bank financial institutions would be permitted an expansion of their consumer and commercial lending powers, and be permitted to offer investment and portfolio management advice and services. The policy statement, however, proposed to continue the ban on links between financial institutions and commercial companies.

The Blue Paper reiterated the need for strengthening the government's supervisory functions. Proposals included a strengthened role for bank auditors, rules for greater disclosure of information to consumers, and insider trading and conflict of interest guidelines.

These policy papers were followed by draft legislation to revise the rules and regulations governing the financial sector, but throughout 1987 and 1988 the government continued to drag its feet in enacting new legislation. Until such legislation is enacted, considerable confusion and uncertainty continues to characterize the financial sector. Foreign financial firms continue to expand in Canada and stretch the spirit of existing laws and regulations. Existing financial firms look for loopholes to expand their services. Non-financial companies desire to purchase financial institutions. For example, in 1989, BCE Inc., Canada's largest holding company with interests ranging from telecommunications to oil and gas, proposed to acquire Montreal Trust, which would be contrary to the government's long-standing opposition to linking commercial companies with financial institutions. When a similar proposal was made to acquire Canada Trust, the country's largest trust company, the federal government was forced to act and announced that purchase of federally-regulated trust and loan companies would be subject to government approval effective August, 1989, even though legislation covering these matters was still pending.

A comprehensive program for financial reform was presented by the Economic Council of Canada in its 1987 report, *A Framework for Financial Regulation*[7]. The Council recommended that each financial institution be limited to the performance of a single major function with each function regulated by a single regulatory authority. In this one-function/one institution approach, a bank would be involved in banking, an insurance company in insurance, and so on. Diversification into other functions would be allowed but only through a financial holding company that would bring together distinct corporate entities performing different major functions. The one function/one institution framework, the Council argued, would keep a clear separation between major functions, which would facilitate regulation and minimize potential abuses. Regulators would determine the range of permissible activities under each function. Each institution would have to maintain a separate capital base to ensure solvency. Transfers of funds

---

[7] Economic Council, *op. cit.*

within a financial holding group would be limited, and the separation of functions would make it easier for the regulator to identify and follow such transfers. The financial health of holding groups would be monitored and they would be required to provide global financial statements on a quarterly basis.

The Council also pointed out that lack of harmonization in provincial policies and between provincial and federal regulations impeded the efficiency of the financial system. This could be overcome by closer cooperation between the governments to ensure interprovincial uniformity of financial institutions and activities. Improved coordination would not only make the system more efficient, it would also reduce the costs of regulation and supervision of the system. Its proposals for regulatory reform, argued the Council, would strike a good balance between enhanced competition, institutional solvency and public confidence, and adequate consumer protection and accessibility.

As the federal government continued to issue position papers and drafts of proposed legislation, some of the provincial governments decided to move ahead with legislative reform of regulations of financial institutions under their jurisdiction. In 1989, British Columbia passed its Financial Institutions Act, replacing earlier legislation governing trust and insurance companies. The legislation maintained the separation of the functions of insurance companies from those of other institutions. It established minimum capital requirements for deposit-taking institutions. Credit unions were brought under the same set of rules as other financial institutions. The Act established a single regulatory agency, the Financial Institutions Commission, to regulate all financial enterprises subject to the province's jurisdiction and to administer deposit insurance.

In 1988, the Ontario government revised its Loan and Trust Corporations Act, tightening the regulatory framework for trust companies in the wake of trust company failures. The Act required that all trust and loan companies applying for a licence to operate in Ontario had to meet certain conditions, including a minimum capital base, and were required to show that the management was competent and the proposed business plan was feasible. It furthermore allowed trust and loan companies to be owned by non-financial firms on the grounds that such firms could contribute to the financial strength of the financial companies. Self-dealing, the procedure by which owners of financial institutions use depositors' funds for unauthorized investments, was restricted. The new law also required that 50 percent of the directors of a trust or loan company operating in Ontario be outside directors, holding no more than 5 percent of the voting shares of the corporation or any of its affiliates.

A major issue of contention between the federal government and the province of Ontario has been the relationship between commercial and financial companies. Ontario favours a policy of permitting commercial firms to buy financial companies, but this is opposed by the federal government on the grounds that such links between the two types of operations would increase the potential for abuses, conflicts of interest, and concentration of power. The chartered banks have strongly opposed any relaxation of the existing controls on the links between commercial and finance companies. It is argued that the two should continue to be kept separate to ensure that depositors' funds are not diverted into unduly risky enterprises of a financial firm's commercial ally.

Joint jurisdiction in the financial system has, in the past, led to numerous jurisdictional clashes between the federal and provincial governments. In some cases, the jurisdictions are clear, as in the case of one securities firm buying another in the same province. But in other areas the lines of jurisdiction become blurred, as in the case of a federally-regulated bank purchasing a securities firm. Another example pertains to trust companies. A federally-chartered trust company is governed by federal regulations, but it is still subject to the rules of the province in which it operates. Confusion results when federal trust regulations have different reporting and disclosure requirements from those of the provinces. The need for open lines of communication and cooperation between federal and provincial regulators is essential for a smoothly operating financial services sector in the economy. This has been recognized and emphasized by the Economic Council of Canada and in various commission and committee studies. It is a crucial aspect for the reform of regulation of financial institutions.

12

THE ENVIRONMENT: POLLUTION CONTROL

Most lines of production and consumption result in discharges of substances and wastes that are harmful to the environment and to the inhabitants of the environment. With the proliferation of these discharges into the air, water and soil, the very survival of this planet is brought into question. Industrialization and the accompanying introduction of new technologies, products, and production processes have invariably resulted in new and more pollutants and seemingly ever more dangerous and toxic pollutants. This has been particularly true in the chemical and energy fields, highlighted by the extremely hazardous waste products from nuclear reactors in energy production. New and developing technologies, however, have enabled society to identify and analyze harmful pollutants from existing as well as newly developed products and production processes. For example, previously unsuspected hazards in various chemicals are regularly being discovered and revealed.

In the last few decades, society has become increasingly conscious of the existence and effects of pollution, and in many instances even alarmed at the tremendous costs to the environment and to inhabitants. The effects on shorelines, fish and wildlife of major oil spills are flashed on television for the world to observe. The deadly effects of nuclear reactor mishaps, such as those which occurred at Three Mile Island in the U.S. and at Chernobyl in the Soviet Union, are clearly exposed in the media. Pictures of dead and dying lakes and streams are commonplace. In this climate, governments have been subjected to ever-increasing pressures to employ various measures and regulations to manage and safeguard the environment.

The need for government action to protect, conserve, and manage the environment arises from the fact that market forces are unable to do so. Elements of the environment, such as air and water, frequently do not enter into market exchange because they are common property. Private property is protected by its owners, but common property is not owned by anyone. Its value cannot be established and it is basically viewed as a free good, subject to use and abuse. The use of common property does not generally enter into the costs of production of a firm or industry. When costs to common property are incurred by a firm through overuse or damage, such costs are external to a firm and are not taken into account by the market. But overused and polluted common property resources, such as water, bring costs to society. If common property is to be protected and managed, it must be done by government acting on behalf of society and serving the public interest.

Types and Sources of Pollution

The amount and toxicity of pollution various with the source. Waste products from industry, the use of chemicals, the burning of fossil fuels, and garbage from consumption threaten the quality of the earth's air, water, and land resources. Air is polluted by carbon monoxide and hydrocarbons from gasoline and diesel fuel consumption in automobiles, trucks, and oil-powered hydro-electric generating plants. Sulphur and nitrogen oxides and other pollutants are discharged into the air from copper, nickel, and iron smelting. Garbage incinerators, depending on the types of waste products being burned, can spew out pollution of varying toxicity into the air.

Suspended toxic materials in the air can pollute the water and soil as they return to the earth's surface through rain. Sulphur dioxide from smelters returns to the ground as acid rain, depleting oxygen in lakes and streams and destroying fish, water-foul, and water plants, as well as harming forests, crops and other vegetation. Industrial wastes and raw sewage in urban centers have in the past been indiscriminately discharged into lakes and rivers, contaminating drinking water. The pulp and paper industry has been a major source of water pollution in the past. Non-organic fertilizers and pesticides used in the farming industry enter the soil and leach into water sources destroying fish and vegetation. Soil can also be contaminated with various waste products from industry and from improperly controlled land-fill sites. The most hazardous contamination can occur from the waste products from nuclear power plants, and technology still has not developed a process by which these wastes can be stored or eliminated with complete safety. Radiation-contaminated soil can be rendered hazardous and useless for decades.

Other types of activities have also caused considerable harm to the earth's environment. The harvesting of forest resources without reforestation and open-pit mining produce soil erosion and a wasteland. Uncontrolled hunting and fishing leads to the depletion of wildlife and the danger of extinction of many wildlife species. Oil exploration in the Arctic threatens the very delicate ecology of that region. The use of propellants or chlorofluorocarbons in spray cans threatens the depletion of the earth's ozone layer, that area of the stratosphere which shields the earth's surface from dangerous rays from outer space.

Naturally-formed carbon dioxide in the earth's atmosphere traps the heat of the sun and regulates the earth's temperature. The continuous and increasing use of fossil fuels, however, has increased the level of carbon dioxide causing many scientists and environmentalists to fear the possible creation of a greenhouse effect. Excessive carbon dioxide would lead to increasing global temperatures. Melting polar ice-caps would raise ocean levels and inundate low-lying coastal areas. A general rise in temperatures would cause an expansion of the earth's arid

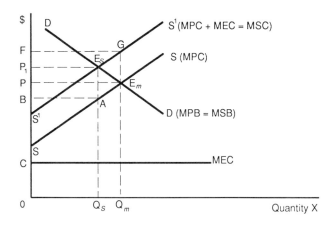

FIGURE 12–1: *Pollution: An External Diseconomy in Production*

regions and deserts, threatening the world's food supply, and life on the planet as we know it.

Pollution As An External Diseconomy

External diseconomies are costs which accrue to society from the production and consumption processes in addition to the direct costs to the individual producer and consumer. They are also referred to as spill-over costs, or third party costs, or external damage costs. They are not subject to market forces and are not priced in the marketplace.[1]

Pollution is an external diseconomy. A manufacturer who pollutes the air or water in the process of production does not include pollution as a cost of production and these costs are, therefore, not reflected in the market price of the goods and services produced and sold. These costs are borne by society in the form of deterioration of the environment, hazards to human health, and depletion of wildlife and vegetation.

Figure 12–1 presents a model of pollution as an external diseconomy in production. Consider some commodity x in which price and quantity are determined by market forces. *DD* is the demand curve for x. It is also the marginal private benefit curve (*MPB*) showing the benefits, at the margin, which consum-

---

[1] An economic analysis of external diseconomies can be found in most microeconomics textbooks and in textbooks on public sector economics. See, for example: David M. Hyman, *Modern Microeconomics: Analysis and Applications*, 2nd ed. (Homewood: R.D. Irwin 1988), Ch. 17; R.A. Musgrave, Peggy Musgrave, and R.M. Bird, *Public Finance in Theory and Practice*, 1st Canadian Edition (Toronto: McGraw-Hill Ryerson Ltd., 1987), Ch.4.

ers enjoy in consuming x. SS, the supply curve, is also the marginal private cost curve (MPC), showing the private costs to the producer of producing additional units of x. Market equilibrium is determined where $D = S$ and $MPB = MPC$ at Em. The supply curve, however, only covers the direct costs incurred by the producer for labour, materials, etc. in the process of production. The external costs of pollution of the environment created by each additional unit of output is shown as the marginal external cost curve (MEC). It is assumed that the external cost of each additional unit produced remains constant at OC. These external costs are not covered by the market price OP. Summing MPC and MEC vertically results in the curve S^1S^1 or the marginal social cost curve ($MPC + MEC = MSC$). Assuming no externalities attached to consumption, the marginal private benefit curve and the marginal social benefit curve will coincide as the demand curve. Equilibrium for society is where $MSC = MSB$ at E_s, and the efficient level of output is determined to be OQ_s at price OP_1. The price paid by consumers now covers the total cost of production, including the cost of pollution. The market has not taken into account the cost of pollution, resulting in a greater output (OQ_m) at a lower price (OP) than that considered efficient for society. At market equilibrium the total damage caused by pollution is represented by the area FGE_mP, the cost of which is borne by society. At equilibrium E_s, total damage cost is reduced to P_1E_sAB, and assuming the cost of pollution is internalized and eliminated the cost is borne by consumers of the product x.

Internalizing the cost of an external diseconomy, such as pollution, requires that the price paid for a unit of a commodity covers its marginal social cost of production. The additional price paid per unit at output OQ_s is E_sA, which can be used to compensate third parties who suffer damages, or it can be used to cover the cost of pollution-control equipment required to eliminate or prevent the pollution. The preferable solution for society would be to prevent pollution.

Problems in Controlling and Preventing Pollution[2]

While there is general agreement on the desirability of preventing or controlling pollution emissions, a number of difficulties and problems arise in attempting to regulate pollution. First, there is the difficulty of identifying the sources of pollution and determining the degree of damage inflicted on the environment. Pollutants are numerous and are generated by multiple sources. Regulatory agencies must possess adequate resources to be capable of detecting pollution and monitoring pollution levels and toxicity. Second, there is the problem of disposal or storage in the case of the discharge of large quantities of waste material or highly toxic material. Municipalities frequently face problems in locating suffi-

---

[2] An outline of earlier pollution regulation and control in Canada is presented in Economic Council of Canada, *Reforming Regulation* (Ottawa: Supply and Services Canada, 1981), Ch.8. A discussion of various measures and policies to control pollution is also presented in Peter Asch and Rosalind Seneca, *Government and the Marketplace* (Toronto: The Dryden Press, 1985), Ch. 12, and in Musgrave, Musgrave and Bird, *op.cit.*, Ch. 33.

ciently large land-fill sites for the disposal of community garbage. An alternative solution is the construction of pollution-free incinerators and waste recycling plants, but these are extremely costly. Considerable controversy has arisen in the selection of sites for the storage of highly toxic nuclear waste products. Communities are fearful that these products will leach into and contaminate the soil and water supplies, and the public opposes storage of these products near inhabitable areas.

A third problem may stem from questions of jurisdiction over pollution. In Canada, jurisdiction in certain areas of pollution is shared by the federal and provincial governments, and both can exercise wide and overlapping powers dealing with environmental issues. It is not uncommon for conflicts to arise. For example, a provincial government may wish to develop a particular resource, such as its forest industry or energy, only to run afoul with federal concern with potential pollution of the water and air. This may occur when both levels of government have jurisdiction in an area and federal pollution emission standards may be set higher than provincial standards. The result may be uncertainty on the part of the industry regarding environmental jurisdiction and pollution emission standards. The issue of jurisdiction over pollution and the need for cooperation between governments extends to the international area. Air and water pollution frequently respects no borders and is international in nature. Witness the issue of acid rain in Canada and the U.S., where some major water sources such as the Great Lakes are shared and industry on both sides of the Canada-U.S. border contribute to their pollution.

A fourth and major concern with pollution is the impact of pollution control on industry and the economy. Some of the major polluters of the environment may also be among the largest producers, employers, and exporters in the country, and may form the backbone of the economy. Legislation preventing pollution or establishing high pollution emission standards may force these industries to incur high costs in an attempt to comply. In Figure 12–1, costs of pollution control equipment would cause marginal private costs of production and the supply curve to rise to S^1S^1. Quantity would be reduced by Q_mQ_s and price would rise by PP_1. The fall in output would be reflected in unemployment of labour and other factors of production. Rising prices make it more difficult for domestic industry to compete in the world market, with a consequent reduction in exports. Costs could conceivably rise so astronomically as to cause the industry to become uncompetitive and to shut down completely. Regulators are, therefore, faced with a dilemma. On the one hand, social concern over pollution creates pressure for pollution-control policies, but these policies may produce a fall in production and unemployment and may retard economic growth. These represent real costs to society and are incurred at the same time that the costs to society from pollution are being reduced. On the other hand, if society is more concerned with immediate economic issues of employment and economic growth, the issues of pollution control will be pushed into the background. Pollution control may require an economic sacrifice which society may not be pre-

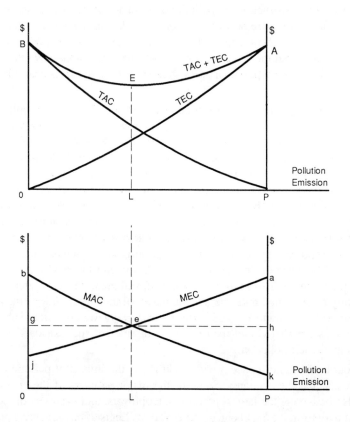

FIGURE 12–2: *Efficient Level of Pollution Control*

pared to bear, particularly if the hazards of pollution are uncertain and distant, potentially affecting future generations.

In many instances, given current technology, there appears to be a trade-off between a clean environment and the economic goals of production, employment, and growth. The government cannot ignore the realities of this trade-off and frequently attempts compromise to minimize pollution subject to the constraints of other goals.

An Efficient Level of Pollution Control

Given the earlier discussed costs of pollution and the costs involved in controlling or eliminating pollution, it has theoretically been argued that it is not efficient to attempt to eliminate pollution completely. In other words, there may exist an amount of pollution reduction or abatement which can be viewed as efficient. Figure 12–2 presents a model of an efficient level of pollution abatement.[3]

The horizontal axis in both diagrams measures the amount of pollution emission or discharge in the form of chemical or biological content. *OP* is the amount of pollution discharged by a given level of output in the absence of any control or abatement efforts. A larger output would move the point *P* to the right, reflecting a greater amount of pollution associated with the larger output. In the upper diagram the curve *OA* illustrates the total external costs (*TEC*) to the environment for different levels of pollution discharge. They are assumed to increase as the amount of pollution increases. With the given level of production, the total damage cost of pollution is *PA*. In the lower diagram the marginal external cost (*MEC*) curve is *ja*, which is derived from the slope of *TEC*. *PB* measures the total abatement cost (*TAC*) and reflects the costs involved in curbing or preventing pollution, such as costs of pollution control equipment. If all pollution is prevented, the total cost would be *OB*. The slope of *TAC* is shown to be rising, reflecting the assumption that generally it becomes increasingly costly to curb the last few remaining units of pollution and to reduce pollution to zero. Corresponding to *TAC* is the marginal abatement cost (*MAC*) curve *kb*. The vertical summation of *TAC* and *TEC* combines the damage cost of pollution with the abatement cost and produces the curve *AEB*, the total cost of pollution to society. At *OP* level of pollution, with no attempt to control it, the cost to society is *PA*. The introduction of an abatement program reduces the pollution level and the external cost, but involves an abatement cost. *AEB* is shown to fall to point *E*, which corresponds to *PL* amount of pollution reduction. Total costs of pollution to society are the lowest at point *E*. *PL* therefore represents the efficient level of pollution prevention for a given level of output.

In marginal terms, in the lower diagram, the efficient level of pollution prevention is where *MEC* = *MAC*. This occurs at e, where pollution emission is reduced by *PL*. At pollution levels between *P* and *L*, the *MEC* is greater than the *MAC*, which means that a reduction in pollution by one unit would impose on society a smaller burden in terms of abatement costs than the burden imposed on society in terms of pollution damage. At these levels of pollutions the net marginal benefit to society from pollution reduction, measured as the vertical distance between MEC and *MAC*, is positive. To the left of *L*, the *MAC* exceeds *MEC*, which means that the cost to society for pollution abatement exceeds the benefits to society from pollution reduction. At these levels of pollution, the net marginal benefit of reducing pollution is negative and increases as the pollution level continues to be reduced. Costs to society associated with pollution and pollution control are therefore minimized when *OL* of pollution still remains.

---

[3] Musgrave, Musgrave, and Bird, *Ibid.* See also Joseph E. Stiglitz, *Economics of the Public Sector*, 2nd ed. (New York: Norton and Co., 1988), pp. 222–226.

While this model suffers from limitations as a practical guide to policy because of the difficulties of measuring pollution emissions and damage costs, the model does serve to illustrate that there are costs involved both from pollution and from pollution control, and where pollution is found to exist, it may not be economical or efficient for society to attempt to try to reduce pollution to zero.

Government Regulatory Policy

Government regulations to protect the environment can be found in a large number of statutes, regulatory agency decisions, and by-laws at the federal, provincial and municipal government levels. Regulations exist covering such issues as the use of chemical substances, the testing of chemicals, air and water quality standards, pollution emission standards, storage and disposal of wastes, and the safety of workers handling hazardous products. At the federal level, environmental regulations can be found in such legislation as the Environmental Contaminants Act, the Canada Water Act, the Clean Air Act, and the Fisheries Act. In Ontario, there is the Environmental Protection Act, the Ontario Water Resources Act, the Provincial Parks Act, the Pit and Quarries Act, the Endangered Species Act, and the Public Health Act.

While these statutes contain many provisions designed to protect the environment, a major difficulty is enforcement of the regulations and compliance by the parties involved. Governments have applied various policies involving either sanctions or incentives, or a combination of both, to obtain compliance with the regulations.

One policy that has been applied involves the careful scrutiny of a proposed operation before a licence is granted. This can effectively be applied to newly proposed industries or plants which have the potential to produce harmful emissions. If, after careful examination by a regulatory agency, it has been shown that the proposed operation has taken the necessary precautions to prevent harmful pollutant emissions, a licence to operate will be granted. For example, the federal government has been careful and rather conservative in issuing licences to oil exploration companies wishing to operate in the far north and in off-shore regions where there is considerable potential for upsetting the delicate ecology or potential for major contamination from accidental oil spills.

The most common pollution-control policy employed by government is to impose penalties on the polluter. These may take a variety of forms, including revoking operating licences, monetary fines, and prison terms. Pollution standards and limits are established and polluters are penalized if they do not comply with these standards. Fines have been fairly widely used and have generally taken the form of a flat levy for each conviction. A daily fine could also be imposed for continued pollution. Alternatively, assuming pollution emissions can be measured, the penalty could take the form of a specific fine or tax for each discharged unit of pollution.

Effluent charges may be applied to achieve the efficient level of pollution prevention depicted in Figure 12–2. Assume a charge of Og per unit of pollution emission. A firm which took no action to prevent pollution would pay a total fine of *OghP*. The firm, however, could reduce this total charge by implementing pollution control measures to reduce pollution to a level of *OL*. Over the range *P* to *L*, the fine per unit exceeds the marginal abatement cost. Reducing pollution from *OP* to *OL*, would cost the firm a total amount represented by *PkeL*. The total fine for this amount of pollution is *PheL*. The total amount of fine that is saved is therefore *khe*. To the left of *L*, the marginal abatement cost is greater than the fine per unit, therefore it is less costly to the firm to pay the fine rather than to try to reduce pollution further once *PL* pollution prevention is achieved. A fine lower than *Og* per unit would cause the firm to stop its pollution-prevention measures before *L* is reached, while a fine exceeding *Og* would cause a firm to reduce pollution beyond the efficient level of *PL*.

In practice, there have been a number of problems in applying a policy of fines to polluters. First, polluters have to be identified, charged, and convicted before the fine can take effect. Second, a relatively low fine may be viewed by a firm as a license to pollute. Third, a relatively high fine and high costs of compliance could conceivably force a firm out of business, resulting in unemployment.

In recognition of the high costs of compliance in certain polluting industries, governments have combined their policies of sanctions with subsidies and other forms of assistance. Subsidies are designed to help a firm cover the cost of pollution-control equipment and other pollution-prevention measures and keep the firm competitive and in business. Other financial assistance could take the form of accelerated depreciation of pollution-abatement equipment for tax purposes, and accelerated depreciation of research expenses to help a firm develop the necessary technology to reduce pollution emissions. Grants and subsidies can also be applied to develop and maintain waste storage and disposal plants. The federal and provincial governments have followed a policy to assist financially municipal and local governments to establish sewage treatment plants. But sewage treatment is extremely costly. The city of Hamilton estimated that it would need $500 million for sewer separation to prevent sanitary sewage from flowing into Hamilton harbour. Saint John, New Brunswick requires $150 million for sewer improvements to prevent an estimated 75 percent of the city's sewage from going into its bay. Halifax has embarked on a $200 million, six-year project to improve its sewage system.[4]

Pollution control can place a heavy cost burden on industry, individual firms, and consumers. Under pressure from government, in January, 1989, some of the largest sources of the pollution-causing acid rain in Ontario announced major plans to curb their pollution emissions. Ontario Hydro announced a pollution-prevention program costing $2.5 billion over a ten-year period. The program included the placement of pollution-control devices known as "scrubbers" in existing hydro-electric plants, and greater reliance on nuclear power hydro

---

[4] *Windsor Star*, Special Southam Environment Project, "Our Fragile Future," Oct. 7, 1989.

plants. The company predicted that the cost of this program would cause an increase of 2.5–3.0 percent in electricity rates for consumers.

International Nickel Corp. (Inco) one of the largest sources of the pollutant sulphur dioxide and acid rain, announced a $500 million program in its Sudbury nickel-smelting plant designed to reduce the emission of sulphur dioxide by two-thirds over a ten-year period. Canada's copper and nickel-smelting industries have for some time been a target of the federal and provincial governments' anti-pollution policies, but the governments also recognized the high cost to these firms of pollution prevention measures. In 1985, in recognition of the burden that anti-pollution policies was placing on the smelting industry at a time when the metal markets tended to be weak, the federal government announced a $300 million subsidy program to assist the metal producing industries in their pollution-control efforts.

In British Columbia, the pulp and paper industry recently embarked on a $1 billion, five-year clean up program to reduce the production of dioxins which are harmful to sea life.

Strengthening Pollution Control

Within the last few years, the dramatic growth in public awareness and concern for the environment has led to a rapid increase in activity to reduce pollution. Consumer activists, environmental groups, governments, and even the polluting industries themselves have increased their efforts to curb pollution. In Ontario, in January, 1987, a new Environmental Protection Act came into effect, with more stringent pollution regulations and much more severe penalties on polluters. Under the new legislation, the maximum fine on a company for polluting was increased from $25,000 per day to $50,000 per day, and up to $250,000 per day if it involved a hazardous waste. In addition to the heavier fines, the new Act introduced prison terms for persons found responsible for pollution. The officials of a company, for example, if charged and found guilty of pollution could be susceptible to prison terms. The government could also suspend or cancel operating licences of companies found guilty of pollution.

Other provinces in Canada have also taken steps to put more teeth into their pollution control laws. In New Brunswick, in 1989, the government passed the Clean Water Act, which set maximum daily fines for any industrial, corporate, or municipal polluter at $1 million. In May, 1989, the government of British columbia proposed legislation calling for the province's pulp and paper operators to reduce toxic dioxin and organic chloride discharges by at least 70 percent by 1994.

In some cases, environmental disasters have prompted more urgent government action. A fire in August, 1988, at a storage site for oil containing toxic PCBs in the Montreal superb of St.-Basile-Le-Grand scattered potentially hazardous soot over the neighborhood, and forced some 3000 residents out of their homes for more than a week. This prompted the Quebec government to establish, within the environmental ministry, an investigative agency consisting primarily of former police officers to investigate and initiate proceedings against polluters and negligent waste-disposal operators and waste storage companies. At the same time the federal and Quebec governments announced a joint program to force about fifty of the worst industrial polluters of the St. Lawrence River to reduce their discharges by 90 percent by 1993.

Many of the provincial and municipal governments are encouraging and helping to fund recycling programs, including the recycling of newspapers, metal containers, plastic products, etc. Such programs are designed to reduce the amounts of trash and wastes that are dumped in land-fill sites or are incinerated.

The stronger sanctions were welcomed by environmental groups who had in the past harshly criticized both federal and provincial government for weak pollution-prevention measures and non-enforcement of regulations. Environmentalists charged that very low fines in the past were frequently viewed as a licence to pollute. It was argued that companies had tended to weigh the costs of compliance with the costs of non-compliance. They procrastinated in introducing pollution-control measures hoping that they would not be caught polluting, and even if detected they would still have to be charged and convicted. The onus was on the prosecution to show that a company in question did indeed pollute and did cause damage.

Numerous cases can be cited to illustrate the limitations of environmental regulations, and to illustrate relatively weak government action. An example is the tar discovered in the St. Clair River near Sarnia, Ontario in August, 1985. The tar found in the water and on the river bottom was traced to the Dow Chemical Company of Sarnia. Following a lengthy investigation, Dow pleaded guilty to four violations of the Ontario Water Resources Act and was fined a total of $16,000. An alternative would have been for the government to charge Dow under the more rigorous Environmental Protection Act, which at the time carried a maximum penalty of $25,000 for each violation. The latter course was not chosen on the grounds that the spillage was a product manufactured by Dow and not a waste material. Environmentalists called the fine ludicrous, a mere slap on the wrist of a huge company. Dow, however, assumed responsibility for removing the polluting product from the river at a reported cost of approximately $1 million and spent another $1 million erecting a barrier between its operating plant and the river. It also spent a reported $12 million to upgrade its monitoring and sewer system at its Sarnia plants.

Another example of the relatively small fines imposed in the past involved the Ford Motor Company of Canada. In March, 1988, the company was found guilty of spilling oil into the Detroit River. Ford was fined $5,000 under the Ontario Water Resources Act on each of three pollution charges.

Municipalities are responsible for regulating industrial discharges into municipal sewage systems. Toxic wastes dumped into sewers, if not treated in sewage treatment plants, eventually reach rivers and lakes. Municipalities must monitor the waste products discharged into sewers for their toxic content and set by-laws regulating such discharge. But the monitoring and testing process is expensive and many smaller municipalities have complained of insufficient resources for an effective monitoring system. There is the added expense of prosecuting polluters and imposing effective sanctions. Often small companies found guilty of polluting have claimed that they could not afford to pay the fines levied on them, and instead of paying the fine would declare bankruptcy. This was a common practice in the United States until 1986, when the U.S. Supreme Court ruled that governments could seize the assets of firms convicted of pollution who declared bankruptcy and use the proceeds from asset disposal to clean up the pollution. Any remaining assets or proceeds would then be claimed by creditors.

Regulation of landfill sites for urban garbage poses its own problems. Ontario currently has an estimated 600 landfill sites, occupying over 100,000 acres of land. As these sites are filled, new sites are required but suitable locations for them are becoming increasingly difficult to find. Furthermore, partly because of the use of toxic synthetics, garbage no longer degrades safely, and causes hazards for using landfill sites containing them. Certain waste products and garbage are being banned from landfill sites but no alternative means of disposal exists. Recently in Windsor, Ontario, landfill sites refused to accept used automobile tires, but automobile dealers and consumers were not offered any alternative means of disposal. In March, 1989, the Ontario government announced that it would spend $225 million over the next decade to reduce by one-half the amount of garbage hauled to landfill sites. The initiatives included forcing industry to introduce recycling programs, encouraging community and municipal compost programs, and providing funds for research and development on new waste-reduction and recycling technologies. In British Columbia, the Environment Department proposed a special tax on non-recyclable consumer goods to help defray the costs of dump sites and garbage collection and to encourage the development of recyclable products.

In addition to the actions of governments to force industry to reduce pollution, increasing pressure from consumer and environmental groups is causing firms to act. Environmental groups have urged consumers to boycott the products of firms known to be polluters, and have endorsed recycled products and the products of pollution-conscious companies. Companies themselves are beginning to realize the value of good public relations as they concern pollution and are beginning to take the initiative in curbing pollutants emitted in their production process. Business establishments are attempting to establish better communications with the public, highlighting and making the public aware of the positive steps that they are taking to control pollution. For example, Dow Chemical widely publicized its plans to recycle 400 million plastic bottles a year. Similarly, Du Pont Canada proudly pointed to its $1 billion, ten-year plan to replace chlorofluorocarbons with compounds less harmful to the earth's protective ozone layer. In addition, a whole new industry has sprung up to develop and manufacture environmental protection equipment and offer pollution-control services, and this waste-management industry has mushroomed over the last decade.

Environmental protection is considered by many people today as a top priority, and many appear to be more and more prepared to put the environment ahead of economic matters when the two are in conflict. This is reflected in public concerns highlighted in the media, activist groups and in recent government policies. In a recent public opinion poll, people were asked whether they favoured or opposed shutting down a major company which provided jobs in their community if that company was polluting the environment. Of those surveyed, 37 percent opposed closing such a company while 60 percent were in favour.[5]

---

[5] *Macleans,* July 3, 1989, p. 44.

INDEX